Cover Down Yuh Bucket

The Story of Sticklicking in Barbados

Elton 'Elombe' Mottley

with contributions by Elvis Gill & Ione Knight

FAT PORK 10-10 PRODUCTIONS

Fat Pork Ten Ten Productions

FAT PORK
10-10
PRODUCTIONS

Fatpork Ten-Ten Productions
PO Box 12, 9 Gordon Town, Kingston, Jamaica
elombe@cwjamaica.com

Edited by Carol A. Pitt and Yejide Maynard

ISBN 978-149-4916-39-8 (paperback)

Table of Contents

Preface and Acknowledgements

Sticklicking is a Bajan form of stick fighting that has its origins both in West African societies and English society. It was distinctly different from other Caribbean stick fighting forms and was well known in Trinidad as Bajan stick. There is no doubt Bajans carried it with them to Guyana, Trinidad, the Virgin Islands and I have no doubt also to Panama and Cuba.

One of the important characteristics about Barbados was the relative isolation it endured in the pre-radio, pre-movies, pre-telephone, pre-television, pre-internet days. The only real communication between Barbados and the rest of the world was through the ships that visited Barbados bringing supplies and collecting sugar or getting water and coal on their way to and from South America.

This semi-isolation allowed Bajans to develop many cultural practices that were completely indigenous. I think of marble cricket and firms, two variations of the traditional cricket game which included coconut branches for bats, tennis or hopping balls or tar balls for the traditional leather cricket balls, and road tennis as a variation of table tennis.

Economic reasons were the basis of generating this creativity. As Barbados has linked with the outside world towards in the last half of the 20th Century, many of these sporting forms have been abandoned for others that we have imported. But most of all, we have exhibited a lack of faith in our own identity as a people. We have abandoned sticklicking and embraced the many forms of Asian martial arts. This is demonstrated without apology by the failure of the National Sports Council as well as the Central Government to recognize sticklicking as a national sport on the same level as the other sports.

I would like to thank the many persons who consented to be interviewed. In particular, I would like to pay special tribute to Elvis Gill (EG) and Ione Knight (IK). As you will discover, Elvis has contributed enormously, almost single-handed, to keeping the art of sticklicking alive in Barbados. His associate Ione Knight, also a sticklicker herself, has assisted him tremendously in keeping the documentation with the stories of various sticklickers alive. I am extreme grateful that they agreed to share these stories with me to include in this book.

Foreword

Elombe Mottley and his co-researchers and writers have presented their audience with a mass of fascinating testaments as to the vibrancy of one of the Caribbean's folk arts. While it is true that this particular art of stick-play is now a moribund skill, what Mottley has done is shown beyond a shadow of a doubt that this art-form did exist in Barbados. The strength of this affirmation comes against a cultural background of the island which had erased the existence of this sport from common memory or mention. Part of the further intent of this book is to encourage the revival of this sport.

Cover Down Your Bucket is a credit to the persistence of those who have sought to recuperate aspects of the lost cultural heritage of a people. The impressive collection of testimonies is furthermore a magnificent monument to the efficacy of fieldwork in the task of such recuperation—the arduous process for the investigator of hunting down information from individuals who recollect past incidents and practices and who have sometimes to be convinced that their personal stories have merit, in fact, that they hold part of the secrets which can unlock the past. The investigator then has the painstaking job of transcribing these memorials, possibly re-checking data with the informants, and then selecting extracts to collate into an exciting anthology such as this is.

The information comes from various parishes of the island, and while most of the informants are peasant or urban working-class blacks, Mottley has also been able to show the participation of some white middle-class Barbadians in this activity. The data also demonstrate the influence of British boxing styles and sword-play on the evolution of a practice which forms part of the cultural legacy of Africa in the Caribbean. Furthermore, this book presents evidence of stick-licking in Jamaica, and the role of Barbadians among stick-fighters in Trinidad, where the practice has had greater saliency, is also evident in several of the accounts here. We may also note that the sport takes a variety of forms throughout the plantation Americas: in Cuba, Brazil, Martinique, St. Vincent and the Grenadines, among several locations.

The size of this volume and the wide sweep of its comparative data speak to the enthusiasm which Mottley and his co-writers have brought to this enterprise. We welcome this addition to the profile of Caribbean folk arts and culture, and the contribution of Barbados to this particular genre of martial activity.

Professor Maureen Warner-Lewis
Mona, Jamaica

Lithograph by Karl Broodhagen

Image Credits

The photographs used in these books were either sourced from my private archives, the Mottley family archives, or were published by the Barbados Government Information Service (BGIS), the *Barbados Advocate*, the *Barbados Annual Review*, the *Barbados Daily News*, the *Nation News*, the *Sunday Sun*, the *Beacon*, the Caribbean Broadcasting Corporation (CBC), the *Trinidad Guardian*, the *Trinidad Express*, the *Jamaica Gleaner*, or from various sources on the Internet. The names of many of the photographers who worked for these media houses never appeared on the photos, but the author acknowledges their work in documenting the history of Barbados. The following is a partial list of some of the photographers.

Art Tappin
Cecil Marshall
Charles Grant
Cyprian LaTouche
Dada Brewster
Darnley Bushel
Erad Brewster
Errol Nurse
Fitzpatrick
Frank Grimes
Frank Lashley
Gordon Brooks Jr
Gordon Brooks Snr
Junior LaTouche
Livy Grimes
Maurice Giles
Mike Williams
O'Neal Oliver
Parkinson
Paul Mandeville
Perce Tappin
Richard Barnett
Ronnie Carrington
Roy Byer
Seth Skeete
Tumpa Greaves
Val Millington
Vondel Nichols
Willie Alleyne
Willie Kerr

Part One

The Tradition

Bussa Revolt, Easter 1816

Tall. Black.
His peppercorn hair sculp'd to his skull
enclosed swollen ears
and met on chin in cane/arrow gray.
His brow, smooth
unlike his gullied cheeks,
verandahed ponds of mustard eyes.
Afrika,
inverted in his flat and bridgeless nose,
ridged the black loam of his face
into lips like sapodilla figs.

He stood erect,
mangrove sinewed arms
swinging from shoulder sockets,
his left hand knotted
round a five foot stick of guava wood
blunted and sanded on flesh and bones
of opposing bodies,
his right hand swizzling
a wet and sweetened wampah
edged the night before on skimming stone.
Bussa spread his balanced feet
on cracked soles
and puffed marl smoke with his toes.

From Bridgetown to Chimborazo
from Bayley's to De Mingo
his name was terror.
To Byde Mill came
this man of men
his marauders

Karl Broodhagen's Statue of Bussa

his black band of warriors,
his freedom fighters
his brothers of the flesh.
Aloft above them
the bloodstained banner of brotherhood
and commitment stood.

Silence at this sight
bent itself round the yard
well and camels prayed.

Sunlight flected dog/stones
in harmony and yard/fowls
unisoned. Then
the quiet. Then the storm
when Bussa's corporal
blew his conch
like Buddy Bolden's horn.

From bush, from tree they came

howling.
From kitchen, from cane they came
believing
to fight the freedom fight
in revolt,
slitting midday shadows in half
and spattering
white colonial house
with black venom
spouting from prisoned wounds.

Afrika called.
A voice had fertilised
the buried drum.
The vegetable beat
of reap had made the ocean's leap.

1970

General Bussa, as he was called by the press of the day, was the leader of the insurgents who attempted to wrest power from the white planters in Barbados on Easter Weekend in 1816. Influenced by the success of the Saint-Domingue (Santo Domingo/Haiti) Revolution in 1804 and the abolition of the slave trade by the British government in 1807, Bussa and his band of warriors launched their attack on numerous plantations in the South/East of the Island.

The insurrection failed and many succumbed or retreated in the face of the fire power of the militias' muskets. Professor Hilary Beckles writing about Bussa—a National Hero of Barbados—in the book *For Love of Country*, quotes one of the British military leaders who said:

> It was about twelve o'clock that we met a large body of the insurgent slaves in the yard of Lowthers Plantation (1.5 miles north of Fairy Valley), several of whom were armed with muskets, who displayed the colours of the St. Phillip Battalion which they had stolen, and who, upon seeing the division, cheered, and cried out to us, "come on!" but were quickly dispersed upon being fired on... One negro was brandishing his sword which my soldiers could not witness without endeavouring to knock him over. Others were armed with pitchforks... [1]

What is significant about these quotations describing the insurgents is the noticeable absence of the weapons of choice—sticks. Bussa and his rebelling comrades seem to have only a few muskets[2] as should be expected. Even if they were many muskets, they obviously did not have the ammunition to use them continuously. Muskets required a complex procedure of loading

1. Prof. Hilary Beckles, *For Love of Country*, Foundation Publishers, NCF, Bridgetown, Barbados, p 16

2. Most infantry were issued with muskets which resembled modern day rifles in looks only. These were muzzle loading weapons which meant the shot and powder were poured down the barrel. The shot and powder came in small greased paper pouches which the infantry man would tear open with his teeth often holding the shot in his mouth while pouring the

and use and it is unlikely that the revolting slave population would have had access to a large quantity of these weapons and the ammunition for them, or would have had experience in loading and shooting them in the context of a battle to the level of considering these weapons as the main weapons of attack or defence.

Their weapons of choice would have had to be sticks, swords (that is, those large knives used for cutting cane—cutlasses, machetes, and wampahs), knives (less than ten inches), iron stakes (used for tying grazing animals in specific areas), other assorted agricultural tools (pitchforks, hoes, forks, etc.) and rocks and stones. All of these weapons are used in close combat and from all the reports cited by researchers, sticks as a weapon remained invisible to various observers. However, it is this writer's opinion that Bussa and his warriors were the ultimate stickfighters.

powder down the barrel. ...The powder and ball was rammed into place with the ramrod and the greased paper provided wadding to keep it there. A small amount of the powder was poured into a priming pan - when the trigger was pulled a flint would spark this through a small hole into the barrel setting off the gun powder and sending off the shot....

To load the musket was loaded vertically, which meant the soldier was usually standing. We get the term "going off half cocked" loading muskets as to load the musket it had to be on 'half-cock' - the cock or 'hammer' drawn back so if the trigger was pulled accidentally it would not set the gun off. Considering that the soldier was spending his time looking down the top of the barrel it was a relatively important safety device. It took at least 30 seconds to load a musket, although this could vary depending on each soldier. There were short cuts that could be taken such as skipping the ramming stage.

Misfires were common and the barrels had to been cleaned of the build up of residue from the powder. Soldiers carried wire brushes with them to do this. They were also inaccurate and the most effective way of firing was en masse at an en masse target.

British muskets were generally known as 'brown bess'. It was a much heavier and longer weapon than the rifle, throwing a spherical ball of 14 to the pound, and the uncertainty of its fire is well evidenced by the expression "as random as a common musket," which is to be met with in treatises on rifle-shooting at the beginning of the century. It would not carry straight for 100 yards, and its effective range was barely double that distance. Such was "the musket, that queen of weapons" as it has been styled, with which the British infantry won all its great victories from the time of Marlborough until the conquest of the Punjab in 1849.

This weapon was in use up to the year 1853. (http://homepages.ihug.co.nz/~awoodley/regency/weapons.html)

Sticklicking in the Sudan, Africa

Sudden death and long sickness!

Ah Mastifay, Mastifay
Meet down by the Croisee
And Cutouter, Cutouter
Meet me down by Green Corner

Well, I waiting for this carnival
To jump up with these criminals
I going to arm myself with a big stick
Any man in town I meet, that is real licks
'Cause I done tell Mammy already
Mammy do, do tie up your belly
'Cause is murder, federation
With war and rebellion
When they bar me by the junction

Ah Mastifay, Mastifay
Meet down by the Croisee
And Cutouter, Cutouter
Meet me down by Green Corner

Monday morning I waking early
Two drink of Vat to steam up my body
And I jumping up like I crazy
I alone go collapse the city

With my razor tie on to my poui
I like a Bajan in the 18th Century
And with my stick in my waist
I chipping in space
Is to spit in ole nayga face

Small Island Pride's *Carnival Celebration*, 1956

Introduction

An early reference to stickfighting among Africans and their descendants in the Caribbean is found in the 1779 lithograph by the Italian artist, Agostino Brunias. Although the focus is on the two stickfighters in the middle, they are actually five more surrounding them. On the left dressed in a pink head-tie is a stickfighter watching another with a red pants with his left hand in the air. Watching the same man in the red pants and seemingly wagging a finger of warning is another stickfighter. On the right of the picture, a man and a woman are holding back another stickfighter who obviously

Brunias' lithograph of sticklicking in Dominica in 1779 (Barbados Museum)

wants to join the fray. Lastly at the back is an older stickfighter in repose, resting on his stick, observing out of the corner of his eyes to make sure the young, aggressive stickfighter does not make any unacceptable moves. Brunias has captured the essence of a conflict between English- and French-speaking groups which is being settled by a stickfight,[3] shades of what was to come in Trinidad a century later as English and French creole speaking gangs squared off against each other in Port-of-Spain.

However, in the Dutch-speaking island of Curaçao, legislation had been enacted against stickfighting fifty years earlier.

> A decree dated April 15, 1720, stipulated that 'free blacks and slaves in and around towns were not allowed to go around with walking sticks on Sundays and other days and hit each other with these sticks'.[4]

The walking stick in Curaçao was called *garoti* or *koko makaku* in Papiamento, the Dutch creole language spoken by the black population. The *koko makaku* was used widely as a defensive weapon and for stick-dancing, stickfighting and the tambu game called 'blood for the drum' (sanger para tambu).[5] Stickfighting was also found in Trinidad and Cuba and came to prominence in both countries in the 19th Century. In Trinidad it was known as *kalenda* and in Cuba as *mani.* In both countries, dance and ritual were involved with the sport and its development and practice was mainly around towns and cities. Usually much of the stickfighting was dictated by the rhythm of the drums, that is, the movement of the feet (the dance) was dictated by the tempo and rhythm of the drums.

---

3. An original of this lithograph can be found in the Barbados Museum's Cunard Collection.

4. www.curacao.com/naam/english.html

5. www.curacao.com/naam/english.html

In Carriacou, the small island off Grenada, stickfighting was known as *bois* (wood) and was found in the villages of Mt. Desire and La Resource[6] while in Guyana it was called *setu*.

> [Setu] involved six or more men playing together using sticks of three and a half feet in length from the akya tree... This contest was sometimes accompanied by a drum and flute, but there was no singing... These sessions were held in canefield clearings, at Christmas or during holiday times, when players from different villages would challenge each other... Sessions also took place in 'the bush', that is, jungle clearing...[7]

In Haiti it was known as *kalinda* or *mousondi*, and in Guadeloupe as *mayolet*. All of these names evolved from specific African languages or more likely from the European languages dominant at the time—French, Spanish, or Dutch. The sport existed in Barbados also and was known as sticklicking.

But where did stick fighting in the Caribbean come from? Professor Maureen Warner-Lewis, in her book *Central Africa in the Caribbean* states that stickfighting in the Caribbean had its origins in Africa.

> Thus, as far as the African diaspora in the West Atlantic is concerned, the sport had its origins in several parts of Africa rather than in one, and it is these variations that led to the further evolution of several transatlantic forms during the period of slavery. These various transatlantic forms must already have been established by the time of arrival of nineteenth-century African immigrants, and these variants must already have constituted part of plantation creole culture. On the other hand, there must have been salient Central African inputs into these West Atlantic forms.... One may therefore hypothesize that in differing West Atlantic locations, morphological elements of African core combat types were either

6. Dr Donald R Hill, Tradition and Trinidad: The 1971 Carnival in Cariacou, Grenada, http://employees.oneonta.edu/hilldr/1971cc.htm

7. Maureen Warner-Lewis, p 200-1

abandoned or elaborated with varying emphases. Yet, given the wide-scale occurrence of migration throughout the Americas in past periods, whether legal or illegal, with masters or as runaways, in groups or individually, the complementary factor of diffusion within the Americas, cannot be ruled out. [8]

Harold Courlander, in *The Drum and the Hoe*, his study of Haiti, writes about observing a battle-dance called *mousondi*:

> The dancing took place around a bonfire. The music was provided by three musicians, two playing Congo drums and the third beating hardwood sticks against a board. Each of the dancers carried a stick about thirty inches long. They moved first clockwise, then counterclockwise, then half of them moved in one direction and half in the other, weaving in and out, holding their sticks like sabers. On a signal given by the older man, they leaped into the air and came together in mock combat. First one would strike and the other would parry, then the second would strike and the first would parry, always in time to the beating Congo drums.[9]

Courlander goes on to say:

> The testimony of older Haitians is that the Calinda was a stick dance, known also by the name Mousondi. In present-day Trinidad there is a Calinda dance which closely resembles the Mousondi; Puerto Rico has its Bomba Calindan; and under another name the 'battle-dance' survives among Negro communities in Suriname.... The stick dance (Battonie) of the Haitian carnival season ...is of more than passing interest for the reason that almost identical dances have been reported from some areas of West Africa.[10]

Joe Hoad,[11] the son of a white planter in Barbados and who

---

8. Maureen Warner-Lewis, p 207

9. Harold Courlander, p131-2

10. Harold Courlander, p 132-3

11. Hoad is from a family of Bajans who loved sports and participated in all types of sports – cricket, football, sailing, table tennis, shooting etc. Hoad emigrated to Australia where he became a Sports Psychologist. He had a stint working with the West Indies cricket team in 2003.

learned the art of sticklicking in the 1940s and 1950s from Stoway Trotman, a legendary Bajan sticklicker, said:

> Barbados stick fighting I believe mainly comes from the tribes of West Africa. There is still stick fighting in parts of Chad, Zimbabwe and I was told by an Ethiopian at Flinders University that it is practiced in the West of his country but it still has variations that are strongly linked to sabre fencing.[12]

Stickfighting did not seem to have a visible or major presence in Jamaica. There is a reference to sticklicking in Jamaica in F. G. Cassidy's *Dictionary of Jamaican English*. Olive Senior, in her book *Encyclopedia of Jamaican Heritage,* writes that:

> Stickfights are also recorded as part of the wake tradition and sticks play a role in dances associated with wakes, e.g. calembe[13] and limbo. Two stick-fighting dances, 'Warwick' and 'Kittihalli', have been recorded. Warrick has been found among the Kumina people of St. Thomas Parish.[14]

Veteran Jamaican journalist Hartley Neita recalls an incident when he was a boy. He had traveled with his grandfather to Linstead in St. Catherine. He said that he had heard rumours about stickfighting, but that it seemed to have been a secret activity. His grandfather left him at the front of a shop and disappeared behind the shop. After a long time, his grandfather returned with a gash on his head. His conclusion was that his grandfather was stickfighting, but he did not have specific proof and he did not have the right to question his grandfather, so he could not say for sure. Folklorist Dr. Olive Lewin, in a conversation with the author, said she saw stickfighting once in Brompton, near Black River in St. Elizabeth,

12. In an email from Joe Hoad who now lives in Australia

13. Raquel Z Rivera, http://www.allhiphop.com/features/?ID=558

14. Olive Senior, p 464

Jamaica. It was part of a Jonkonnu version of an English play.

However, Brian L. Moore and Michele A. Johnson in their book *Neither Led nor Driven: Contesting British Cultural Imperialism in Jamaica, 1865-1920,* wrote:

> Free fights also took the form of "sticklicking" ("stickfighting" in Trinidad), a sort of ritualistic social contest. For instance, at a "Queen's Party" that was held at Juno Pen, a few miles from Annotto Bay, to celebrate the August (emancipation) holidays in 1899, a fight occurred with sticklicking or "roast-wood", a name given to the sticks. By the time the fight had reached its climax, several people had been knocked down, speechless, with blood flowing from their wounds (principally in the head) "like water". Then many of the Annotto Bay folks, who seemed to have had the worst of it at Juno Pen, determined to have revenge as soon as the Juno Pen people went into town: "Having met them as desired, a fight again ensued at a place called 'Marking Stone,' near the railway station, on Thursday night, followed by another on Saturday evening which resulted in many more going to hospital, and the arrest of about nine of the 'ringleaders,' and noted 'warriors'." By the turn of the century the Jamaica Times declared, "Sticklicking is becoming a pastime"; in Kingston in October 1902 there was a big sticklicking at Tower and Church Streets that lasted for about forty-five minutes. Sticks, stones and other missiles were freely used by the combatants.[15]

Stickfighting in the Caribbean also absorbed European and Indian influences. Both European and Indian stickfighting seem to have long traditions. African stickfighting was dependent largely on historical circumstance. The extent and influence was primarily political and depended on which island or territory the various Europeans powers exercised authority in. Trinidad, which was ruled by Spain, France and England, reflected these cultural influences. In the case of the English territories, these influences came from three

15. Brian L Moore & Michele A Johnson, p. 156

different sources: English, Irish and Scottish forms of sticklicking. The presence of a larger number of English persons, both as planters and as militia members, most likely created some influence in Barbados as we will see later. The influence of

Indian stickfighting has been most prevalent in Trinidad in the post-emancipation period.

> It appears that from the time East Indians began to arrive in Trinidad (1845), African-Caribbean stick-fighting traditions (including absorption of European and Amerindian techniques) met those of the Indian subcontinent. Day notes this rivalry in the late 1840s, reporting: "A fight between the two races is a most ludicrous spectacle; for the physical inferiority of the Hindoo, is amply compensated by his superior strategy, and a well-organised combination amongst themselves. Whilst one is engaged stick to stick with a negro, another will creep between the legs of his countryman and pull his antagonist down. It usually requires white interference to put an end to the fray." [16]

And in Guyana:

> [A] young Indo-Guianese boy, Mohamed Zahie—alias Midnight Man—was convicted of leading large groups into business and homes to expel the employees. Armed with a stick, he directed the "operations" of a crowd, some of whose members had a band. (His possession of an alias hints at his participation in centipede or other quasi-criminal gangs.)[17]

16. John Cowley, p 66

17. Juanita de Barros, p 151

So whether visible or not, stickfighting existed in the Caribbean from the earliest days of settlement and it also would have existed in Barbados.

Barbados was unlike other Caribbean territories. Every square inch of land was owned and occupied by plantations. There were no crown lands. There was no possibility of maronage and establishment of isolated villages separate from the existing ruling group.

There were militias stationed all around the island to protect the planters, their crops and their land. Even after emancipation they were forced by law to live in the tenantry of the plantation they worked on. As a result of fear of the large numbers of blacks, many of them unemployed, the ruling classes, as a matter of course, started encouraging the migration of workers to other territories.

Barbados was not a recipient of post-emancipation 19th Century African immigration like many other Caribbean territories viz. Trinidad, Guyana, Jamaica, Cuba, Haiti, Grenada, Carriacou, and St. Kitts. This importation of free Africans along with the existing maronage helped to reinforce and re-invigorate African traditions in those territories. African-creoles in Barbados were evolved from the epitome of a creole culture born in slavery and maintained in the post-emancipation period by the oppression of the white planters. Added to this, Barbados remained an English colony from settlement until Independence in 1966. The dominant Anglican Church linked to the plantation openly demonstrated its racism. What this meant was that there was a general absence of words and phrases from other European languages in the Nation language of Bajans, yet in many areas it did not affect the Africanity of blacks in Barbados. Studies have indicated that like other peoples in the Caribbean, Bajans utilized African syntax structures in their use of and indigenization of language as well as literal translation of traditional African languages.[18]

African religions have all but disappeared in their traditional forms in Barbados. However, the religiosity of the African-creole population can be seen in the plethora of small churches distributed across Barbados in every tenantry or village. They expressed the concept of adopting the strong God of their conquerors and, like their traditional counterparts in Africa, any individual who feels he/she can be a healer or communicator or interpreter between his/her fellow man and the Higher Being, can establish a shrine or altar or church and gather those who are willing to follow his or her leadership into a congregation. This phenomenon can be found across plantation America represented by the one-door store-front churches in urban areas and a plethora of small churches in every community and village.[19]

The perpetration of the idea that Barbados was 'Little England', stemming from the attitudes of the white planters in the earliest

18. "...The linguistic and social forces originating particularly in sub-Saharan Africa have also played a striking part in that development; so striking indeed as to raise the question whether their influence has not been much greater... For a better start let the reader look at items like cut-eye, hard-ears, suck-teeth, etc – Caribbean compounds of English words as labels of Caribbean particularities of behaviour for which the etymological explanations are found in African languages. They are folk-translations, in word and deed, of African cultural 'modes'." (Dr Richard Allsopp – Dictionary of Caribbean English, Oxford University Press, 1996, p xxxi-xxxii)

19. "An outline of African Religiosity includes some vital elements, such as a cosmology in which God is central and is the Creator of humans. The group affirmed a basic theological declaration of African Religiosity namely, that GOD EXISTS. For example, the Ewe say "Mawu li" (God exists), the Akan " Nyame wo-ho" (God is there), the Yoruba "Olórun m be" (God exists), and in Swahili "Mungu yupo" (God exists, is there). This religiosity affirms the value and respect for life. It is expressed in vibrant liturgy in which symbols, art, music, dance, etc. predominate. It places a high degree of value on women, both on their own merits as persons and as nurturers of life. The spiritual and the physical are interconnected...

The complex area of religiosity is still prevalent in the use of charms and magic for success in examinations, football matches or sports, law courts, business transactions or search for good jobs. Likewise, witchcraft and sorcery are a social reality that affects many and leads sometimes to serious accusations and fights in the family and community. However, the work of the traditional doctors (medicine men and women) finds parallel in the healing work of the founders and "prophets" of the Independent/Indigenous Churches days of settlement, particularly in the late 17th Century, seemed to have prejudiced scholars as to the worth and contribution of black Bajans throughout history. Because of this lack of understanding, few scholars chose to study Barbados and the Bajan way of life as has been done in several other Caribbean territories.

For example, Bajan folk music was never recorded, nor were cultural expressions such as Landship or sticklicking ever studied or written about in depth until recently. There are, however, a couple of exceptions: the work of Jerome Handler *et al* on aspects of slave life and the short work of Elsie Clews Parsons, whose collection of traditional folk tales and riddles was published in the 1920s. A few Bajan scholars have recognized these omissions and have struggled through the years to make the rest of us aware of these unheralded elements: Hilton Vaughan, Gordon Belle, Cicely Parkinson-Squires, Frank Collymore, Dr. Henry Fraser, Trevor Marshall, Dr. Aviston Downes, Dr. Curwen Best, *et al.*

It is difficult to pinpoint the exact time when sticklicking started in Barbados, since those who recorded the history of Barbados never gave credence to the many cultural practices of blacks. To most contemporary writers, the life of blacks was of little interest. Unless their activities crossed the paths of whites, they were ignored. So stickfighting seemed to be completely invisible and was never mentioned in any of the historical books. Perhaps there were reports in the newspapers about it, but so far none of these reports have surfaced in the studies done on Barbados. However, we know

(that have branched off from Mission Churches and one another). The motto of these Churches would be: "We heal, therefore we are." They focus on healing and exorcism, which is an expression of partnership with traditional religiosity in moments of crisis...

Space and time have not vanquished expressions of traditional religiosity in places like Jamaica, Trinidad, and Tobago. In Haiti and the Dominican Island, these elements manifest in their own local way, like the Voodoo." (John Mbiti - The Contributions of Africa to the Religious Heritage of the World, http://www.wcc-coe.org/wcc/what/interreligious/cd37-14.html)

that sticks, among other improvised and accessible weapons, were used by Bussa and his cohorts in the rebellion of 1816. We can also extrapolate from information about stickfighting in surrounding territories, e.g. Trinidad, Virgin Islands, and Guyana, where there were reports of Bajans using sticks for fighting, the extent of sticklicking as it existed in Barbados.

The art of sticklicking has been known to black Bajans and utilized by them for several generations. Many a watchman carried a stick whether he worked on a plantation protecting factory yards or agricultural fields from praedial larceny, or in urban areas protecting commercial buildings. This stick was not for decoration or to use as a third leg for walking, but as a weapon of self defence. The black enslaved population assumed that ground provisions (potatoes, yams, cassava, eddoes and other vegetables) were theirs for the taking. They did not conceive that this action was stealing, but instead saw it as an extension of the overall arrangement of being the property of the plantation. There was no distinction of ownership between them and the produce of the land. So beyond the actual consumption of these victuals, some were taken illicitly to town to be sold. Many plantations used to send their trusted slaves with such provisions to be sold in town, so it would not have been difficult to add to the official inventory along the way. Watchmen were required to protect fields from night raiders. This arrangement became more critical after emancipation. Plantation management felt it prudent to use watchmen in these circumstances, especially since watchmen were introduced into Bridgetown from 1762[20] and maybe other towns (Speightstown and Holetown) and waterfront areas (Six Men's Bay, Oistins and The Crane).

Small Island Pride, the Grenadian born calypsonian, refers

20. Pedro Welch – Slave Society in the City, Ian Randle, 2003, p 163

in his calypso *Carnival Celebration*, that as a stickfighter he was going to behave like a Bajan stickfighter in the 18th Century. By this he is implying that 18th Century Bajans were noted stickfighters and by doing like them, he was going to collapse the city by licking all and sundry with his stick. Indeed, his self-acclaimed bold-facedness was unprecedented as he challenged two of Trinidad's most notorious and legendary stick fighters—Mastifay, to meet him at Croisee, and Cutouter, to meet him at Green Corner. Pure grand charge and bravado! It is ironic that Small Island Pride would choose to mention a Bajan sticklicker in his calypso when Grenada and its sister island of Carriacou were also noted for stickfighting.

Small Island Pride

In the 1840s and 1850s, planters in Barbados felt the pressure of having large numbers of blacks living on their plantations in what was known as tenantries. This pressure became more critical as sugar went through its cycle of low prices and with the 1816 Bussa revolt still strong in their consciousness, planters encouraged blacks to seek work in other Caribbean territories. Many Bajans as a result headed to BG, (British Guiana now Guyana), Trinidad, and the Virgin Islands. In BG and Trinidad, they joined other migrant workers that were being brought into the region to help work in the sugar industry. These migrants were coming from India, China, Madeira and West and Central Africa. This migration by Bajans was to continue for the remainder of the century in addition to newer destinations—Panama, Cuba, Brazil and the USA. For the purpose of this study, we will focus on the migration to Trinidad, the Virgin Islands, and to a lesser extent BG.

The Bajan immigrants were people who fled from the plantation fields or had been living in the burgeoning urban tenantries that were developing in and around Bridgetown—Carrington Village, Bay Land, Kensington, etc. [Tenantries were established around a piece of land as opposed to a barrack-yard which was based on a room in a yard or building.] Many of these men hung around the wharf looking for work unloading cargo from inter-island schooners and other ships. [Barbados also had other ports at Holetown, Speightstown, Six Men's, Oistins and The Crane.] In most cases, they found it difficult to get work. Out of crop season was also pretty hard for men as they were mainly utilized during the reaping of the crop. Women did most of the maintenance on the fields. John Cowley, in his book *Carnival Canboulay and Calypso*, points out that the economic situation in Barbados and the Eastern Caribbean was such that by January 1870:

> Migration from smaller islands (including Barbados) [had] increased pressure on accommodation, jobs and all other aspects of survival among the poor in Trinidad. Unfortunates were seen as an incomprehensible underworld, and feared and loathed accordingly. Thus the diametre came to be made up of stickmen, singers, drummers, dancers, prostitutes (another meaning of jamette), bad johns (swashbucklers), matadors (madames), dunois (jamette rowdies), makos (panders), obeahmen (practitioners of magic) and corner boys. All were associated with a culture that revolved around the barrack-tenement yards of Port of Spain and similar locations elsewhere in the island. Migrant groups competed with one another, and more established settlers, for territory. At the same time, the diametre flaunted themselves (especially during the masquerade) to sustain their identity and draw attention to their plight in a society in which they were decried." [21]

In Barbados, it was easy for a man to get access to an inter-island schooner and disembark more or less where ever he wanted in the Caribbean.

21. Cowley, p 72

Most of the Bajans immigrants were reared in the rough and tumble world of the Bridgetown Careenage. A travel writer (and a postcard) 50 years later described children on the wharves of the careenage as wharf rats. What he was describing were children whose daily living was a scramble for survival. Bajans found a world in Trinidad where survival of the fittest was required. They had no attachments; no family, no women, no rootedness. They were free to take what they wanted if they could. They were bad and people knew it. The French creole-speaking population corrupted the word Bajan to 'bad john'. The authorities blamed Bajans and other migrants for many of the problems that developed around Port of Spain, especially at carnival time. John Cowley quotes the report from the Colonial Office investigation of the Canboulay Riots of 1881, which stated that:

> The bands are a creation of quite recent times, and they are largely fed by immigrants from other islands, the number of whom is constantly increasing. [22]

On another occasion when a group that the police said was composed of 'rogues and vagabonds' held a drum dance or bamboula in the yard of a Congo man on Easter Monday:

> The participants were described subsequently as members of 'the two notorious bands' of Arouca. They were 'composed not only of the riff-raff of the creole population, but also of Barbadians... of the worst type.' [23]

The English-speaking Bajans were in a culture milieu that was primarily French-speaking, reflecting the historical circumstance of that country. The British colonial government had several disputes to deal with on an on-going basis. For example, the British

22. Cowley, p 2

23. Cowley, p 122

rulers were Protestant/Anglican in a country that was dominated by Roman Catholicism. The French creole elites did not warm to the British officials. In this state of continuous conflict, the common folk organized themselves to survive. Again Cowley reports:

> During the last quarter of the century the diametre formed themselves into self-perpetuating units. Such bandes, like plantation slaves before them, were divided into English-Creole- and French-Creole-speaking groups. In the 1870s, the English Creoles were principally migrants from Barbados who had come to Trinidad in search of work. [24]

He quotes the *Port-of-Spain Gazette* editorial of January 12, 1884 that it was:

> ...the ruffiantly bands, organised by the most desperate characters, men and women; thieves, vagabonds, prostitutes [who] took possession of the town from midnight on the Sunday preceding Ash Wednesday. It noted how 'in former days no Police Force was required to control the cannes-boulees'. Blame was again apportioned to 'the large immigration of roughs from Barbados and other islands. [25]

But what made the Bajans so bad and so much hated? I can only conclude that they were bold, brazen and licked stick with a vengeance. Here's Cowley again describing a confrontation in 1891 known as the Arouca Riot.

> Between 8:00 and 9:00 on the same Tuesday morning, the principal stickmen came down the road and stopped in front of the police station. They parried their sticks, sang 'diametre songs', and shouted 'sortee, sortee, come out and we will give you

24. Cowley, p 135

25. Cowley, p 99

> something', and 'if you come out today we will give your flesh to the birds'. This bravado lasted about fifteen minutes, after which they retired to the yard of 'Simeron' and set themselves up with bottles and stones pending an expected fight.
>
> Police reinforcements were dispatched from Port of Spain and, after their arrival, two parties were sent out 'unarmed' to look for the stickmen. In the ensuing court case, one witness reported that the police carried long sticks (which seems likely), but this evidence was rejected. The party led by Superintendent Sergeant Fraser encountered the band at 'Simeron's' yard and were routed. Fraser was knocked to the ground and his blood said to have been drunk by 'Bulbul Tigre' (one of three fighting names adopted by Arthur Augustin). Fraser however escaped with his life. [26]

Cowley noted that "most black policemen were from Barbados and doubly disliked."[27] No wonder the police were armed with long sticks!

In December 1891, there was a battle between the English-speaking band Canelle led by Gooty, and a French-speaking band Typean led by Eli. Cowley summarizes the report in the press:

> One Man is another fighting name mentioned in the newspaper report. This may have been One Man Bisco whose exploits were commemorated in song. Bisco was remembered in 1919 as a 'notable stick fighter' and in the 1950s as 'the greatest terror in Canboulay.' He was an exponent of Bajan stick (a similar sport to Stickfighting kalenda, from the English-speaking island of Barbados). This fact, and his membership of the Freegrammars (in which he was recalled as having been its 'second king') suggests he was one of the many black migrants drawn to Trinidad from Barbados. [28]

As I stated before, Bajan immigrants also went to the Virgin

26. Cowley, p 122-3

27. Cowley, p 83

28. Cowley, p 126-7

Drawing of Labourers' revolt in Virgin Islands in 1878 taken from Prof. Isaac Dookhan's - *History of the Virgin Islands of the United States.*

Islands—St. Thomas, St. John and St. Croix. Professor Isaac Dookhan recorded in his *A History of the Virgin Islands of the United States* that:

> Barbadians began to arrive between 1860 and 1861 and, in addition, a small number of freemen from the Dutch West Indies migrated to St. Croix after they were emancipated on July 1, 1863; by 1864 as many as 1,700 immigrants had arrived from Barbados and St. Eustatius. [29]

In October 1878, there was an Agricultural Labourers' Revolt in St. Croix. According to Professor Dookhan, "Sticks were the only weapons carried, and fire was the principal means of destruction."[30] After arresting 403 labourers and a trial of 18 months, 336 were freed, but:

29. Dookhan, p 226

30. Dookhan, p 230

> ...the trial revealed active participation of the newly arrived immigrants from the other West Indian islands. Of the so-called leaders, two were from Barbados, and one each from St. Eustatius, Antigua, St. Kitts and Jamaica. Among the other participants imprisoned, eleven were from Barbados, nine from Antigua and four from other islands. However the only four women imprisoned were native born. [31]

When the emancipation/apprenticeship period ended in 1838, all the Caribbean territories with the exception of Barbados suffered from a shortage of labour on the plantations. As a result, many of the territories, especially the larger ones, started to import labour from India, China, the Madeira Islands and Africa.

> West Indian planters, including those in British Guiana, also began importing contract labourers from abroad. Bound to the plantations for up to five years and liable to harsh penalties for violating their contracts, these workers were to provide the inexpensive, plentiful estate labour the planters craved. Immigrants—mostly indentures labourers from India, Portugal, China, Java, and Africa—migrated to French, Spanish, Dutch, and British territories in the Caribbean; in the British West Indies, of the approximately 536,000 immigrants who arrived between 1834 and 1918, about 56 per cent went to British Guiana. This included close to 80 per cent (or 32,216) of the 40,971 Portuguese migrants to the British West Indies; 55 per cent (or 238,909) of the 429,623 Indians; 75 per cent (13,533) of the 17,904 Chinese; and about 35 per cent (or 14,060) of the 39,332 Africans, most of whom were from West or West Central Africa. [32]

British Guiana was one of these countries. It was originally made up of three colonies owned by the Dutch: Berbice, Demerara, and Esequibo. These colonies only became British in 1803 and finally amalgamated in 1813 to form British Guiana.

31. Dookhan, p 231

32. Juanita de Barros, p 21-22

British Guiana had slave revolts in 1763 and 1823. But after emancipation "Indentured labourers [rebelled] some eleven times between 1869 and 1913. Georgetown rioted four times in the early post-emancipation period—in 1856, 1889, 1905, and 1924".[33] The 1856 and the 1889 riots were caused by dissatisfaction of black Guianese over how they were treated by the Portuguese merchants who operated stalls in the public markets. There was a general feeling that the Portuguese merchants were dishonest. However, the riots of 1905 and 1924 were a result of labour agitation for better wages and working conditions.[34] In these riots, sticks and throwing of stones were used.

> They also attacked any Portuguese in their path, throwing stones and "beating them with sticks." [35]
>
> (A)nd, in one or two instances, some Englishmen who attempted to protect the Portuguese were hit by sticks and other weapons. [36]
>
> Likewise, large groups of labourers, "armed with sticks and beating drums," entered the manager's houses at Plantations Providence, Peter's Hall, Diamond, and Farm and forced the servants to leave. The crowds in 1924 were described as festive. Those in Georgetown, whether participating in the house and business invasions or watching on the sidelines, "danced and shouted" and waved sticks in the air. [37]

The activities of the crowds in 1889, 1905, and 1924 resonate with traditional festivities. People carried sticks (similar to the swords of Jonkannu?) and danced and sang (as they did during Christmas festivities and, indeed, as they did in Africa, suggesting that continent

33. Juanita de Barros, p 138-9

34. Juanita de Barros, p 139

35. Jaunita de Barros, p 141

36. Juanita de Barros, p 141

37. Juanita de Barros p 146

as a source of cultural inspiration). But crowd behaviour in 1905, and particularly in 1924, also echoed other traditions, particularly, stickfighting. In both 1905 and 1924 members of crowds were armed with sticks. These, of course, were the 'centipede' weapon of choice, but their use, particularly during disorder in the streets, resonated with stickfighting. Descriptions of the confrontation in 1924 irresistibly suggest a stickfight: the members of the crowd at La Penitence Bridge were armed with sticks and were dancing, beating drums, and waving flags and banners.[38]

All of these quotations come from Juanita de Barros' study of Georgetown from 1889-1924. Her primary sources were mainly colonial office documents—reports from the Governor, the Colonial Secretary, the Commissioner of Police, *et al.* These reports seem devoid of details that would indicate who the stickfighters were.

For the purpose of this paper, the question needs to be asked. Were Bajans involved in these riots and if so, were they some of the persons carrying sticks and involved in stickfighting? Let us look first at the question of Bajan involvement. We note the role that Bajans played in Trinidad and the Virgin Islands during the latter half of the 19th Century. Bajans seemed to have acquired an aggressiveness not usually displayed in Barbados.

When the British government took over the territories of Berbice, Demerara and Essequibo in 1803, very few, if any, Afro-Guianese had English names. Black people's names were a corollary of slavery and plantation life in the colonies. If the colonial power was England, names tended to be English. If it was France, then the names were French. It was the same for Holland, Spain, Portugal and Denmark. The advent of the British so late in the history of Guiana did not give them enough time to breed African women like their planter

38. Juanita de Barros, p 150

cousins in other parts of the English-speaking Caribbean.

Bajan workers, then with their English names, invaded BG from the 1840s onwards and it is reasonable to assume that those persons with surnames like Nurse, Scott, Greenidge, Williams, Bowen, Cox, Archer, Marshall, Russell, Murray, Rollins, Ford, Reid, Brown, Thorne, Browne, Payne, Smith, Jordan, Davis, Osborne, Carrington, Holder, Thomas, Lewis, Edwards, Drakes and Critchlow were Bajans or children of Bajans. All of these names were names of persons involved in the riots, the carrying of sticks, and were at some point charged before the courts for disorderly behaviour. Critchlow was definitely a Bajan and was founder of the British Guiana Labour Union (BGLU), the main force behind the riots of 1905 and 1924.[39]

Besides the riots there were a number of gangs operating in Georgetown using sticks and stickfighting. These were called the centipede gangs or the more colloquial 'santapee gangs'. Santapee gangs were made up of poor men and women who in their youth were known as wharf rats 'thieving and scavenging on the docks'.[40]

> The members of centipede gangs shared with the rest of Georgetown's poor more than economic insecurity and the constant threat of unemployment: they also shared residential and recreational geography. Centipedes were associated with areas of working-class residence in Georgetown, particularly with Tiger Bay, an area of riverside wharves and warehouses. Both gathered at street-corner rum shops, loitering about the street. [41]
>
> Centipedes were signified by their possession of hackia sticks (produced from an extremely hard, local wood).[42] Police, local

39. His son Critch Ivan (Ivan Critchlow) was an impresario and promoter who lived in Barbados from the fifties. In discussions with the author he confirmed the existence of Bajan sticklickers in BG.

40. This term was also used to described Bajan boys whose photos appeared on several 19th Century postcards

41. Juanita de Barros, p 90

42. Also known in Barbados as ockya-stick (Dr Richard Allsopp),

> political leaders, and, indeed, "respectable" observers relied upon the presence of these weapons to identify gang members. The significance of sticks was codified in legislation (anti-centipede laws usually mentioned them) and invariably cited in prosecutions. Yet these weapons, useful as they were to members of the superordinate classes, played an important cultural role among the gang members themselves, who employed them in a kind of ritualistic, mock-ferocious fashion that alluded to both Afro- and Indo-Creole traditional cultural practices. The origins of stick-carrying and stick-wielding are uncertain, but suggest the influence of both Afro-Creole and Indo-Creole traditions. During the period of slavery, slaves in some parts of the Caribbean carried sticks, a tradition retained in the post-emancipation period.[43]

De Barros cites the case of two rival gangs fighting to control their own territories.

> A 1924 battle between two urban gangs illuminates the importance of place. The rival gangs were the Berlin Team (captained by Percival "Beast of Berlin" Greenidge) and the Peppersauce Team (captained by Ezekiel Williams), and their 1924 clash ended in the death of the latter's captain.[44]

It is also interesting to note that throughout the period of these disturbances, the colonial government boosted up the police force in order to deal with the various gangs. Many of the members of the force were Bajans. As a matter of fact during the 1880s, the majority of policemen were Bajans. In 1881, there were four times as many Bajan non-commissioned officers compared to Afro-Guianese creoles. The same applied to privates. By the mid 1910s, Bajan police dropped to about one-sixth of the number of Guianese police.[45] When the 1889 riot occurred, "Barbados sent a man-of-war and sixty-five men at British Guiana's request."[46] The same support

43. Juanita de Barros, p 91

44. Juanita de Barros, p 93

45. Juanita de Barros, p 44

came from Barbados in 1905. However, there was a great deal of mistrust by the white colonial authorities who wanted whites to protect them. They supposedly settled for Bajan police with the hope that they would not join forces the Afro-Guianese agitators.[47]

> ...Caribbean historians have noted the preference for the use of Barbadian police throughout the region—a preference which, according to [Howard] Johnson, was influenced by perceptions of Barbadians as a "martial race". [48]

There are many questions arising from this information. Did these Bajan policemen use sticks like their counterparts in Trinidad? Were there Bajans in these stick-fighting gangs? Many of the Bajan migrants to Trinidad and the Virgin Islands were of the same ilk that went to Guyana. Were there sticklickers among them also? In Bajan sticklicking the term *satu* is used to describe a formal stickfight. Is this a corruption of the Guyanese word for a form of sticklicking called *setu*?[49] Dr. Richard Allsopp, in a personal conversation, suggested that setu may be a Hindu word which would indicate the Indian influence on stickfighting in Guyana. This fact of Indian influence on stickfighting in Guyana was noted by de Barros.

Finally, over 60,000 Bajans migrated to Panama to work on the Canal. My grandfather and a great uncle were among them. It would be very hard for me to believe that those Bajans did not carry sticklicking with them. I saw Tuk Bands, donkey belly and maypole dancing being performed in Havana, Cuba at CARIFESTA 1979. I heard some traditional Bajan songs and also heard the pleas of these Panamanians for closer relationship with Barbados.

46.Juanita de Barros, p 153

47.Juanita de Barros, p 153-167

48.Juanita de Barros, p 182

49.Professor Maureen Warner-Lewis, p 200

In concluding this introduction, the following points can be made.

1. Bajans were prominent in the underworld culture of Trinidad.

2. Bajans were involved in stickfighting and gangs i.e. Kalenda and Canboulay in Trinidad, and most likely the santapee gangs in Guyana.

3. Bajans earned a reputation of 'badness' and were disliked by the social establishment in Trinidad.

4. Many Bajans were also policemen in Trinidad and Guyana and they would also fight with sticks.

5. Bajans had a form of stickfighting that was different from Trinidad stickfighting, kalenda. The Bajan form of stickfighting was referred to as Bajan stick or sticklicking.

6. Bajans seemed to be very aggressive outside of Barbados.

7. Bajans were considered a martial people.

Stickfighting in Grenada.

Stickfighting in Trinidad between Joey Hamilton and Gilbert Frederick in the 1980s

Sticklicking competition in Barbados

Bajan Sticklicking

"...we gine block evry blow dem can pelt
like a sin Andrew stick man..."

Kamau Brathwaite - *Sun Poem*: "Hereroes"

What, then, is Bajan stick/licking and is it different from Trinidad stickfighting also known as kalenda?

Bajan sticklicking is similar yet different from Trinidad kalenda. The similarities between them are the shared art form that requires good eyesight, good footwork, strong wrists and hands, and a certain athleticism. Kalenda had certain rituals associated with it. The use of music, especially drums, singing and dancing were an integral part of this ritual. Music too played a significant role in sticklicking, but was never integrated within the art form like kalenda. Music through the dance hall, singings and service o' songs provided the occasions for ramps (sticklicking fights) to take place. According to Colvin Brathwaite, a sticklicker who went by the name of Mud Soup:

> "They used to have dances down there every Saturday Night. We would go there and dance and watch so much sticklicking. Sticklicking and service o' song, they used to have on Sundays. Dance Saturday, service o' song and sticklicking on Sundays."

Many of the locations identified by sticklickers or observers were invariably dance houses (dancehalls) or community centres where some form of music and dancing took place. Of course rum shops and village spaces were the stomping grounds for the ubiquitous Tuk Bands which were almost always present. Gullyboar talks about the legendary Edwy Taylor, the drum maker, drummer, masquerader and Tuk Band leader:

> "Now, the month of December that man Edwy Taylor—these people should be highly recommend. He used to got the whole of Christ Church pon he back. In the month of December two or three weeks before Christmas you would see he down dey in Water Street, yuh see Edward come up wid de band. (He died in the Almshouse.) He got a son yuh call Bumma - Archie Bumma (Potato Mout). He is a cousin to these children by mother and Edwy gone right way up to the Engine House Hill and Mr. Mottley, when Edwy tek up dah drum and kittle and coming back down the people running from all over the bridge and ting, yuh know where duh gine end up, all the way down Maxwell Hill and gone down Top Rock and come up Maxwell long road to hit back through to Oistins. Dah is coming to Christmas."

Magical protection from an obeah-man was also used by some kalenda players.

> One informant who 'played stick' while old African people were still alive would go to his grandfather to secure protection for his fights. His grandfather would give him a 'guard', or amulet, and hold prayers to ensure his success. In Grenada, 'ranging stick' was the term for drilling the stick head and infusing it with ingredients. These activities were done to defend the stickman against fighters with bad stick: men hit you a stick in those days, you blow like that and worm come from your nose" [50]

In sticklicking, obeah seemed to have been used. Sticklicking master Elvis Gill describes one 'use' of obeah in the preparation of a stick, although he does not give details of the process or how the powers were invoked.

"Then if you preparing the stick to damage or injure the person

50. Prof Maureen Warner-Lewis, p 209

without causing any bruise blood or anything, when you done swinge it and everything, instead of using linseed oil, yuh use urine pee. Now wid dat dey claim dat yuh can hit a man and he won't even swell up."

But Aberdeen Jones, the formidable Gall Hill, Christ Church sticklicker, related that most Trinidadians believe Bajans' prowess at sticklicking was due to obeah:

> "Duh say dat some fellows got de ting yuh call obeah. When yuh brek a lash heah, one heah, the main stick hit yuh heah. One stick. Dah was de saying. You know all we do in Trinidad, dey say yuh like obeah. Yuh get whuh ah mean. But I never believe in dat shite doah. The only obeah I believe in gawblineyuh is de food in we mout to eat."

Aberdeen is a little bit disingenuous, but there is no doubt that the obeah (wo)man was a ubiquitous figure in Barbadian society up until the middle of the 20th Century and was consulted by the general public on a regular basis to solve a variety of personal problems. Here is Aberdeen again:

> "You, I know fellows who use to go tuh a man for some obeah to play cards. And dah man will gi yuh obeah tuh play cards and becrise play wid he and he cyan win a cent. Ah use to dead wid laff...."

However there is no way of including or excluding such details with respect to sticklicking. Obeah was another invisible practice that is unknown to and un-pursued by scholars and other writers.[51]

Obeah as a magico-religious practice was prevalent in Barbados even though it was against the law. In the early 1970s, while campaigning for parliament, one of my constituents was an obeah-man by the name of Black Ben. Black Ben not only gave me and

51. My bother Elliott is a lawyer who qualified in 1961. Many of his clients brought summonses burnt at the corners, with burnt notches along each side and throughout the document. The document was also wet and slimy from being sewed up in a crapaud's (frog) mouth.

the others accompanying me advice on how to protect ourselves, but he chased us from his home at dusk because he said he could not protect us from some of the spirits that were visiting him. Later in the decade, I was in a televised debate with the then Bishop of Barbados, Drexel Gomez, and an obeah-man named Racketeer Clarke. The Bishop refused to acknowledge the existence of obeah. Clarke made the point that members of the congregation of St. Michael's Cathedral would leave the church on Sunday nights and come over to his place near JK Hunte shop, where the Central Bank is now located, to get bush baths and other treatments and/or protection for the following week.

In the eighties, I hosted a program on radio called *At the Stand-pipe*.[52] On one particular night my guest was a well know obeah-man from the city. The switch board was jammed with calls from listeners who wanted advice from and information on how to reach him. On another program, *Duppy Dust*,[53] which dealt with cultural matters, people called to solicit information on how to remove 'spirits' from their homes. I put them on to an obeah-man from Pinelands, who openly practiced the traditional science.[54] Pharmacists in Barbados were also expected to treat customers' psychic ills and maintain their well-being. Many of them were considered obeah (wo)men based on these practices. If this practice still existed in the last quarter of the 20th Century, then what was it like in the 19th and early 20th Centuries? There is no doubt that sticklickers would have been among those who sought magical powers to assist them.

52. At the Stand-pipe was aired on CBC Radio and mirrored what people would discuss when they met at the stand-pipe to collect water.

53. Duppy Dust was on Voice of Barbados. It dealt with black culture on the basis that physical residue was dust and spiritual residue was duppy. So all pas cultural expression including books, records, etc was combined to tell a story.

54. Prof Vincent O'Neale studied in Haiti, Africa and India and continues to practice in Pinelands, a large working class community in St Michael, Barbados

Of course, the use of a wooden stick is a necessity to both forms of stickfighting. Kalenda sticks were made from cog-wood, yellow poui, gasparee, anaree or sour-guava. Sticklicking

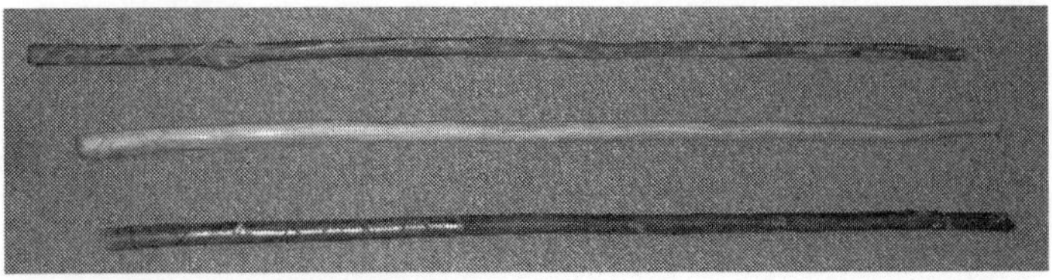

Sticks prepared for fighting (Elvis Gill)

sticks were made from common or wild guava, black willow, rad wood, baywood (wild bay leaf), calimantis, ockya or long sage. In both art forms, sticks were about 80-100 cms (32-40 ins) long. Sticklicking sticks were selected on the basis of weight, strength, shape and colour. Weight was important, in that sticks should not be so heavy as to tire the arm and shoulder of the sticklicker. The grain of the wood was important to its strength and sticklickers preferred to use young saplings of the right size and length to be converted into fighting sticks.

Sticks for kalenda were sometimes prepared in particular ways.

> There were secret formulas for cutting the wood and preparing a stick. One method was to cut a stick when the moon was weak and the night was dark. The bark was then peeled off and the stick was pushed into the heart of a rotting banana tree trunk and left there for seven days and seven nights. It was then taken out, covered with tallow, and buried in a manure heap where it cured for fourteen days. After this, the stick was removed and was bent and rolled. It was then concealed in a dark place for seven more days before it was considered ready for use. [55]

In Barbados, sticklickers would have several sticks and these were prepared in different ways depending on their intended use. Elvis Gill outlines the various preparations.

55. www.silvertorch.com/its%20a%20fact/various-2htm

> "Yuh cut yuh stick and put it pun an open fire, green as it is and rub [on] engine oil—used engine oil. Years ago dey used to use linseed oil pun it but you'll find that engine oil is readily available now so yuh use de old engine oil dat work in an engine, rub it pun de stick and swinge it thru de open fire. When yuh finish dat, yuh cud skin it de same time or yuh cud put it down two or three days and then skin it. If it got in any bends, yuh set it to tek out de bends. When yuh done skin it, den yuh get linseed oil and rub it and polish it and keep working wid it to flex it and straighten it all de time. And yuh keep doing dah till... The more linseed oil you put pun it, the more sturdy it becomes. If you do it, use linseed oil every week pun it. After six or seven months, it is a proper stick. It ent gun flake, it ent gun break."

For special performances:

> "Like stage performance, or you gun do a show, yuh do the same ting wid it but de only ting yuh do, is then put it some place cool or humid or bury it in sand and let it stand dey for a week. All de time if the sand dry out, yuh wet it, yuh wet de sand. But if yuh got it in a humid area dat is cold, when you done, yuh tek it out, yuh linseed it and den you cud start using it."

The prominent Jamaican consultant, Dr. Trevor Hamilton, who grew up in St. Elizabeth in the small village of New Market, described the use of sticks by members of the community. Although in his time the science of sticklicking was less than artistic, he described the preparation of the sticks, usually wild guava and packy (calabash tree) using methods similar to those in Trinidad and Barbados.

> "The length of the stick was important and the curing of it. The guys who really did it were professional, but the guys who would do it with a little more finesse were the guys who would actually treat the stick. The guys would tell you that the fresh stick is not as penetrating whether you beat a horse or a man. You would normally cure the stick, so you would cut the stick and you would cure it, cure it... You can use the sun or hang it

up in the smoke in the outdoor kitchen where you have wood-fire smoke going up like how we used to dry the tobacco. So you would normally dry the stick for 14 to 21 days before it is used for whatever it is supposed to be used for. And it's cured. It is a way to bringing out all the moisture."

"...They used linseed oil the same way we used to use linseed oil, mostly, to give the stick some flexibility. In fact when I was growing up we used the linseed oil for the stick, for the bat. It was something we used which gives some kick."[56]

Bajan sticklickers speak a lot about sticklicking styles. These styles were made up of a number of sciences which were primarily influenced by British boxing rules and regulations that developed over the latter half of the 19th Century and were probably brought to the island by sailors and members of the militias. These styles were: Tom Johnson, Queensberry, Donnelly, Sword, Creole, and Swab. It is important to emphasise that the art of sticklicking preceded these so-called sciences that evolved in Europe, and it seems that the acceptance of these sciences by blacks was their way of seeking legitimization of the art form. Black Bajans have consistently done this in the face of the dominant and domineering authority of the white power structure. Bajans have a term for this. It is called "cutting and contriving." Tuk drummers used it for generations by pretending to use European rhythms, especially the march, to camouflage their persistent use of traditional African rhythms.

Many sticklickers define themselves as practitioners of one or more of these styles. Maybe some of these techniques were used

56. See Appendix B for the whole interview

in the past, but by the end of the 20th Century it was difficult to distinguish one from the other. However, in attempting to unravel the differences in these styles, a number of things are evident. Tom Johnson, Queensberry and Donnelly all relate to boxing. Tom Johnson was named after Tom Johnson:

> ...the bare-knuckle champion of England from 1784 to 1791... [who was a] ...courageous and skilful fighter and was regarded by his contemporaries as having plenty of 'bottom' i.e., ability to take punishment." [57]

Bare-knuckle boxing:

> was little more than "street" fighting, anything is fair, and the last one standing won. Betting was heavy on these events. Often the bout began with cudgels and the first round of betting was on "first blood" at which point the match changed to fisticuffs, with further betting on the final outcome. [58]

Johnson was known to fight 62 rounds before he won the fight. You will note in the last quotation that boxing may start with cudgeling before moving on to fist fighting. Cudgeling is a form of stickfighting using a "short thick stick as a weapon."

Queensberry seems to be more associated with boxing rules created by the Marquis of Queensberry to govern boxing contests of endurance. There were probably introduced after 1865. These rules specified that rounds should last three minutes long with one minute of rest between rounds.[59] In kalenda, you could not hit below the waist, while in sticklicking, to quote Aberdeen Jones, "Barbadians brek from yuh toe nail to yuh eye broo [brow] and if yuh doan be careful de cap of yuh head gone too!" Head cuts in Kalenda

57. Jack Anderson: *Pugilistic Prosecutions: Prize Fighting and the Courts in Nineteenth Century Braitain.* http://www2.umist.ac.uk/sport/SPORTS%20HISTORY/BSSH/The%20 Sports%20Historian/TSH%2021-2/Art3-Anderson.htm

58. http://www.georgianindex.net/Sport/Boxing/boxing.html

59. See Appendix E

were drained in the 'blood hole'. In sticklicking it was "hell, heaven or de hospital."

Donnelly science was named after Ned Donnelly who styled himself as the 'Professor of Boxing to the London Athletic Club'. A former boxer, he published a pamphlet called *The Art of Boxing: The Manly Art of Self Defence* in 1886. In 1898, R.G. Allanson-Winn and C. Phillipps-Wolley published a book called *Broadsword and Single-Stick, with Chapters on Quarter-Staff, Bayonet, Cudgel, Shillalah, Walking-Stick, and Other Weapons of Self-Defence*. In chapter IV, Phillipps-Wolley described the art of the single stick as he thinks it should be practiced. Describing the first position, he wrote:

> And now as to position—the first position from which every attack, feint, or guard, begins. Ned Donnelly, the great boxer, used to tell his pupils that if a man knew how to use his feet, his hands would take care of themselves. And what is undoubtedly true in boxing is equally true in fencing. "Look that your foundations are sure" should be every fighting man's motto. Take trouble, then, about the position of the feet from the first. [60]

Here then is the relationship of Donnelly to sticklicking. We can also surmise that Donnelly science is therefore more associated with the broad sword/single stick style.[61] This style was a combination of the use of the English tradition of the sabre and the French style of fencing. The sabre used the side of the weapon and the rapier

60.http://ejmas.com/jmanly/articles/2001/jmanlyart_Phillipps-Wolley_1101.htm. Also see Appendix I, p. 290

61. These books were expensive and not widely circulated or available to the average person. However the knowledge of the techniques would have found currency with the men of the military, sailors and seamen, and sports men in general.

used in fencing used the point. Single stick style combined both techniques. That is the basis of Donnelly science.

Creole science represents the indigenization of all the influences combined to create a national or regional style. Sticklickers were influenced by fighters from across Barbados, first and foremost, absorbing defensive and attacking moves according to their effectiveness. These may include the flamboyance of different sticklickers and their individual idiosyncrasies. Like language, creolity develops out of national needs, and sticklicking developed a particular style that is known as Bajan stick or sticklicking. Swab is a creole style that is dependent on how the stick is held—at the end like a walking stick. Essentially it allows for twirling of the stick above the head and in front of the body. A sticklicker by the name of Prince describes it this way:

> "Rain could be falling and when them sticklickers start to swirl their sticks over their heads, you could shelter under them like an umbrella."

Regardless of the science or style used, the aim of sticklicking is to target various parts of the body and force the surrender of your opponent.

- Head – front, top, and sides
- Body – front, sides, and shoulders
- Stick hand – upper arm, fore arm, and knuckles
- Leg – thighs, knees, shins, and toes
- Crotch – testicles

Sticklicking has a number of names for the various lashes/cuts/chops that are delivered in the various sciences or styles: head lash, waist lash, shoulder-plex or shoulder-clutch, knee pad, strollop or waterline, knuckle or sliding, wet lash, sudden death & long sickness, ear bang, long seven or open seven, creole joint, overthrow, and the knife. In kalenda for example, you could not hit below the waist, but in sticklicking anything goes. Striking at the crotch was not an accepted target outside of Barbados, but in Barbados a lash to the crotch was called a strollop and was used quite often.

A formal organized sticklicking competition was called a satu. Competitors were judged according to set rules. They were judged on:

- Science and technique
- Response and accuracy
- Flair and style
- Control
- Speed
- Dominance
- Subduing
- Disarming

The most essential part of sticklicking is defence. There is a defence or guard for each targeted area. Informal battles were called ramps and could take place literally anywhere.

In the early part of the 20th Century, kalenda and the structure of stickfighting in Trinidad evolved into more individual contests taking place in stickfighting yards, with such names as Lacu Harp, Lacu Pebwa (Breadfruit Tree Yard), Hell Yard, Toll Gate, Behind the Bridge, Concrete Yard, Mafoomba Yard.

In sticklicking, there were no marauding gangs or bands, but there were organized ramps or satus (setu was the name of such fights in British Guiana) at Easter, Whitsuntide, August 1, Christmas, and New Year's Day. There were other occasions at singings, service o'

songs, outings, fairs, and agricultural exhibitions. Sticklicking also took place on Saturdays or Sundays in various spaces—plantation yards, rumshop yards, open pastures, crossroads like De Mingo in St. George, theatres and community clubs or dance houses. However, sticklickers generally could fight at any time in defence of the weak and disadvantaged. Most of the time, however, they fought informally for all sorts of reasons: grudges, to protect a friend, for a bottle of rum which was the usual prize in contests at and around rumshops, and/or to defend or obtain a reputation.

Early kalenda fighters were organized into bands or gangs along social lines. In some cases as we saw above, these gangs could have been based along language lines—French-creole or English-creole speakers or organized along communities or occupations like clerks and 'jacket men'. In sticklicking there were no gangs perpetuating themselves, but they may have been organized around communities—Silver Sands or St. Phillip (cf Fish Soup vs Cane Juice) or ad-hocly for a specific purpose (cf Aberdeen Jones). Generally though, sticklicking was more or less organized around occupations. According to Trevour Bay Brown, an 83 year old informant:

> "The fellows used to play in grades. They had masons, carpenters, agricultural workers [and so on]... Agricultural workers couldn't play the masons or carpenters as the masons felt that the agricultural workers was below them."

This was perhaps a practice from earlier times, but by the latter half of the 20th Century, these class distinctions became very blurred. Druggists, jewelers, plantation managers, sportsmen and other persons in the middle classes also pursued the sport.

In both kalenda and sticklicking, players exhibited a certain bravado and indomitable spirit. In the quotation from Cowley about the Arouca riots in 1891, the principal stickmen challenged the police to come out to fight:

> "Sortee, sortee, come out and we will give you something, [and] if you come out today we will give your flesh to the birds." [62]

In Barbados, Gullyboar recalls how in the 1940s one Albert challenged him through the plantation manager:

> "Mr. Ward tell you that Albert tell you [he gun] gih yuh flesh to the birds in the air and yuh bones to the dogs of the earth."

Those who are familiar with the bible would know that these words are similar to those exchanged between David and Goliath before their epic fight. Aberdeen Jones relates how he broke up an organized celebration for Princess Margaret in the 1950s in front of the police:

> "And when the first fellow in front rush to me and I do so and so, half laying down there and half laying there like sparrows. And de rest of de fellows dat got de band [Steelband], nuh, standin up wid de band so, and de police... Dat time Garfield Sargeant was de corporal at Oistin's. I seh 'if you come cross heah. Your share heah fuh yuh. Yuh cud come lil further...' "

Stickfighters in Trinidad had very colourful names, nicknames that reflected something about their character: Bulbul Tigre, Bengy Moomoo, Codrington, Grammar, Magamoutch, Nedzie, Pappeto, Ramsay, Soucatau, Simeron, Sonny Bo, One Man Bisco, White

---

62. Cowley, p 122

and Blue Turnbull, Bundo Maybone, Johnny Zizi, Eli Walke, Black Prince, Fredi Mungo the dentist, Mongobush, Chitambi, Cutouter, Mansley, Willie Dolly, Peter Ejan and Mastifay.

Sticklickers in Barbados were no less colourful: Arnold Greenidge, Audley Carter, Dynamite Rock, Lightning Vaughn, Battling Sardine, The Million Dollar Lash, Tauties, Tee Campbell, St. Simon Shadow, Sorry Boy Pilgrim, Ten Pound Callender, Gifted Callender, Sunny Garner, Gullyboar, Stoway Trotman, Hopper Lashley, Joe Hoad, Bomey Harewood, Eagle Blackman, Snotty Man Bispham, 98, Mice-in-the-Tot, Ajax, Knocka White, Youngster, Buhbup, Boysie, Israel, Moonie, Willie Jude, Cheetah, Colvin Sargeant (a woman), Pin Parris, Avery, Devonnes, Butting Sardines, Curds, and Dandy Mr. St. Hill.[63]

Sticklickers practiced in many different ways. Like boxers, many did shadow sticklicking. St. Simon Shadow talks about Tee Campbell of Belleplane, St. Andrew who developed a lash called the knife.

> "Campbell, this man knows stick to such a height that he eventually develop a lash in sticklicking. And how he practice this lash. He took a cord and a piece of bag and tied the two ends of one stick overhead in a tree and he begin to ramp wid it like a punching bag. And brother when he invented it he tried it out. This is a lash that is a murder lash. You can believe it. When this rack back and throw the stick that he was using at the one that was in the tree, an use the lash, the stick came down by one end and left one hanging in the tree. And that lash was eventually called the knife. The name alone is enough to get yuh believe as men go."

Folklorist and musicologist, Peggy McGeary related this story about her father Curry Jones in Speightstown, St. Peter:

> "My father use to do sticklicking and as a youngster I used to see

63. See Appendix A for a list of sticklickers, their occupations and where they lived.

> him putting the stick in various positions which made no sense to me but he used to be saying words to the effect hory tillyah trury zompah zaie zoo. They were eight words but those are the ones I could remember. I am not sure I have them in the correct order except for zompah zaie zoo. He was always putting the stick in different positions. He was always doing something and I don't know if it was a way of remembering which movements to go through or what. His name was Archibald Jones. They used to call him Curry Jones. He lived on Church Street in Speightstown, just below the Wesleyan Holiness Church."

From these two examples we can see the extent to which individuals created their own specific ways of developing the art form. Over the years, much has been lost because of ignorance, neglect and low evaluation. What follows is but a small sampling of those who remembered and shared their experiences and knowledge of yesterday's Stick Gods.

Ngolo stick fighters in Africa

Sticklicking in Barbados

Kalenda (Trinidad & Tobago)

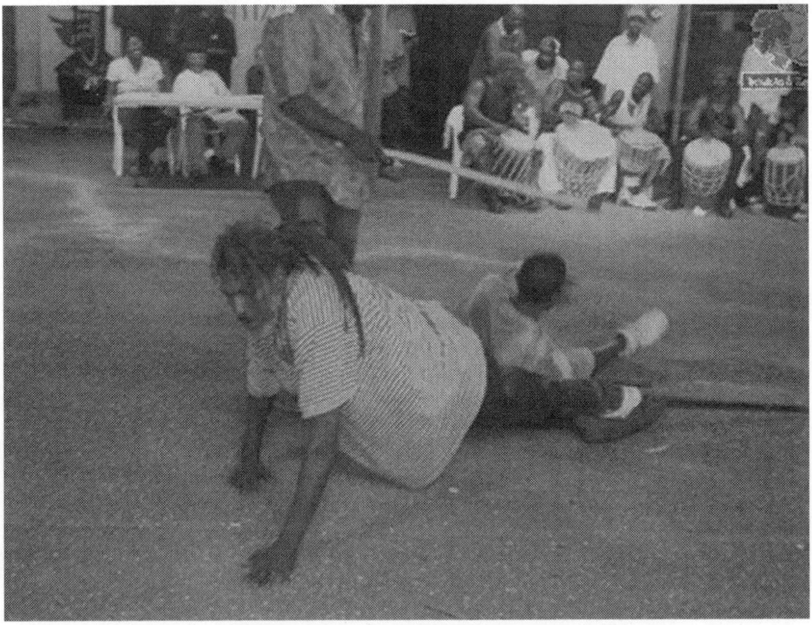

Kalenda (Trinidad & Tobago)

Kalenda (Trinidad & Tobago)

Kalenda (Trinidad & Tobago)

Sticklicking in Barbados

Part Two

Stick Gods: The Interviews

Stick Gods!

The two decades of the 1940s and 1950s were not substantially different from the earlier years of the 20th Century. Although the Barbadian possessed the type of social structure that typifies an isolated island, it was dependent, by and large, on its people's intellect, knowledge and education, and environment. This education they imbibed as it came from England. This education conditioned the imagination of all islanders about the gloriousness of their European (white) owners. These methods were helped by the use of the bible with its projection of white Gods, and the Parish church, its liturgy with their windows of white icons, and reinforced by the images and physical presence of those who governed—the Governor and the Legislature of Planters and Merchants.

From the early years of the post emancipation period, black Bajans were traveling by the thousands annually, not only as seamen, but as specialist professional cane cutters, moving around the Caribbean working in Guyana, The Virgin Islands, Trinidad, Panama,

and Cuba. These men took practices bound up in their Bajan-ness, practices that came from their day to day living habits and rituals. From time to time, they would fall back on these habits and rituals, leaving lasting impressions on their hosts. I have chosen to look at a few of these practices—Tuk music, masquerade dance and sticklicking.

Many of these men brought back new knowledge, not with imaginary beliefs, but with concrete images of other blacks and other people (other than white), and different environments. We know they learned many new techniques in their work. They learned many indigenous songs from the places they visited which were shared with their families and friends when they returned home. Much of this knowledge was shared in conversations and story telling in the community. Some of these communities were isolated from each other and were like islands in a sea of sugar cane.

Most people had no transportation to go from one place to the next. It wasn't until later a that few people were able to acquire a cart drawn by a donkey, mule, horse or ox. Even though there was a train, its route was strange, which made it useless to the majority of blacks living in rural villages. Some people used the train to reach certain points. They would then walk the remainder of the distance, but that was in the afternoon. After dark, you had to walk from Bridgetown to the country. My mother used to tell me about the many times in the mid 1930s when she walked from Bank Hall to Speightstown after a dance.

This isolation was a very important condition that helped define the character of the community as well as the character of the individual people—their speaking patterns, their songs, their sporting activities, their religious preferences, and so on.

The introduction of radio broadcasting in the 1930s reinforced this bias of anti-self thoughts created by the formal education systems in primary schools. It was the same with books used by British school boys and was the same within their environment. It was this same belief that made the bible valid. A few pictures of real or imaginary white people served to concretize the stories. By this I mean that radio programming from the earliest years of broadcasting in Barbados delivered all British content, this way extending what was given to us in schools with sounds and songs. Church and secular music, with the help of radio, challenged the validity of indigenous music by deprecating and/or causing people to abandon our indigenous music, which now became known as Banja, tarnishing it as a less than worthy pursuit for decent people.

The same thing can be said about short wave radio. However, it must always be remembered that an individual's imagination has no bounds and is influenced by the environment to which he/she was exposed. However, cinema was the first to offer concrete images to replace one's imagination. Most of these films were from the United States, bringing in for the first time the pernicious propaganda that would come to dominate Barbados for the last quarter of the 20th Century through television.

It is within this context as a young boy around 8 or 9 that I saw my first movie. It was one of those swashbuckling movies called Captain Blood, starring Errol Flynn. This was soon followed by The Adventures of Robin Hood, also with Errol Flynn. What was interesting was that Flynn played these swashbuckling roles sword licking all over the place against great odds, and coming out the winner. My friends and I used to think of Errol Flynn as a sword licking god. Over the years we identified many other actors as sword licking gods. Although from early we played cowboy and crook, and police and 'tief', we never imitated sword lickers using sticks and sticklicking.

The first time I saw sticklicking was in the late 1940s on CIVIC Day[64] in Queen's Park. Every year after that we would watch the art form there, but never got near the sticklickers because of the crowds. I saw the satu at the Roxy that Joe Hoad organized in 1955 or 56. It was only after my return to Barbados in 1966 that I was determined to visit every village and speak with people to see if I could identify who or what was Bajan. I recorded a few of these encounters and have been able to preserve the voices of these people whose memories and activities span the major part of the 20th Century.

One of my first visits was to St. Simon Village in St. Andrew. Even in the late sixties, St. Simon, like Boscobel, was still considered to be 'behind God's back'. After touring the village and visiting with the Smiths and the Vaughns, I was about to leave when I saw this elderly man sitting on a short stool, his legs crossed and a shiny stick in his hand. This gentleman turned out to be the man I call St. Simon Shadow.

Since that time, I interviewed Rupert Yarde, who was one of my idols when I was growing up, not as a sticklicker, but as a mason. He was a friend of my father and when he 'had up his grogs', he would be talk about various ramps that he took part in. I never paid a lot of attention to the conversations until after the interview with the St. Simon Shadow. Rupert was from Hothersal Turning, St. Michael.

I decided to do one more interview and that was with Aberdeen Jones. I spent two afternoons talking with Aberdeen, who not only talked but demonstrated quite a few moves with his stick. When

64. CIVIC Day was celebrated each year on New Years Day by the CIVIC Friendly Society which had over 45, 000 members. My father Ernest Deighton Mottley was one of the CIVIC's founders.

I finished the interview with Aberdeen I thought I had enough material for my work. However, when I started to prepare material for publication, I realized that sticklicking was not only practiced more widely than I thought, but that I had substantial material for a book.

Coincidentally, I was approached by a friend called Chris Griffith, the then Manager of the Saneitation Department. He said he had in his possession a small manuscript of stories about sticklicking written by a staff member, and asked if I would mind having a look at it. I agreed and subsequently met the authors Elvis Gill and Ione Knight.

When I settled down to read and listen to all the interviews, I realized that quite a few people were involved in the sport of sticklicking. From the reference to Trinidad and the stories from the various sticklickers in Barbados, I realized that we were spanning the whole 20th Century. Many sticklickers recalled that it was their fathers or uncles or older sticklickers who trained them. Many recall seeing older sticklickers at various ramps in a wide variety of venues from rumshop yards, the public roads, in dance houses, at singings and dances. Sticklicking seemed to be a village sport and was taken up by people who were successful at their professions of masonry, carpentry or agricultural work.

Many times, many of the interviewees would talk about a 'Master Workman', men who were on top of their game. Many didn't hesitate to define who they thought was the greatest sticklicker or Master Workman. These stories are about real people who existed, but who remained tied to their small communities where they were respected as Stick Gods—masters of their art form.

Many of us never got the chance to see these real 'Stick Gods' as their fans, admirers and contemporaries called them. We will never see them now as swashbuckling heroes, but we need to respect these Stick Gods. They were some of the the great athletes of their time. They were not thoughtless ignoramuses, but brilliant performers of a sport that was invisible to many and deprecated as something of little value. These are some of the stories about the Stick Gods. I hope they will be remembered by future generations who will take them to the screen to really become like the swashbuckling movie heroes of the past and our Stick Gods of the future.

Nuh rain water cyan wet me!

Elvis Gill is a sticklicker. He is the founder of the Barbados National Science of Sticklicking and the Sticklicking Martial Arts School in 1987. Although born in St. Joseph, he now lives in Bibby's Lane, St. Michael, an area known for a number of notorious sticklickers. He has researched sticklicking and is currently working on a technical book that will assist those who wish to learn the art of sticklicking. My interview was conducted at the National Cultural Foundation (NCF), West Terrace, St James, Barbados, on Saturday, October 17, 2004. He was interviewed by EM.

EM: I was asking you something just now about these drawings or whether or not you have kicking in sticklicking...

EG: Kicking, butting, anything that you deem to break the attack. Donnelly is the science of the combined system in that sticklicking, wrestling or judo, whatever you might call it, boxing and any other [techniques] that you could think about whilst playing stick. So basically wuh yuh do is strike the person. If de body strike at you, you block and then you incorporate anything else you can get incorporate, once the person is close enough [for you] to get the advantage.

EM: Now in a lot of my interviews, I have also come across Johnson, Queensbury, Broad Sword/Single Stick...

EG: ...which we call sword

EM: Rupert Yarde call it Broad Sword/Single Stick that he learn, and then I heard Rupert talk about Donnelly, which I thought was D-O-N-N-A L-E-E, and in St. Simon, this was back in 1969, a man called The Shadow talked about Donnelly, and I could not find any reference to the two except to a boxer called Donnelly who set up certain rules [for boxing in the UK]. I just want to make this clarification.

EG: You are actually right 'cause it was a boxer that start sticklicking and he combine the two.

EM: ...and the feet, 'cause the use of the feet was critical

EG: He combine the two, so dah is how come yuh get dah. Queensberry is rules...

EM: I don't quite understand the differentiation between Queensbury as a sticklicking technique and Queensbury, the rules.

EG: Queensbury is like if you gun do Crop Over and you want to do a good demonstration, you use Queensbury which is a more florid flamboyant play, a lot of style and twirling and acrobatic stuff, if yuh can get it work. But not to take anything from it 'cause it is just as dangerous as Johnson. Johnson is the science primarily created to beat the sword.

EM: Which is part of broad sword/single stick [science]?

EG: Yeah! Any person wid any kinda sword or sharp edge is the object, Johnson method primarily should be able to beat it. It only matters how skilled each person is.

EM: Most of these you are talking about are really guards – defensive positions also.

EG: Each science got dey lessons. Queensbury got five lessons. Johnson got seven. Donnelly could be a combine of all plus the martial arts, the boxing aspect or any other tricks you could work. Then yuh got swab. Swab got three lessons. This is holding stick like...

EM: ...quarter?

EG: No, quarter is Queensbury. Holding it like a walking stick and maneuvering movements out of that. Then yuh got sword which is primarily the same movement as fencing, using the point.

EM: Creole?

EG: Creole is going back then to the martial arts. It is a combined system of the martial arts. This was explained to me by my master instructor, Browne—Lemuel Browne. He was from St. John. He dead now. He had two brothers. He explained to me they also had a book wid sticklicking. I cyan remember off hand what the name was. It is seven something.

EM: What I gathered was that there were seven defensive moves, seven lessons...

EG: When I say lessons, lessons mean seven positions that you would learn to defend yourself. When you set up yourself, the position that you hold, determines whuh lesson you get.

Wuh I can tell you 'bout my science 'cause I does practice it is that the first three lessons got three positions. So yuh got position one, position two, centre guard, left side guard or right side guard or open guard, depends pun if yuh is a left-hander or right-hander, the guard would change.

Sometimes, you may use high seven which got three guards. It is forward, down and back. Eventually when we start to show positions, then you will see what we talking about.

The only lesson that got four positions is the fourth and the fourth position is that usually when you fight all the rest is waiting pun yuh opponent or capitalizing pun yuh opponent. Put it this way. You drop in any other position. You can leggo a lash or you can leggo a strike, regardless of however you want to term it. But you don't have the full control to defend a skillful repeat to you. But when you drop in the fourth position, when you leggo a lash, and he repeat, you got full control to deflect, to block, to do anything. So that is basically fighting thing that the majority of the people that learn Johnson, when they get to the fourth lesson, they hardly go past the fourth cause they could fight at that point.

Yuh can gi' lashes and tek lashes and the rest would just only enhance the fourth position.

EM: Some men said there were seven positions, and then three from Queensbury and three from Johnson which would give yuh thirteen lessons.

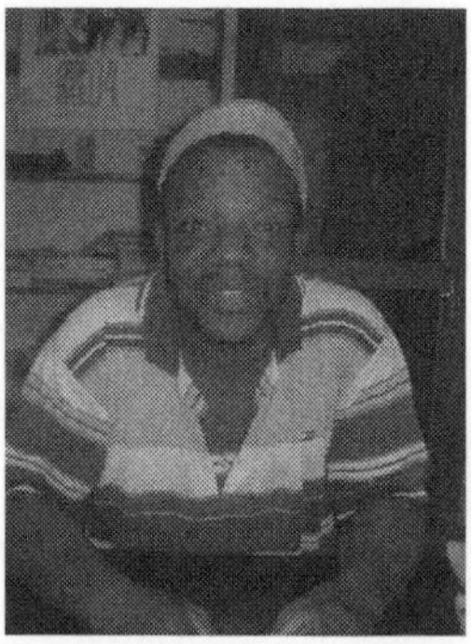

EG: Dah is when it combine, 'cause the majority of de sticklickers used to combine Queensbury and Johnson.

EM: Which I suspect is how creole evolved because it is improvising and also using whatever traditional 'ting existed.

EG: But if you brek it down, Queensberry got five lessons. Sword got six lessons. But like I tell you, although yuh say position one and two in whatever, that position one might got two positions in it or it might got three positions in it. Very seldom it go over three. I got positions home for the sword. I have not, this is what I've been trying to do ever since, got a pure Queensbury man. Never meet one.

EM: No and I can't find the information on one. I can find information on pure broad sword single stick. But what Bajans call Johnson and Queensbury and creole crisscross. I remember Rupert Yarde tell me yuh could come wid Tom Johnson or Johnson Tom, he ent nutten to do wid that, he gun tek yuh apart because all the techniques, yuh don't know which using or wuh gun use or wuh it is. Some men started off learning a particular form and end up in another.

EG: But I got de full Johnson 'cause de man dat taught me gi' me de full Johnson. Plus duh had a fellow in Christ Church, I think he must be dead by now name Ninety-nine, he was featured in de paper a couple years back.

EM: Ninety-nine or Ninety-eight?

EG: Ninety-eight. He had a million dollar punch.

EM: ...call de million dollar lash...

EG: He used to boast by it and I went and play he. And when he bring de lash, I counter it. He say, "Who could ever teach you dah?" And when I tell he, he say "Oh dah is my buddy!" He say man you good, you good. I used to go round challenging schools in martial arts, sticklickers and I use to get frustrated quick cause the NCF did a workshop with a man teaching sticklicking. I come and watch it. Man wuh you teaching is folly! Wasting people money and time! So he get angry and me and he went thru two sessions and then Addy Forde call me to do the workshop fuh dem. 'Cause Addy tell me a young man like you! At that time I was about 25-26.

EM: These are your drawings showing grips, balance.

EG: These are aspects of throwing the stick, how to line it up. And yuh can't line it up unless yuh line it up with two fingers. Anything else yuh ent gine get it line up. Right? It doesn't matter if the person in front of yuh or not.

The next one is call walking the stick, yuh pelt it and it tip from end to end. And it bounce back. Actually I see it happen in the road in St. Joseph. A fellow Joseph Holder and a fellow pull off he hat and he say "Boy bring back that hat" and the fellow start to run way and he pelt de stick at he and de stick walk and trip up the fellow, man.

A stick got six ends. Wuh it really mean? Yuh hear a lot of sticklickers say, "Man a stick got six ends, and when I get in Queensberry third, nuh rain water cyan wet me!" But a lot of people does talk 'bout it and I does talk to a lot of sticklickers and when duh tell me dah, I is ask duh wuh de six ends is. Man you is a sticklicker and doan kno'? But the joke is wuh it is. You got an idea or wuh?

EM: The two ends....

EG: Yeah

EM: ...the sides, you tell me

EG: It is wuh de stick cud do, practically wuh de stick cud do. Wuh you tink de stick cud do is de ends. Not really top and bottom ends, wuh de stick cud do.

EM: Side lash? Shoulder Plex? Strollop?

EG: Dem is areas, but you go ahead, we gun get there just now. This is Queensbury double section and it show yuh how yuh defend and how yuh put yuhself against a wall...

EM: ...and nuhbody cyan get at yuh at all

EG: I had a challenge at work when de fellas at work realize dat I did doing sticklicking. Fellow [who does] cut coconuts, "man I get my collins..."[65] Ev'ry morning I come in he aggravate me, ev'ry morning he aggravate me. This morning in question me and de wife had a noise, so I gone in and I ent [in] nuh good mood to start. I say wuh! Get de so-and-so collins and come. Wuh eva' you get you teking, wuh eva' I get I tek. He come out wid de collins and say, "you ready?" and swing. When he swing I do so and cut, trollop and come up all over he face. He do so [and shake]. I seh, "Man I ent hit yuh!" I just wedge de stick [and] walk. He seh, "But how you get dey?" I seh "Right now I ent feel so good. Me and de wife had a quarrel." He seh, "Man you guh long, you guh long." And from dah morning he never trouble me. All he is tell de fellas, you see he, he dangerous, dangerous.

---

65. cutlass

EM: In dis age, people doan' know nutten bout stick. But 40 years ago ev'ry watchman in Barbados used to walk wid a stick. Old men yuh know. Barely bend. Doan' even risk think that because he is a old man wid a stick. Dem fellows clean yuh up man. When de gun came in in de 40s and people had access, dat is when stick begin to dead out. Evry'body use to play stick.

EG: You can play, block and then trap de person by falling down without dum. Dah is trapping. Without even realizing wuh yuh doing. These are the potato licks, that is when you in de open and yuh got more dan one person playing yuh, yuh buckle up, drop yuh two foot and block.

EM: Aberdeen Jones tell me about gangs, his gang of sticklickers in Oistins in de fifties dat brek up the reception for Princess Margaret. In Guyana, you may find three, four, five men fighting at a time. And if a man hit you, you can hit a next man. But it was a open sort of thing but I din' know it existed here in Barbados whether you could be fighting more than one man at a time. I mean in a ramp or satu.

EG: Yuh know de police does do a tattoo when de year come so they invite us. So I tell de fellas let we get into it. I think wid my training gine pun stage it do not be a prearrange situation as such, all does happen is when yuh playing, how I is train yuh, if de first set of licks you send, three lashes, four lashes, five lashes, when my turn, I send de same. Wuh you does know is how much lashes coming at you. If is 3, 4 or 1, you send back the same amount but yuh doan know which part duh coming. So like dat yuh got to block dem. Duh got a few people and duh is prearrange every move and when yuh mek a mistake pun stage yuh got to back all over cause it preset. I is avoid the presetting.

But we did dat, and it wasn't a preset ting and de fellows get carried away man and I is de body dat did getting de blows. I get some good blows dah night but I still defend myself and come out.

Back to wuh de stick can do. Punching, tripping, dey is different types of sticks, what you gun fight and what aspects. This one is when yuh hear de men bout how duh gun pop out yuh belly button, always this shape or close to this shape wid a little circle at de end of de stick so that when yuh push and grabble, it lock yuh skin and pull. But yuh cyan do it wid a plain stick. Dis stick is fuh cutting. If you is a person that want to fight, you can cut de person. Talking bout directly cutting dum like if yuh had a knife, yuh shape de stick dah kinda way, a bevel edge dat when you pull, de strike could rip de shirt and cut you. So yuh have different aspects so! The normal aspect you will see would be normal stick wid ends cut off square and round off decent.

EM: What wood do you use for mekking sticks?

EG: My personal choice is black sage, I like black sage. Guava, black sage, wild bay leaf, calimantis, black willow, a kinda tree, when it small it small, but then it is grow in a tree wid some fruits that is drop dat de birds would normally eat. Dat is the trees dat I know bout.

EM: How do you prepare the stick when you cut down a small sapling tree?

EG: This is next aspect of it. It is all depends on what you want from de stick.

EM: Explain that to me.

EG: OK, you can prepare a stick fuh fighting. First yuh get it. Yuh normally would cut it over the length you want.

EM: Usually what length that is?

EG: Well the average length is three feet three inches, a metre, normal walking stick length. Then it depends pun how if you doing Queensberry and you doing it among folks. Yuh get it extend four feet, cause yuh want enough for double deception which is double hand, each hand would got piece to block and so forth. But if yuh ent doing that and you even get yuhself in trouble yuh could still do that wid the normal size stick.

Yuh cut yuh stick and put it pun an open fire, green as it is and rub it wid engine oil, used engine oil. Years ago dey use to use linseed oil pun it but you'll find that engine oil is readily available now so yuh use de old engine oil dat work in an engine, rub it pun de stick and swinge it thru' de open fire. When yuh finish dat, yuh cud skin it de same time or yuh cud put it down two or three days and then skin it.

If it got in any bends, yuh set it to tek out de bends. When yuh done skin it, den yuh get linseed oil and rub it and polish it and keep working wid it to flex it and straighten it all de time. And yuh keep doing dah till...

EM: How long dah may last? A month? A week? Two weeks?

EG: No! It is on-going preparing. The more linseed oil you put pun it, the more sturdy it becomes. If you do it, use linseed oil every week pun it. After six seven months, it is a proper stick. It ent gun flake, it ent gun break.

EM: When do you start using it as a stick?

EG: You cud use it as a stick three days after you done skin it. You can start fighting wid it. But it all depends on how serious you is wid dis stick, because if it is a nice stick and you really want it, yuh don't fight wid it until you want to.

EM: Dah is wuh I mean. How long then?

EG: It is up to you. You want tuh know when you gun tek it up to fight wid it. After three months you could fight wid it. And every week you linseed it 'cause the linseed oil goes into the stick and harden it, make it tempered. That is strictly fighting stick. If you doin' a stick for performance.

EM: What do you mean by performance?

EG: Like stage performance, or you gun do a show, yuh do the same ting wid it but de only ting yuh do, is then put it some place cool or humid or bury it in sand and let it stand dey for a week. All de time if the sand dry out, yuh wet it, yuh wet de sand. But if yuh got it in a humid area dat is cold, when you done yuh tek it out, yuh linseed it and den you cud start using it.

Now when you start wid dah stick, we could sticklick here and the village down below there could stand and hear – plix plix plix. Cause yuh prepare it for echoing. So de more echo, de better.

Then if you preparing the stick to damage or injure the person without causing any bruise blood or anything, when you done swinge it and everything, instead of using linseed oil, yuh use urine pee. Now wid dat dey claim dat yuh can hit a man and he won't even swell up.

So dem is de aspects dat I know. I try all de rest besides de urine because I got nuhbody yet. All de rest I try and wuh Brown tell me I realize it work.

EM: Who is Browne again?

EG: Lemuel Browne is one a my instructors primarily wid the Johnson science.

EM: He was from St. John?

EG: Yeah! Greens. Browne used to play sticklicking but he was never used to be as much in the public eye. He brother used to go round and fight but he never used to really. He would play too. You would find he would get into play effing he brother went any place and lose and den duh boast too much, den he would get involve because he is a more aggressive player.

EM: He wasn't a jacket man as they say, meaning dey had some suit man dat would back off de jacket...

EG: Wuh he tell me is dat he never used to ting 'cause he would be too aggressive when he start to play. In his lifetime he only teach five people.

EM: And you're one.

EG: I is one 'cause he tell me his temperament was when yuh go in a ring to fight he never used to go to fight fuh money, he go to show how good he is. So he say he never used to hold back. If yuh cyan hold de blows don't come in cause he seh in he time when he start to trow down some licks, you feel like a hundred pong weight coming down pun yuh. And ef yuh buckle at all, he never ease up. Sometimes men used to have to tek he off yuh. So he say dah is why he won't play. Is only ef he brother then get lick and the person start to brag nuff nuff nuff, then he would get involve. But otherwise he never really play. I get real licks from he too. And is a good ting too for the simple reason like I was telling you about Tull, Louis Tull uncle. He live in Bibby Lane, Canewood Bottom. He name Donald. Dey use to call he Deaf Donald. He couldn't hear good. He is de first body dat start to teach me. But he had a combined system. When yuh go by him he used to tell yuh "When I teaching you and licks get too much, back me." But the time you turn round and back he yuh get three or four lashes before he stop. The only good ting about him is that he never used to drink. So yuh did lucky. But Lemuel used to drink. He used to cyah a mini rum and whilst he training he drinking. By the time dah mini rum done, now he ready to share licks. Yuh used tuh get real blows.

EM: Anybody else teach you?

EG: Joseph Holder. I started wid Joseph Holder when I did about sixteen. Youngster. But his wife get vex and tell he dat ef he want she wash he clothes he would stop from teaching me sticklicking, dat ent nutten fuh nuhbody. Dah is vagavunism.

EM: He was from St. Joseph.

EG: I raise and see he at the Sugar Hill area. So I had stopped. Then after I done wid Lemuel, then I went back to he and me and he talk stick and I show he the lessons I get.

EM: How old you were when Lemuel and all dese fellows were teaching you?

EG: Thirties, Thirty-two, thirty-three.

EM: You ent start before that? What make you decide to learn stick?

EG: I used to see a fellow name Marshall and Joseph play years ago. I was about 8 or 9, 10 years. I did one of the fortunate ones cause my fadda did known then as a bad man.

EM: What was his name?

EG: Son Gill. My old man did never a sticklicker. He was a gun specialist. I was about 8 years 9 years.

EM: This was wuh year?

EG: I born in sixty. That was the early seventies. Whilst de young fellows pun de road would run home de lil boys and ting, nuhbody never used to trouble me. Dah is Son Gill son. Cause de old man would come an deal wid yuh. He never use to ask nuh question. So whilst pun evening and ting when de sticklicking start, the older fellows would run way de lil children I was de only one used to really stand and watch what was going on.

EM: Where most of the sticklicking ramps or satus used to tek place? Wuh you call dem ramps or satus?

EG: Ramps because satus is a organize way. Two fellows just come and play dah is only a ramp. Satu is a organizing ting wid betting and ting. Mayers Corner, yuh used to get dah regular, where de old Three Fives did, in dat area in de middle of de road.

EM: Who were your contemporaries dat learn wid you at de time?

EG: Not many.

EM: You learn from the old men!

EG: I observe it. I did like it. My old man had a couple of lessons and it surprising yuh know he never teach me. I got a nephew and he teach the nephew. 'Cause he tell me I too aggressive. I did a more aggressive person. I use to fight everyday at school because of his reputation. When yuh home OK, but when yuh gone to secondary school, other different areas come in and den people get to know dey point at yuh, point at yuh. I use to fight from the time I went school. The only time I stop from fighting was when I went at Metropolitan. I did fighting at West St. Joseph from de time I went dey till I left. When I was suppose to go in fourth form is when I left. Fourteen years and still fighting. Is only when I come in town I stop from fighting. But he use to get complaints 'bout me all de time. He tell me I too violent and I never tell he wuh de real reason I use to fight ev'ryday. He reputation. People used to say "You fadda bad. You tink you fadda bad!"

He shed blood!

Dandy St. Hill was an old man who years ago used to watch in the road. He was a champion sticklicker. Dandy was a very thin and fragile looking man.

In those days they used to hold championships that would take place under boat sails. They would get canvas sails and put up a tent. On bank holidays, that was a big thing. There was a shopkeeper who used to put on these big shows.

One time, this champion player from St. George came down in an old truck with his supporters to challenge Dandy. Dandy was like an early Muhammad Ali, and he used to predict how long the fight would last.

That day, he predicted that the fight would finish in round three. So all of his supporters had bets on him. The St. George champion was a big strapping man, a man something like Goliath and Dandy stood there like David.

The fight started with Dandy very fragile and moving slowly and the St. George man coming out like a hurricane, raining blows from all sides. Dandy blocked most of them. But one of them went through and put a cut on Dandy's head.

So Dandy supporters started to worry because of the physical strength of this man because he seemed to be a good sticklicker too. There was relief when the referee rang the bell for the end of round one. During the break, they put alcohol to soothe the cut on Dandy's head. Dandy's supporters began asking "Dandy, how long the fight is going to last? You gine to do it in three rounds?"

"No!" Dandy answered. "He shed blood."

As the second round opened, the St. George champion came in raining blows from all sides. And Dandy making a move that nobody saw. He slid the stick through his hand into the St. George man's mouth and had his tongue pushing back in his mouth, choking the man. The fight was finished in round two with the St. George man defeated. Somebody let go a gun shot in the air and 'fight for days' took place. Now this fight took place in the Fitts Village [St. James] area and the truck driver from St. George caught up with some of the men he brought in Eagle Hall. Man, let me tell you something, Fitts Village is more than two miles from Eagle Hall. So, you can image how fast dem fellows run.

Elvis Gill

The Hoop Stick

"One night I was up the road, and me and my brother was skylarking. A fellow take up his stick and challenge anybody to sticklick he.

My brother said, "You can't play he, you know."

The man had a hoop stick. When he fire the lash at me, I break. When I break it, I catch he cutting. So I move away. I went in. I ground my stick. When I moved one way, he moved the next and when I pulled him over on the stick, he foot couldn't touch the ground.

He passed red water and had to go to the hospital."

David Brathwaite

You could not wet me with a bucket of water!

Joe Hoad is a white Bajan whose roots and friendships cross all class and colour barriers in Barbados. He comes from a plantation family of sportsmen. His father, ELG Hoad, played cricket for Barbados and the West Indies in the 1930s. While he himself was a table tennis champion, a cricketer and all-round sportsmen, he was also an avid sticklicker who earned the respect of the fellow Stick Gods of his time. He migrated to Australia with his wife and is a practicing sports psychologist and coach. It is from there that he responded to my enquiries and sent me this email.

Barbados stick fighting I believe mainly comes from the tribes of West Africa. There is still stick fighting in parts of Chad, Zimbabwe and I was told by an Ethiopian at Flinders University that it is practiced in the West of his country but it still has variations that are strongly linked to sabre fencing (when I watched "The Last Samurai" I saw several moves that were identical to things I learned from Edwin Yard, Arnold Greenidge and Bobby Osbourne).

I first got interested in stick fighting when I was told that my brother Ted was learning the art from Stoway Trotman at Applewhaites, and I soon learned that every parish had a stick fighting master and many villages boasted their own champions.

* Elwin Lampitt, a white fisherman from St. John (his brother was Wes Hall's grandfather)
* Arnold Greenidge and Audley Carter from Christ Church
* Abraham "Dynamite" Rock and Lightning Vaughn from St. Thomas
* Thelbert Blades (Battling Sardine) and Jerome King (The Million Dollar Lash) from St. Michael
* Tauties, the lighterman from St. James
* Tee Campbell from Belleplaine, St. Andrew
* St. Judes Joe from St. Judes, St. George
* Sorry Boy Pilgrim from St. Lucy
* Ten Pound Callender from the Orleans, Bridgetown
* Gifted Callender from Searles, Christ Church
* Sunny Garner from Blackmans, St. Joseph
* Inspector Nicholls from St. Andrew
* Edward Prescott from Jackson, St. Michael
* Fitz Simons and Brad Cadogan from the Garden, St. James
* Rupert Mapp and Bobby Osbourne from Roebuck Street, Bridgetown
* Edwin Yarde from Bibby's Lane, St. Michael
* Stoway Trotman from George Park, St. Phillip
* Gillie from Hothersal Turning, St. Michael
* Barlow Woodruff from Porey Spring, St. Thomas

These were all skilled stickmen, but there were others like Jack Ashby (the druggist), my brother Ted and Mr. Olton who owned a store in Tudor Street who could all play stick and give you a good practice, but would never compete in a "Satu" (stickfight).

Elombe, this is a start, if you want to know about the fights that took place during my time I will have to check in my diaries between 1948 and 1963, but I have them somewhere. If you want to know about the seven positions of the art I would have to do drawings for you with explanations. When I fought Major Tulloch (who was head of the Barbados Regiment) in Cecil Warner's backyard, his sabre fencing techniques were very little different to stick licking, also the Melville Island Aboriginals and the Pitinjatjara Aboriginals have stick fights. There are also a large number of stick fighters in the north of Portugal and Indian policemen are taught stick fighting. There is a book by an Indian author Lalall Balkasoon on *The Stick Fighting Art of Self Defence*.

One of us getting old and forgetful. Rupert and Edwin Yarde is the same person and he lived in Bibby's Lane not Hothersall Turning and he was a carpenter not a mason.[66] He and his friend George Gollop made a wardrobe for me when I first got married and it was a beauty. He also had the nickname "Bird", as he fell off a roof and got up and walked away without a scratch. He was a wonderful man and a friend of your father's. He used to talk about [how] ED Mottley was not only Ernest Deighton but it meant "Every Day Money". We all used to drink and eat pudding and souse or cow heel at Hoyte's shop in the Turning on Saturdays after cricket.

Aberdeen Jones had a club in Gall Hill that held stick fights, he had been taught by Arnold Greenidge. I was at his club one day playing table tennis and he brought in two sticks and asked me if I wanted him to turn my white ass red. I did not want to fight,

66. Rupert Yarde was a mason who built houses for my father and was very close to the family. Edwin was a carpenter and was Rupert's cousin.

but thought the people there would think me a coward if I did not spar. He threw lashes like a madman, but in those days with stick in hand you could not wet me with a bucket of water and I broke every lash, cut through his guard and dropped a lash in his big guts. One of his sons who I knew from Foundation School cricket team, laughed and he turned away from me and beat the boy so bad he could hardly walk. He also ordered me out of the club and told me never to come back. He is probably the only human being in all my living days that I can say I did not like.

Marshall and Joseph Youngster Holder

"There was a man who was married to Pead [Pearl?] Rudder. I think his name was Marshall. He was a sticklicker too. The first sticklicking that I ever saw was between Youngster and Marshall, when Marshall used to wear his white cork hat.

And always when Youngster made the move and drop the lash, Marshall would push his cork hat out. And as youngster hit the cork hat, Marshall would give him a water-line (lash to the waist) and the fight done.

Youngster promised himself to get a remedy for that. So he would go into the back yard and practice for him. And when Marshall come back the next two Sundays, Youngster play he.

And when Youngster do so and conk down on the cork hat and when Marshall look for the water-line, Youngster step in and jerk up the hat and gave him a lash on top of his head and blood start to spout all over the place.

That was in the late 70's going on to the 80's."

I doan' skylark wid a stick!

St. Simon Shadow was a very small man when I met him in St. Simon, St. Andrew, in about 1969. He was as black as the ess of spades and when you looked at him casually from the distance his appearance was that of a silhouette. Neatly dressed in a pants and shirt, the sleeves rolled up above the elbows, he wore an old felt hat with a sweat band that was discoloured by the sweat of many days in the hot sun He sat on a small bench outside Dottin Rumshop, his legs crossed at the knees. He wore a pair of shoes whose soles seemed to have been half-soled by the shoemaker many times as the uppers had numerous cracks along the instep. He also had a stick in his right hand which he was forever caressing with his fingers. Perhaps he gave me his name but I can no longer find my notes with it, so for the purposes of this book I call him the St. Simon Shadow. He was interviewed by EM.

SSS: If you had to learn stick, as far as I may know, the man is going to tell you what you can do. He gine show you the position and then the right way that he is going to practice you. He will tell you you are going to begin your practice as from tonite. He come back and he ask you if you remember the positions that he showed you [how] to hold your stick. You tell him yes and he tell yuh hold de first position and start from there. He show you what lashes you are to break. That is lesson one.

When you get to the end of lesson one he will tell you that you have come to the end of that. Eventually when you throw a game that night, he tell you to show him the lashes the same way he was showing you. If there are any mistakes it will be eventually corrected.

As soon as you get thru' with the first he is going to practice you the second. He will show you the positions, then he show you the lashes. Go thru' it again and eventually he will turn back and tell you well show him on what position he pass the lashes to you and you will give him a explain. And yuh get yuh mistakes cut out as well until yuh get down to the third and from there yuh go right down the same very way.

EM: That's when the lashes start?

SSS: Yuh won't get the lashes unless yuh really gine have a ramp. That is that both of you will be playing now like two champions. Instead of learning, now you would be playing like two champions. Well suppose for instance you use a lash that is not thrown in the right form, he will eventually ask you to correct it. And if yuh doan be able to correct it, he coming back and show you the way in which you should use this lash because in using a lash in the wrong direction or in the wrong manner, the man that you playing liable to get in on you. See what ah mean... and you wouldn't be able to make no cover for that and that gone home.

And then eventually yuh may get hot, and the man may get just as hot as you are or hotter. And there you gun get ruff and tumble licks. See. But apart from that if you can get thru that third lesson as he teach you, you go from there to the fourth. Ah mean yuh cyan have all of this in one night, mark you well, because it going take you some time to learn these lessons.

And then from the fourth yuh learn the fifth. From the fifth then you come down to the sixth. And when you get to the sixth, you go right thru the sixth and then yuh normally get a ramp thru 1,2,3,4,5,6 to be champion, see. And from there then you get the seventh. But when you get down to the seventh, you run thru' again from one down to seven ramping it right thru'. You would be brekking yuh licks and exchanging. He sharing lashes, you sharing lashes. You break lashes, he break lashes. Well anybody who mek the mistake wid lashes lose.

Then I doan' know, but some people say that yuh pelt lashes in the first lesson. I pass ev'ryting. Then along the lines you come down and as far and as fast as you advance, you find that there are different licks in between there. Yuh get lashes call Creole.

EM: What is Creole lash?

SSS: Creole licks is joint licks. All de joints of the body. And the position for the stick is this. [One quarter up the stick with heel protecting your elbow]. But remember if you doan know what yuh doing yuh cyan keep the stick dah way. Number one a man may throw a lash over the end of this stick and slide it down and eventually on yuh knuckles. Yuh won't be able to block any licks 'cause yuh cyan represent yuhself. That is a sliding lash. See. If you cyan control that yuh have to hold it like this [Upside down with the quarter up in de air].

EM: You cyan lick anybody with the stick in that position! How yuh gun get dah done?

SSS: That is what you think. Lashes can be shared in all directions. Lashes in all directions, brother! Yuh know when yuh have a good peas and rice? Lashes like that. They are joint lashes. Yuh find a man one over here and one over there, one over here, one over there. Then eventually he get down to the ankle and he come back up. This is the dangerous end. I can put it here push it here stab yuh in de eye wid it I can wreck yuh kidneys anytime yuh think. The seven lashes I told yuh about, dey is Johnson licks. Johnson licks, Johnson science.

EM: Why Johnson?

SSS: That is what I came along and was told. I doan know who is Johnson. The other is Donnelly/Queensberry. Those are the Donnelly/Queensberry, Johnson and the Creole. Dey all bad! The Johnson is the science that yuh get seven lashes in the first lesson. That is why I told you that just now that I pass fuh thirteen. The Donnelly/Queensberry and the Johnson is seven and six together. But the man who only preach bare Johnson knows nutten 'bout de other six. Seven in Johnson and three in the others learn de first lesson in thirteen lashes. So if you get a man dat only practice Johnson seven and he meet on a fellow who practice Johnson, Queensberry and Donnelly together, when he get to seven...

EM: What about creole?

SSS: Yuh get de Creole in either one of de lessons. If you meet a man dat practice the seven, bare Johnson, he would also have de Creole along wid dat. But then when he meet a man that have Donnelly, Johnson and Queensbury together, when he get to the end of his first lesson, seven lashes, I doan' know what he is going to do about the other six. Because mark you, he won't have any remedy for them. He won't have the slightest bit of remedy. Well the next ting dat happen in the seventh lesson, there is a position called the open seven or long seven. Well it's a position with both hands extended and the stick across the ear. While that position is like that, you are inviting your man to come in.

EM: Why is the stick across the ear?

SSS: You have it by the quarter and the right hand is up and left is also out here. That is the position of the seventh. The seventh open to the extreme then. You are inviting your opposition to come in. But if he attempts to come in, and doan try to be good, something is going to happen inside here. But this is what I always know. No time you see a champion throw out his arms like that in an open seven, and rack back, I won't advise a man to venture. Try and get the man off that position. As a matter of fact change your position and get the man off that position. Try and move him.

Now let me tell you 'bout this man Tee Campbell. This man knows stick to such a height that he eventually develop a lash in sticklicking. And how he practice this lash. He took a cord and a piece of bag and tied the two ends of one stick overhead in a tree and he begin to ramp wid it like a punching bag. And brother when he invented the lash, he tried it out. This is a lash that is a murder lash. You can believe it. When he rack back and throw the stick that he was using at the one that was in the tree, an use the lash, the stick came down by one end and left one hanging in the tree. And that lash was eventually called the knife. The name alone is enough to get yuh believe as men go.

EM: Where he hit yuh?

SSS: That lash is a lash for any part of yuh body. Remember I said he invented the lash. And therefore to have an opposition, yuh cun learn anyting about dat one. That in nuh plan. And eventually, if this lash land, yuh in trouble.

EM: Now when you starting, at what point in a stick fight yuh have de cross sticks on the ground? At the beginning?

SSS: Dat stupidness nuhbody doan worry about nowadays. When yuh gun have a ramp, dat is Johnson science. Nuhbody does worry about dat nowadays. You gonna march. You and your man march. He have his stick in his hand. You have yours in your hand. Marching with the cross, it can also be dangerous. Because let me tell you this, let's say that you are opposed to me. I doan' want my stick. March you round. You have to be very active and by so doing if you are faster than I, you are going cross your foot upon your stick and draw mine. You doan' fight to get yours. You cross your foot and make a half turn sudden when yuh going [around in a circle]...

EM: Who on top?

SSS: Either one can be on top. But you must get one and keep one on the ground. You are not going to fight to draw yours. You gun fight to draw mine. Stand up on yours. When you draw first and you are seeking for a knockout, well I am in trouble unless I really have the techniques depending on this. [Holds up arms bent at elbows exposing the triceps at the back of the upper arm]. You may tell me now that this cyan take licks. But would be as much as you know!

EM: You can use that to absorb lashes?

SSS: Of course you can. Providing you know what this [the fleshy part of the hands]. If you at all push this to stop a lash, yuh doan' contact it and push this to the lash, the man gine to attack you again and brek dat if it doan' come back down. Otherwise than that, from the time he grabble the stick, you find you can't get the one down there, doan' go down. Stand up and put your hand in de air. He cyan lash yuh. That come that you surrender.

Sticklicking have rules too yuh know. If you meet a man that really in tune to be severe, without the rules being read, you can get lashes from round one to round all because this man is not going to be waiting back. From the time the bell ring, this man gun be eventually licking straight and regular. He won't gi' you time to break a lash. But as long as the laws are being read, yuh have to break and pull yuh position. And then both of you will meet from corner to corner.

EM: Who determines the winner?

SSS: Well yuh have judges [who] determine the winner by the number of lashes scored.

EM: How long a round last?

SSS: Approximately 2 minutes. Sticklicking is good, sticklicking is bad. I go back to say again that if you intend to learn sticklicking, yuh have tuh make up your mind to take lashes. Do not think within yourself that you are going to sit at a desk and write with a pen. Another thing, if the person who is going to teach you this science... please let me go further, if they know exactly what they are going to teach yuh, they must first show you how you will have to hold your stick. When you hold a stick they must then eventually show you the position that you must stand in, and what position you hold the stick in. Because yuh cyan just go and take up a fellow that doan' know anyting and expect him to hold a stick like a man that knows what he is about or to hold it in a position as one who has been taught already. As I have told you, as long as you are not equipped, you cannot put this finger where you see I have mine. Otherwise that finger will eventually get what it gone up there for. Another thing, in holding your stick, and the man practicing you to break lashes, one in one out, one in one out, you have to be sure that at no time your stick doan' slide. Would you like me to show you?

When you doing lessons, this quarter is left behind here [to protect the elbow] this quarter position it protects the wrist. When you are playing in other lessons, you leave that quarter behind here. You play mainly from the wrist....

A man playing you the second lesson or the first, he will eventually throw a lash at your wrist. You have that stick in the air, that quarter is to protect that wrist. In the creole position, yuh not a one hand man yuh use all two.

EM: Who teach you to play stick?

SSS: I doan' know who taught me. It is just something I fell in love with and where ever I know fellows playing, I got myself in place to learn.

EM: What type of wood you used for your stick?

SSS: Rad wood. It doan' be heavy. Duh had many sticks dat we used to use Rad wood, bay wood, black willow, long sage. I have seen an overthrow, a lash coming from the air to the floor, awesome, landing here [on the skull]. There are remedies for those. Doan' tink and believe dat the judges doan' have a cover for them. There are covers. Listen, understand me carefully, a man that is practicing you, he can't use those lashes until he has gotten that far in showing you how to block lashes. He has to learn you the defence before you can start to do that.

I doan' skylark wid a stick! I am going to tell yuh why. Yuh burn my skin, I get cut. I don't skylark. Dey got some fellow who take pride in trying to burn yuh. I am the type of man who would leave my guard open and let yuh burn me. Because if you find me wid a open guard and you burn my skin yuh have to find a cover. Cover down yuh bucket or otherwise I gun put de tot in it. So I doan' skylark!

I have a brother see, and this is no joke, he learn as far as number three lesson, but ah mean he learn more than me 'cause nuhbody ent learn me nutten. And the man who taught him to play stick, let me tell you something brother, there was another man in the area that was teaching boys stick and they made a challenge to each other. I learn to understand that my brother was the furthest in advance with this particular man he was learning wid. And the other fellow who was the furthest in advance with the other man, and the man that taught my brother told him to clean him early. And they were lashes 'pun this man. Mash him up early o'clock. Those were the two first lashes that I told you about - a shoulder clutch and a strollop. Draw one down and bring the other up. This man would have been finish for life. My mother thought it too hard.

He saw where about he had the two lashes clear clear clear to land but it was not good enough to just end a man career like that. But brother let me tell you something, he pay for it. He paid for it. The next time he been back to execute the practice, the man started to practice him, and this was a lot to do wid it, while practicing you should always learn to see the positions that the man put his stick and what lashes in store. My brother told me that the man throw a city point at him, one outside the book, and it was too fast for he to ever cut it out wid the stick and the only thing he could do was quarter the stick and tek it on the wrist... and he done stick from dey.

He had practice up to number three lesson, and if you learn three and you got the third lesson good, you can represent yourself as a man. When you get thru' the third lesson, you have gone thru' the hardest in the book. In the third lesson is licks all round your kidneys, all around yuh chest and de waist, you are getting lick on the chest all under your arms all down the rest of your kidneys. You have to have both hands on the stick. The man I told you about in Belleplaine, Campbell, he doan have a right and left, just a right, the left hand is as fast as the right. Doan' fool yuhself when he hold both ends on the third and you looking fuh de right, he lash yuh wid de left and slap in yuh skin. Yuh have to be physical, yuh got to keep moving, yuh have tuh have de footwork.

The Old Man in de Rum Shop

"Two fellows was drinking rum in the rum shop, and this old man come in with his stick and sat down and watch the two fellows drinking the rum. The two fellows drink all the rum and wouldn't give him any. The old man got up and put two lashes, one a piece, on them. One man said, "Old man, I going for my mother." The mother came and the old stick man put a lash pon the mother.

The man get up and said to his mother it is time to go, *Come mother, I get one and you get one too.*"

Four little rack

Rupert Yarde was a mason or, as he would be described in his day, a Master Workman. He was born and lived all his life in Hothersal Turning, St. Michael,. He worked with my father, Ernest Deighton Mottley, as a Master Workman building and repairing various houses. He also worked on local government buildings. He also taught me the fundamentals of coral stone, how to cut it and how to use wallaba wood splinters, and how to make white lime. He was a member of the group of three (with Sunna Barker & Joe Tonkey) who accompanied EDM to Harrison College when an English teacher by the name of Derek Fowles kicked my brother Elliott during a PE class. He was a sticklicker of extraordinary skill and class. He was one the Stick Gods of his time. He was interviewed by EM at sunset in the mid seventies at his favourite rumshop in the Turning while dressed in a three piece serge suit.

EM: Rupert, where you learn sticklicking?

RY: Where I learn it... right here in de [Hothersal] Turning,

EM: Who teach you?

RY: Two people. Bomey Harewood and Edwin Yarde. Bomey Harewood... that dead, and Edwin Yarde that dead, my cousin. I learn broad sword and single stick, hear... I learn broad sword and single stick.

EM: Wuh is the difference between the two?

RY: I tell yuh wuh I learn but other people learn Tom Johnson and Donnelly.

EM: Wuh is broad sword?

RY: Step, break, cut!!!

EM: How? Ah mean wuh is that?

RY: Well yuh pull yuh position and if you are up, you advance. You is to cut. But the fellow is off, he is suppose to break. But as he break and he hear click, he got to cut, that is, he step and break. And as he cut, you got to take care of yourself too. That is broad sword single stick. But they got anudder ting they call Cudgeling and another ting called Tom Johnson.

One time I was playing a man there who playing he come to me wid someting call Tom Johnson. I tell him my first card. I tell he it could be johnson-tom-cut, and he make a cut here fuh my jaw. When he make de cut, I get back and stop the hit. Boy I ent telling yuh nuh lie and he make the same cut again pun dis side and I gi' he back the same way. Gi' he back the same way and I tek up de foot and ford it and cross cut it. So when I cut and cross cut yuh he thought it couldn't come from me. Not with much intentions, but the father was going to stop back in here fuh me.

EM: You ever lick stick seriously? I mean fight, I ent talking bout mekking sport? I talking bout real lashes.

RY: Yes, because when yuh start mild, if you seeing some usual crowds, yuh know tings can get hot. For instance, my cousin Edwin Yarde had a satu [just] before yuh get to Bibby Lane. Stoway is to come. Harold Trotman. This boy Hoad come.... Bomey Hill is to come. Bomey ent come. I gone up dey, dah is true and when I gone up dey now, I see de people outside at de window. At the then time it was only 12 cents to come in...

EM: Where was this?

RY: Bibby Lane! It was a rumshop. I cyan remember the name. I say wait, this is my cousin satu, yuh know. I saw Hoad come down wid a boy. Yuh always keep a boy wid about 5 or 6 sticks. Like duh varnish kind a ting. He's de champ. Hey, I gone up dey, a fellow called Gilly that dead too, waiting pun Bomey. Bomey ent come.

I tell Edwin, "Man you is my cousin, I gun open de house." I gone to Hoad. I suh, "You cud lend me one a yuh sticks? I gun open, dis is my cousin satu." He suh, "You gun open wid a master like dat wun dey?" I suh, "Yeah." I went and he lend me one uh de sticks and tell me doan brek it. I telling yuh. And I went in dey and becrise dis man fire all kind a cross lashes at me and I brek dem. When I fire a cross lash at he, he name Gilly, he dead now, my cousin Edwin suh, "Gi' it to me.... gi' Rupert to me. Wuh you tink I wanna do wid yuh?" And me and he fire one.

One time he mek a cross lash cross de foot, I gi' he a scratch. Oyyyy!!! and when yuh hear de shout, be'crise you doan' know dat dis man put so much lashes in my ass... my cousin dat did learning me, yuh. He suh, "Man, I still want you as my friend 'cause we learn wid de same people." I suh, "You want who to be you friend? Skipper I done wid dat, come let we drink some rum."

I suh, "Yuh gun gi' Mr. Hoad a practice?" Hoad suh, "I ent practicing wid Edwin unless Stoway come 'cause Stoway tell me doan play Edwin Yarde cause if yuh touch he and yuh burn he yuh gun find licks all over yuh body." Da was Hoad yuh, Joe Hoad. Yuh mekking sport, yuh! Joe Hoad come down heah playing cricket, watching cricket, and I deah under the gallery "Come Yarde, come try out de stick!" I suh, "Boy, we ent into nuh stick now."

EM: The old man use to lick stick too?

RY: Who?

EM: Daddy...

RY: No, he ent know nutten bout nuh stick. He was up in heah when me and Stoway and Bomey and ting mek bricks at that corner over there.

EM: Tell me someting, you know de old man as a boy up here? Wunna grow up together up heah?

RY: Whey?

EM: In De Turning? Up in Bibby's Lane?

RY: Nuh Bibby Lane, right dey so whey John Mottley is. Not Bibby Lane. My mudda use to wash he clothes. My mudda and Dots Alleyne did dey. John Mottley's aunt, Dots Alleyne and my mudda Betty use to wash Ernest Deighton Mottley clothes. We use to call he Babs. [He] cut my ass in second standard for misspelling geography.

EM: You knew his brother Bunny too?

RY: He brother? No, that get kill? No.

EM: How old the old man was when you know he then?

RY: How yuh mean how old he was! He taught me at second standard at St. Mathews School.

EM: But you din' know him when his family live in Lears?

RY: I never know he up in Lears. I know he heah. But he was ever up in Lears?

EM: John tell me that he father, John's father, come from Lears.

RY: I ent talking bout John father. I doan' know anyting bout John fadda.

EM: When he left living in de Turning, he went to the States or he remain living up heah?

RY: When he leave, he went to Lower Estate turning keys wid Dowding like a bookkeeper.

EM: You remember wuh year dah was?

RY: Nah. Not me I cyan remember wuh year dah was. In them times, a teacher at school, (wuh even the headmaster higher dan he) never use to get any money. Furthermore, so da wasn't any money so he went to Canefield to be a bookkeeper under Dowding, old Dowding dat dead.

EM: Where he went after that?

RY: He went to America. One time he did come back heah with a lorry dat get mash up in Waterford Bottom. You ent know nutten 'bout dat in de first place. It get mash up in an accident in Waterford Bottom. Yuh tink he did sweet!

EM: Greame Small was a friend of his. He was from up heah too?

RY: No, Green Hill! Graeme and your father went to America together. Wuh beat me is dat Graeme come back heah and me and Graeme and your father talking. They say they gone in a place in America, and your old man and Graeme in America got an apartment doing. And Ernest tell me, "Man Rupert, when we done the Jew man won't pay me my money." He suh someting gone wrong. This man got dis lotta hair all de way down heah [pointing to he belly]. I suh, "And wuh you do?" He suh, "Man I draw a match and light he beard and he send and call de cops." Dah is you father, yuh. When de cops come now, first body he gone to is you fadda and ask he wuh happen. He suh, "Listen I do some work fuh him and he refuse to pay me and he start to push me out and he was smoking and I was smoking and he beard get lit." And the cops say pay him he money. And the man pay dem and duh left. Boy dah is why I like he.

EM: The old man was bad? Whey he get the name Rugged from?

RY: He get de name Rugged 'cause he used to do anyting 'bout heah. He wasn't bad to lick down nuhbody nor nuh fighting an ting, but what I mean is he din care fuh nuhbody, he tell anybody wuh he like. Yuh hear wuh I tell you, not vagabond bad, but tell yuh wuh he like. One time, Friendship did heah (all a dis was Friendship), and the same Bomey Harewood, the stickman, did de watchman, and some potatoes did dig and duh say Babs did dig dem. So Dots, he Aunt, call he when Bomey went and mek de noise. So Dots suh, "Babs, you dig dese potatoes?" "No Dots." She ask he again, "Babs you dig these potatoes?" The watchman suh dat he dig them, yuh know. "No Dots." She ask he the third time, "Babs you dig these potatoes?" He suh, "Dots, you are a blasted fool." Dah is you fadda. I done wid dat. Come let muh show yuh someting...

EM: Wuh yuh showing muh?

RY: Ah gun call Hopper. I got on dis big three piece suit of gabardine, yuh know, waistcoat and every fuck. I inside hearing de talk and singing and so on and so on. But outside I hearing click click, in de yard. Click click! And ah ent know Big Syrup gone out there and interfere wid somebody in the district and get a lash. He come inside and tell me, Rupert man, come out heah and represent muh. I suh, "Represent yuh wid wuh?" He suh, "A man just put a lash in my ass an I tell he I got a fellow in deah." "You ent see how I dress? And I ent gine out deah tuh play any stick!" He suh, "Man doan let down de Turning." I suh to muhself ah got in two grogs but ah seh ah coming.

I pull off de jacket and de waistcoat an' gi' somebody deah and I gone out. When I gone out in de road, dey got a shop up pun a hill up de road. When I gone out in de road so, a fellow come an' gi' me a stick but I ent know I gine run in trouble. A fellow come. I mek a lash at he yuh know and I tell he watch out I coming. When I mek a four little rack at he so and he brek, he head cut off and he cut up.

Ah ent know that de boss suh "Hey go up dey to Victor house and bring two pairs of sticks an' gi' me he." Dah's one of de fellows dat learn to box. Oh jesuscrise! Ah say well de boss coming now. But I gun keep eye. You know stick? If you know certain positions, you see de eye, you see dis, watch dis, put yuh eye pun dis [the stick]. And de boss come and tell me walk [march in a circle] and I walk like a watchman. From the time I put down a crossing walk, he come and do so to me, look, Tom Johnson first. I suh it could be Johnson Tom. I cut and step back. An when he went up and when I put a lash in he ass, he suh, "Who learn you?" I call ev'ry sticklicker I did know in Buhbadus. But he ent know. He suh, "Come leh we go up heah at dis shop."

When we lef de shop de man din' have a pint a-half bottle of rum. Billy suh, "Yuh see ah got to walk bout wid good man tuh protect muh." I suh, "You playing de ass. You walk 'bout an put yuhself in trouble. Run yuh rasshole self in trouble and den men got tuh rescue yuh rasshole." This hand is like rasshole lightning. But when I cross the lash pun de man, yuh know, I look 'way from he like so like Edwin used to learn me, and I look 'way so and when he mek de brek, he did wrong and I cross cut he. "Come let we go up heah man," he suh, "who learn you?" Man I call everybody I did know learn me. But dah time dese two did good. I ent fooling yuh. Yuh know when dey did good. I had a good fucking pair a hand by muh side. Gawblindmuh, yuh mekking sport!

One time I used to do some shite. The only other man dat had two good hands was Harold Greaves (Drakes.) Lemme gi' a joke! But the joke is we gone to work, Harold working wid me. But I ent know dat me and Harold is to play de Sunday. A man call me in de week and tell me "Boy Harold uncle got he dey practicing to cut yuh ass de whole week in de back of Carrington." Harold uncle is who help to learn me too. I say awright. Yuh know me, I play fair.

I gone godblast me up Bibby lane tuh Edwin and get a few lashes. Skipper I got a friend, although he work wid me Bomey gun feel glad that Harold gun cut my ass. Right! When de day come and he start to wrestle and ting, we hold one another and shove off, shove off de stick. Well I gi' he third he had tuh guh back and gi me a position. And when I did make the cross shot I did sorry dat Harold use to work wid me. I did sorry.

Let me gi' a joke. You never hear the joke wid me and Bomey the master. Bomey is the man that did learning me. One time he got Pa Massiah down dey at Miss Humphrey. We drinking rum and ting, had Son Richardson and every time he tek up the wood as Sonny brek out, he brek in and he get touch. So he suh, "Thelbert, come fuh de stick." I suh, "Pa after I hit Bomey (all we got in we grogs but you know me) he dangerous." He suh, "Come fuh de rasshole stick." He getting on. Bomey tek up de stick and he put heself cutting rack pun me and ting and I suh tuh muhself, it is this wild shite is get me offset yuh know. I 'pon de perfect stand. Godblindyuh want me mek a cross cut and I tek up de stick and when I cross cut I see blood coming done heah. Gawblinmuh Bomey eye get cut. And yuh know wuh he do? He went to the hospital.

A couple of weeks after, he come tuh dah shop when Prince was in um. All de gents in deah. He suh, "Yuh cut me in me eye and put me in de hospital and yuh won't gi' me nutten, and if yuh ever tek a stick in yuh hand, son, ah gun blind yuh." I suh, "Gawblindyuh, you cyan blind me, not wid a stick". I did get hot 'cause we owe Willie dey. Come go. I gine tek out de rasshole, I grab Willie stick. Oh shite it is granite. I snatch Willie stick and went in de yard wid Victor and all de giant men and ting.

When he come, he tell me drop. I suh, "Man, me? Is you who should drop. Not me, you gun blind me. Drop!" He do so and he walk round. He tell me drop. I suh, "No you is de body to drop. You gun blind me. But I heah." But he smarter than me, but I ent gun drop cause he is de boss. Man I ent dropping at all. I still awright heah, I still awright. But I did anticipating if he drop and he do anyting that I woulda gone up and do my little ting first and then cross cut. But the question is he walk round. And when he walk 'round and I won't drop, he stop and suh, "Gi' me a pint-nuh-half." and I suh, "Dah is wuh yuh is to do, leh we drink." Gawblindyuh, he walk 'bout de place and suh he gun do wuh! I did waiting fuh he rasshole. I was watching dis right hand wid dah stick in um. I did waiting fuh he cunt and if he did mek a mistake he woulda see who get blind.

Goodnight.

Ta-pa yuh good

Vernon Hopper Lashley was another sticklicker and a student of Rupert Yarde. In this interview with Elvis Gill (EG) and Ione Knight (IK), he recalls some of Rupert Yarde's exploits.

Man there had some good sticklickers in those days. I remember Edwin Yarde from Bibby's Lane. He learn Rupert who was his cousin. He learn him because of Bomey Harewood, the watchman at Friendship and then Lower Estate Plantation. Bomey was very, very good with a stick. He was the best 'round here.

Edwin learn Rupert to keep Bomey quiet. And it turn out that Rupert was faster, three times faster. Bomey turn 'round then, and learn a boy to call he uncle name Harold Greaves to take care of Rupert. And Harold was very good at what he went to do. And it turn out then that Harold was the only one to control Rupert.

But he didn't last too long all because of rum. Those was the days where you play a touch for a pint and a half of rum. The fellows used to gather and claim that they was the best and they would play for a drink. Everybody would claim that them is the best. So the easiest way of breaking it down was to say 'All right you is the best, I better than you man. I will play for a bottle of rum'. Every touch was a bottle of rum and they would play that way. Every time a fellow got touch he had to call for a bottle of rum. It was their way of training against one another on weekends. On Saturday evening or Sunday, mostly Sunday mornings you will see many a sticklicker come along with his piece of stick.

You would hear Rupert Yarde say, "I don't have a cent in my pocket, but I want a rum to drink". He would get a joke out of that because his hands was fast. And regardless of what you do he will hit you, and you would end up having to buy him a bottle of rum.

I remember he had a friend live down here, a fellow called Pa Massiah. He was a big, long, tallish fellow. The two of them was good, good buddies. Man, Rupert couldn't get Pa hit at all, at all. Rupert would say, "Ta-Pa yuh good." Ta would reply, "I better than you."

On this day in question, I don't know what happened, but when Rupert moved, his hand was like lightning and Ta-Pa cross cut the same time, and all I see Rupert do is flick the stick and touch him behind his head and cut him. The blow didn't look no way mysterious the way it happened. Pa said: "Bring the bottle of rum and let me get one." He wash the cut with the rum, and everybody told him that he would have to go to the hospital to get stitches. I remember at the time Pa sister Molly Massiah told Rupert, "Yuh bitch, yuh, yuh cut yuh best friend with the stick. That man is yuh best friend and yuh cut he."

I wudda stand 'pun he!

Prince Albert Prescod was a sticklicker. He was a former blacksmith who operated a popular rumshop in Hothersal Turning, St. Michael, during the seventies. Rupert Yarde taught him how to lick stick. He was interviewed by EG and IK.

Rupert Yarde learn me some stick. Oh my God. I think that I used to only stand up because I had a good mind. Rupert was a terrible man. One Saturday evening, that man made me break so much lashes. I had a shop up there in Hothersal Turning. We had the back where yuh could play and thing. That man force me down between the toilet with licks coming from all sort of kinds of ways and all I doing is breaking. I telling myself, "Well I ent Stoway, how is it that all I doing is breaking. I ent Stoway".

The man would not ease up at all, at all. And I remember that I fall back between the toilet and rest on the paling. When I rest on the paling, he fire and I break it. I break and cut. When I cut, he step out and I showed him the sword.

He said. "Why you didn't stop me? I would kill you down in there if you didn't stop me." A friend of mine just come from America was standing in the shop door. He said that he didn't holler for me because if he had holler for me I might have look at him and get hit. So he stop in the shop door. He said, "I'm going to buy you and carry you back to America with me. You down here selling rum and can play stick. Man, I can get money for you up there."

"No man," I replied, "I only learn this here to take care of myself if anything. Carry long that old man." Me, he and Rupert went in to the shop and drink some rum. My friend asked, "Rupert, you were going to kill he just now down in the comer?" "If he can't get me off, I wudda stand pun he," Rupert replied.

I satisfied with what Rupert show me!

Vernon Hopper Lashley was interviewed by EG and IK.

Patsy Ward was the last man that I played. And because of him, I made a vow that I would stop playing stick. You know, when people don't know what you have in store, I don't believe that they should get one-sided and put down other people.

He always used to tell me, "That stick-break nonsense that Rupert show you ent one damn use. Come up at me, man, and leh me show you some Queensbury this and Queensbury that."

I told him, "I don't want to learn no Queensbury."

He asked me, "You got another one of these 'bout here?"

I was at the front of the shop standing up and he calling me for a piece of stick. And he gone out in the back in the yard looking for another piece of stick.

When he returned, he said, "Come and let me show you what I mean."

I said to him, "I don't want to see what you mean. I satisfied with what Rupert show me."

A bit irritated, he said to me, "I is see you and Rupert play, and you and Sonny."

I used to play Rupert Yarde and Sonny Wilkinson 'cause them know my movements. Rupert would lash you if he get there before you, but not Sonny. Sonny would hold the lash.

He added, "There is a lash that I see up to now you is play and can't get it break."

I replied, "You don't worry your head about that. What is this lash that I can't break? Show me."

Quick so. He send a lash at my feet. I said, "That is the lash that you talking about? That is a joke lash, you idiot. Nobody don't regard a foot before they hit your belly. That is a joke lash". He said, "Then I going to learn you to block that."

From the time that I was training, I never could have get back to block my foot. So I built up a thing for that move, so I never used to worry about it. Because my eyes was so good and my hand was very quick, whenever it would come I always cut it down in the second position. He came back and hit me on the foot again.

I said, "Man, what you doing? I got something for that." He said, "Show me what you got for it."

He didn't pay me any mind. And when he send the third lash and I hear pix, I was up. All I hold back the stick, all I do, he got cut and the blood start to flow.

Angrily he said, "Man, you cut me." I told him, "Man, I told you that I got a play for that. I don't bother my head about going back to cut back to break."

I never played him again because I know that he would be looking for a chance to get revenge and cut me back.

Hot licks at the Roxy

Sonny Wilkinson was a sticklicker. He played Rupert Yarde and was one of the Stick Gods. He was interviewed by EG and IK.

EG: I know you got a lot of stories on sticklicking.

SW: I ever did like it from a little boy. They used to lick stick in Suck Hole Gap, the gap by the [Hothersal] Turning [St. Michael]. They used to play down thru' there. The men, you know. Little boys used to gather round them while they playing. I was one who used to be around them. I did really like it.

After I get to find out what this thing was all about, I heard talk 'bout an old man named James Prescod. He was a middle-aged man at the time. He had learn wid a famous man by the name of Edwin Yarde from Bibby's Lane [St. Michael]. He also learn my oldest brother too. So, after I grow up a certain way I find out that I still like this thing. So I told him that I like it and would like to learn. Prescod tell me, "After you get a bit more mature that you can walk about by yuhself, come over and the same way that I learn your brother and Edwin I will learn you."

So seven of us started off going out there and after the boys got a little burning and thing they back out and stop, but I continue. I gather a lot after going through with he, and I develop a lot for myself too. You does have to get a technique for yourself, yuh understand. The same Hopper, me and Rupert used to give him practice.

EG: You mean Rupert Yarde?

SW: Yes. He learn the same science too. Rupert was Prescod cousin and he had learn Rupert.

EG: Do you remember some of the fellas you used to play?

SW: Me? I play a lot of fellas... lots of fellows. I play a fella from Belle Gully [St. Michael] at the Roxy.

EG: You mean the Roxy Theatre in Eagle Hall?

SW: Yeah! It is now a supermarket. This was in 1954, some way about there. That was a long time ago. I had not too long come back from the States... U.S.A.

EG: That was a satu or ramping when you play at the Roxy?

SW: This was for the congregation. Instead of showing pictures they pay to see people play stick.

IK: How regular this used to take place?

SW: I only took part that time. Let me tell you how it happened. There had this white fellow. His name was [Joe] Hoad. He was one of the Hoads from Vaucluse [St. Thomas] son. And he was going round in the districts like the Turning, Jackson and the Belle Gully, you know, gathering somebody to represent the place that they lived.

So the same time he was up there, it was a Sunday and I happen to be up there that Sunday, although I wasn't living up there. I mostly was in the Turning. So, a few of the fellows decided that they would go. But after the time came, they didn't go down.

One fellow name Gillie say that he didn't go because he was too old, but he went to watch the fun. I even pay to watch it too. When I got there, I didn't see any of the fellows who arrange to go. So I decided I was going to watch. But it so happen that they had somebody from all the districts except the Turning. And somebody point me out to Hoad and say that I was a Turning man. I decide I would play after talking to him.

I went then and play some fellow from the Belle Gully. Me and he had the place so hot they called for us again. At that time I wasn't no slow man. I had the place hot. We had the play that they wanted to see. Only thing I was sorry after I did it, though. My hands was too quick, we playing the science all the time. So after he done, we round out and finish everybody start clapping and clapping and call for us again. We went back and play and he start to exaggerate then with his Creole [style]. And I told him to change his position... You know Creole?

EG: Yeah... the stick is straight down and you just holding it like you walking with it.

SW: I hitting the stick down and telling he to change, change it from this 'cause I know that he can't hit me with no Creole and I don't want to hurt he. The man wouldn't change. He wouldn't change. And when I went to cut he, a cousin of mine down in the theatre, shout out, "Don't do that!" People did bawling, man. We had the place hot, hot. I tell yuh, it was hot licks at the Roxy. But you know me. I ent ask 'bout no money and didn't wait bout fuh nothing. 'Cause after I finish, I mek fuh home, I was living down the hill at that time.

From yuh toe nail to your eye broo!

Aberdeen Jones was a cocky, rambunctious man and an aggressive sticklicker. He was one of the Stick Gods of that Gall Hill, Lodge Hill, Water Street area, an area that produced many, many sticklickers. He operated a shop in Gall Hill, Christ Church. He was a community organizer and served as a policeman in Trinidad. Opposite his shop was Club Randall which he operated as a dancehall and community centre. He was interviewed by EM sometime in the early seventies.

AJ: I is a Bajan in Trinidad. One carnival in Tunapuna, in front the police station, a crowd of people gathered. Two sticks lay down and I is persuade to tek up one. The people warn me not to take up one. The warning of the crowd saying, "Don't take up that stick Bajan because dey ent no rights for getting cut up in carnival season." I say I must try this cutting up to see how Trinidad people is cut up. Trinidad people dem plays Creole. I say I play Creole.

EM: Creole is how yuh hold de stick?

AJ: No, Creole is from the belly come back up. Yuh can't hit below yuh belt most like when yuh boxing. See. But the Bajan men lick stick from your toe nail tuh yuh head. Where ever the stick rest yuh receive it. Yuh unnerstand wuh ah mean. So when yuh go in front of a man, yuh going straight to hell, heaven or hospital if yuh don't break right. So when I mek the first march wid de man, de man trow the stick outta he hand and declare you must be the winner 'cause he cyan brek below the belt 'cause he doan' know 'bout dat. But we Barbadians break from yuh toe nail to your eye broo. And if yuh doan' be careful the cap of yuh head gone too. And I win de match so. Easy as drinking tea!

EM: I thought the Creole style also had to do wid how yuh hold de stick?

AJ: No yuh see. Dey doan need... This is Creole science, see. They breaking from heah so tuh heah [to the waist]. Bajan science is different. If a Bajan man playing out of different sciences, a Creole science man is there. And de licks coming at he any kind a how, he can save. And when a Creole man t'row a stick at you, you cannot trow yours at him. But when you are playing in the Bajan styles, any time that you like tuh pass licks you can pass it if you feel that the man that you crossing gun mek you win de fight, you cross him. His lash may not be nothing so great, and you may give him a lash to put him out. You know wuh ah mean. You may be able to rest your stick down in heah. In de shoulder-plex [points to neck/collar-bone area]. You may be able to rest your stick across the knee pads. And by so doing those is dangerous places. Yuh understand. So if a man burst a water-line lash at you, you see, or strollop...

EM: ...up between yuh legs...

AJ: If a man fire a strollop at you, dat ent nuh lash at all. Dah is lil children lash. So when a man fire a strollop at you, you only raise the strollop and the same time you raising the strollop you cross his knee and you win de fight 'cause he cyan move agin. Anybody hit you cross heah (the knee) yuh gone. Yuh unnerstand wuh ah mean.

Then you try to knuckle him. If you can get a stick lash cross heah, the knuckles of a hand, the person got to drop their stick because duh hand cannot hold their stick.

EM: I thought yuh grip the stick from the quarter? Backwards?

AJ: No, depends... depends, on the way you choose to play. You play from how-so-ever you believe you can win a man. Suppose you believe you can win a man in the long seven, you cud play him in de long seven. Yuh unnerstand wuh ah mean. Suppose you cud come back again by playing him creole. That is our first lesson. Again in the first lesson line. But that is when de ting cool. But when it hot yuh ketchin de long seven man all of dem is licks 'bout yuh chin gine up to Greame Hall. Yuh unnerstand sometimes yuh collect down in dey so and den yuh face up in de air. Yuh cyan see back down till yuh laying down.

EM: What is the opening ritual?

AJ: Suppose in case that the Trinidad men generally play so... We stop dem from playing so. If you are stronger than me in defence, you bring me to your command. The body that is strongest, bring to their command. Well when I gine playing wid a man and I ketch he as he come out he dey, I gone wid he too. I markin he. But when de congregation look at me ...and say "wet the man", I done wid dat. I doan want to hold dis end no more. Dis end representing your backside. Den I gone long down dey. Becrise when you see me down dey look out for sudden death an' long sickness. And ever time

I change a chop, dah is a chop coming up dey by you neck all the way out here. Dah is a sore! And from the time it rest in you neck, I got it back dis way... You cyan get hit! You frighten! Yuh unnerstand what ah mean! Practice makes perfect!

We had a get away. We playing a man and a man fire a head lash at you. Head lash in my day din nuh lash. Head lash in the days of this same man Now Carter, dah was waste like. When a head lash leggo, and you do so look... see dis foot, dah is de person dey, dey pelt a head lash at you, it break de same way as a sword, gone long down dey, see. Dah's a waste lash and de same way it breaking you coming right away around. And yuh know whey dat lash land... 'cross the knee pad and he gone!

EM: Wuh is he defence? When he trow dat waste lash at you an he miss, wuh is he defence?

AJ: Miss! He cyan miss. When you brek a lash from a man, your stick cannot be using 'cause you breaking the lash wid de stick. But when he pelt a head lash at you, you are doing two things in one. You are wasting his lash and using your stick too. So this is wasting the lash. In a quick space of time, your foot step dey which draw you nearer to him. Yuh coming down wid de lash which break de same time, cross the knee pad, he ent nuh more use. Yuh unnerstand wuh I mean? He gone; cyan come back.

EM: Who is the best sticklickers you know in the last 40 to 50 years?

AJ: One of the top notch sticklickers we had was a fellow name Arnold Greenidge from Lodge Road [Christ Church]. Simmie Best, Gifted, George Newton. Dem so was Stick Gods. Dis lef hand man from up dey in Lodge dat learn de lil' red fellow... Leon Small. But anyhow, those was the Stick Gods. I have had fetes heah wid dem dey playing. Men come from all about showing fuh nothing cause we only want fame. Flatform tall in de air man. The last fete I had here wid de flatform tall in de air was estimated at 6,000 and odd people by the Advocate.

That time I was a Goddard [supporter]. That time Goddard had belong to the House of Assembly and also Talma. And I gun tell you, as God made my life this time, we had it on a carnival day. And when we land dey, I went and tek up de men and I notify them. Any man at all with a pair of eye, come pun de flatform fuh sticklicking. And I am specifying I won't like no man from whey I live to come. Any stranger. Who ever like come. If yuh out fuh mekking sport doan come up. And a fellow come up.

I won't lie to tell you, from the time that he come up, man all you cud hear was the two sticks wrestling. That time I was in form too. And the two sticks wrestling. And all you cud hear from de people yelling "Oh God! Oh Lord! Oh Lord!" Look like I gun get cut up bad. And I gun tell you when I finish and get down, Mr. Goddard call me. And I went to him and Goddard was crying.

I seh, "Mr. Goddard, wuh yuh crying so fuh?"

"Aberdeen man, I thought you did get cut. Who de man is dat you were playing wid? Whey he from?"

I seh, "I doan know him!"

He seh, "Aberdeen, and you did playing him?"

I seh, "Man wuh you talking. Duh got a man wid a pair a eye I frighten fuh?"

He tell me call him to see if I get him and I send a boy to call he. Goddard gi' he fifty dollars. Earnestly bejesuschrise! He seh he did never see nutten so and I had $150 fuh meself one. Man dem was days, man! But dese doan encourage yuh tuh do nutten. Yuh unnerstand wuh ah mean. Dat was 1970 all down in dey. The politicians use tuh spend money in dah day. Dese doan spend none.

EM: When you setting up a fight wid a man, yuh had tuh cross de sticks first on de ground?

AJ: Two sticks so, [cross on the ground] and yuh march [anti-clockwise in a circle] and de same time yuh march he cut back down and you cut back y'own and we gone long licking...

EM: ...and he doan stand pun yours?

AJ: Ef I cut back mine quick enough that you ent got de stick in yuh hand, yuh ass is mine too. Gawblindyuh yuh ass gone!

EM: Did the fighters say anything?

AJ: During de fight? No. But I gun tell you I seen in Port-of-Spain the blood like water, man. You doan know on morning the train coming down and de better part of the people on the train is sticklickers coming from Point to wet Port-of-Spain crowd. If duh win, duh tekking train again and gine to Sangre Grande... And um ent nuh law because from the time, it in front the police station. From the time dat you go and tek up a stick yuh is a man responsible fuh yuhself.

Duh used tuh say dat some fellows got de ting yuh call obeah. When yuh brek a lash heah, one heah, the main stick hit yuh heah. One stick. Dah was de saying. You know all we do in Trinidad, dey say yuh like obeah. Yuh get wuh ah mean. But I never believe in dat shite doah. The only obeah I believe in Gawblindyuh is de food gine in we mout to eat.

You, I know fellows who use to go tuh a man for some obeah to play cards. And dah man will gi yuh obeah tuh play cards and becrise play wid he and cyan win a cent. Ah use to dead wid laff.

EM: Did you ever play stick at Civic Day?

AJ: About Civic. They got Civic Day[67] and I went and tell Mr. [CB] Layne dat he doan gi' me nutten wen he got Civic Day

67. Civic Day was held on the first of January every year in Queen's Park in Bridgetown by the Civic Friendly Society which had 45,000 members at its peak.

and if I got my fete I gun mash up Civic. So he tell me I cyan do nutten wid Civic. Go on Aberdeen, do wuh ever you like. And dat day, yuh know who was in de Park, he and [Ernest Deighton] Mottley man. Gawblindyuh, the people up here like corn-rass-hole-grain! The next day The Advocate had in an estimate of 8,000 people. Mine was freeness and he wun yuh had to pay to go in de [Queen's] Park. Ever'ting mix up—tug-o-war pulling, greasy pole, potato eating, a man eating 50 pounds of potato, two pounds of raw salt fish, and a gallon bucket of sweet water and rum. Boy you mekking joke! Dem was days.

Wuh you tink Layne tell me? Any Civic Day I having on sports, Mottley tell me must tell yuh yuh must come to he fuh someting. As man I tell dem I doan' wan' nutten I only wan' show dem wuh I cud do. I cud rack duh.

Duh got fete in Oistins and I mash dum up, man. The first main stay fete that I mash up in Oistins, the princess coming heah. Duh giving a thousand dollars to each parish. Dat time it was the vestry. Well Goddard propose me second by George Ward. Awright and duh propose different people. When duh done duh give the casting vote between me and Garnes in St. Lawrence. And what happen Mrs. Talma seh Aberdeen gun gi' good sport but he gun got nuff of de money. But Mr. Goddard and dem get up and say dat it doan matter whuh a man got after he gi yuh good laffing and good sport. Wuh de shite yuh tink happen? Duh gi' um tuh Hugh Garnes. I ent know 'bout nutten yuh know. Goddard come up heah when he done in a flood of tears. The only ting dat ent coming out he eye was water.

He seh, "Man Aberdeen, man you should get some of de money, and she gi' Hugh Garnes. What yuh gine to do? I seh "let me mash it up den." George Ward was here de same time. Harry Ward. The three was here. Dey seh, "Aberdeen mash it up. I gun help yuh mash it up." And duh make a lil' brief fuh I to spend at 10 people, 10 chosen people to give help to mash this sport.

When de day come dat de Governor wife at that time sharing prizes at the vestry union, and I gun tell you, wen I get coming down the road, I meet a crowd coming up from Oistins, and dum telling me doan guh tru' Oistins, Oistins too pretty. Dey got about five steelbands down dey. Dah time I carrying four steelbands. Dey got five steelbands in Oistins and the Governor wife was sharing prizes: boat race running, tug-o-war pulling, and ever shite. I seh I ent gine in Oistins but I mash um up tru' Oistins. Dey seh but dey gun be a noise. Den another crowd come to me and tell me dat duh now change up the program pun yuh. Putting one band behind the next and playing dat duh gun mash you band. You band ent gun have nuh hearing.

Dem ent know wuh I got dey, dem ringing dat I got a one man troupe. I blow de whistle. I stop my band and then call up my police. Dat time I had police. All dem bad men I got fuh police. And I bad too! Dem bad and I bad but I wusser dan dem. I seh boys dis a fight today coming to we. Duh seh wuh happen? I seh doan' matter wuh happen, you see me lickin' everbody lick. An duh gone long laffing. Duh seh awright, we in fuh dat. And I coming down de road by de district council, and hear de band coming up meeting me "All day all night, Miss Mary Ann." And I call pun my band to change down to Mary Ann too. And I marching wid dese shepherds dat did third mortar dat did seize up pretty. And when the first fellow in front rush to me and I do so and so, half laying down there and half laying there. Like sparrows. And de rest of fellows dat got de band, nuh, standing up wid de band so and de police.

Dat time Garfield Sargeant[68] was the corporal at Oistins. I seh, "Ef you come cross heah your share heah fuh yuh. Yuh cud come lil further." Band all de time! And since I tell you so, she send and call me. The Governor wife. Since I tell you so, I seh I ent going. And I went and I wont lie to tell you she seh dey ent no band cud beat you. And you are the first person coming in. You will come back for your prize. I seh Mistress I doan' come back. Give me what so ever you giving me now. She gi' me two hundred dollars in a envelope when I open um. Dat was my prize. And I gun tell yuh she ent hear anudder band 'cause nuhbody ent left in Oistins. I bring all duh up heah. The very shopkeepers be'crise did up heah. Yuh mekking joke!

The very man now that is Governor General of Barbados,[69] he went dey at a bar I had and seh, "Aberdeen bring anybody and let dem call fuh wuh ever duh want." I never see anyting like dis since I born. Boy you mekking sport. You ole man was up heah too, you know. De Princess Margaret went heah. It wasn't de first time she went heah. Duh had de vestry at dat time. I doan mean in Barrow time. It was Adams time. I won't lie to tell you, Oistins like the fete was de Monday, when you see Saturday, Oistins sweep down wid

68. Garfield Sargeant, who later became a lawyer, a member of Parliament and Deputy Speaker of the House of Assembly.

69. Deighton Ward, Brother to Mrs. Talma, who became a member of the Federal Parliament, a Judge, and then Governor General.

so much flags it turn yuh stomach bone. I went all tru town and cun get none to buy. I say dem ent gun have more flags dan me. The Sunday, I send down dey by Mr. Rock and get two long bamboos and put knife pun de end of duh, I seh boys come and help me get some of dese flags. Night time we guh down dey and cut duh out. I had more flags dan dem when duh done. And people bawl fuh murder man. All de way down had flags. Flags all de time! Wuh! An' ever minute Goddard pun de telephone, telephoning fuh buses tuh come and bring de people and cya' duh. Next day people seh bout heah cyan get. Boy dem did days!

Theophilus 'Tee' Campbell

"During the 1950's, the art of stick licking was practiced by some men in the rural area of Belleplaine, St. Andrew. A few of those men who readily come to mind include Theophilus 'Tee' Campbell, Conrad Worrell, Horton Dixon, Pearlie Hunte and Eustace 'Nanook' Campbell.

These men would gather by Pearlie Hunte's shop on Sunday mornings to practice their craft and it was widely accepted among them and others who gathered to watch, that 'Tee' Campbell was the best of them.

It was a joy to watch these men practice their craft and to appreciate the skills they possessed whether in defense, attack, the movements from left to right, or the get 'ready' stance. Nanook would often challenge Tee and one would never forget one such morning when Nanook attempted to block a lash from Tee that was destined for the knees, but did not see the swift movement that caught him on the head and opened a cut. Tee then twirled the stick and positioned himself to attack again just in case Nanook felt like continuing.

These Sunday mornings sessions would end with a lime at Pearlie Hunte's shop with pork chops, corned beef and serious 'beverage' resulting in 'ole' talk, arguments and lively discussions on any topic and ending with very unsteady feet on their way to the respective homes, mumbling and planning how to defeat the master craftsman, 'Tee' Campbell. "

Andrew Campbell

Cane-Juice wash Fish-Soup in licks

Sticklicker Prince Albert Prescod tells this story to EG and IK who interviewed him.

Let me tell you something, Christ Church and St. Philip was known for sticklicking. When you see fellows go to a dance and a fight take place, any stick that's around, a real sticklicker is going to drag it in his hands. A real sticklicker only have to get in a corner, and he will lick every one of them. We talking bout a real dance hall fight. And you can't get in to him 'cause he own de corner.

Those Penny-hole people and Silver Sands people, when there had the dancing house in Silver Sands, dey used to have real sticklicking going on up there. And they would come down and ramp. One fellow, I know he good, was a small man, but nuff man. He would lick them up bad, bad, bad, and all of them would have to go to the hospital.

One of the real good sticklickers was a man called Aberdeen [Jones] from Christ church this man was Clyde Jones—the funeral—man brother.[70] He had his own crowd.

Silver Sands people used to laugh at the St. Philip people. Now, St. Patrick, the upper part of Christ Church by the oil fields was considered part of St. Philip. So St. Patrick's people or the St. Philip people couldn't come down to Silver Sands without getting their

70. Aberdeen's nephews are Sydney and Ken Jones, founders of the band Troubadours International.

tail wash in licks by him. And he used to make sport of them. They used to call Christ Church people Fish-Soup because they lived by the sea and they would call St. Philip people Cane-Juice. And they would challenge anyone saying that Cane Juice couldn't beat Fish Soup.

Now in those days there had a lot of rivalry between sticklickers from different parishes. So, on bank holidays they would keep competitions to see who the best sticklicker was. The fellows would put on a big pot and cook. There would be lot of food, nuff corned beef and sardines and some of the food would be thrown away cause there was too much food to eat.

Man, people for so down there to see the fellows playing. And licks sharing! Them tekking their blows, and breaking and breaking. But this particular Sunday in question when Cane-Juice played Fish-Soup, the Cane-Juice people wash the Fish-Soup people backside in licks. And the people holler for so. You can imagine how them people got on. The Fish-Soup people was so shock they didn't know what to do. So the Cane-Juice people showed the Fish-Soup people that even though they thought that they were weaklings and couldn't fight, the Cane-Juice people show what weakling could do. So that day the joke was on the Fish-Soup people.

Sticklicking is a pretty thing to see, but you have to know what you're doing. Rain could be falling and when them sticklickers start to swirl their sticks over them heads, you could shelter under there like an umbrella. That is what is called sticklicking. It pretty for days!

Flesh to the birds of the air and bones to the dogs of the earth!

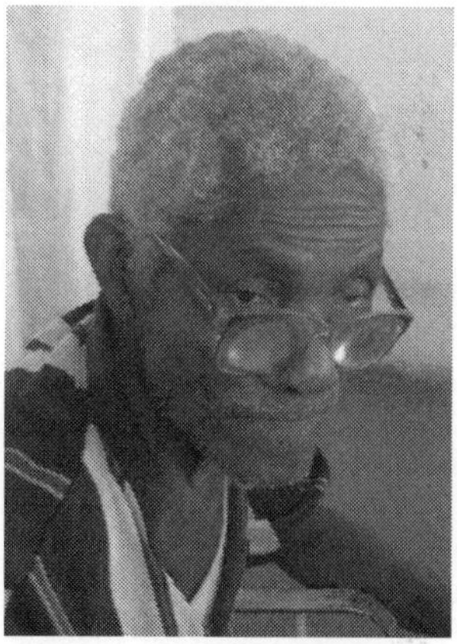

Dudley Nathaniel Walcott aka Gullyboar was a sticklicker. He was a mason and a Master Workman in his own right. He lived in Lodge Road, Christ Church, an area that produced many Stick Gods of which he was one. When I met him in 2004, he was 94 years old and blind. He however possessed an indefatigable spirit. He was interviewed by EM.

EM: What is yuh right name?

Gully: My name is Dudley Nathaniel Walcott.

EM: Yuh were a carpenter?

Gully: Mason. Man, I am a mason.

EM: And they call yuh what?

Gully: They call me Gully.

EM: Short for Gullyboar?

Gully: Uh uh. Being that I cudda play de stick good, that I din frighten fuh nuhbody, yuh know, so dey gimme dah name – Gullyboar.

EM: I want to know a little bit about the sticklicking and wuh style yuh used to use?

Gully: Well, I generally used to play the sword exercise. The sword exercise is what yuh would call seven lessons. Yuh count from one, two, first lesson, second lesson, third lesson, fourth lesson, fifth lesson, sixth lesson, seventh lesson.

EM: What was the first lesson?

Gully: The first lesson is what yuh would call point seven. That seven lesson is one hey, one dey.

EM: One to the right....

Gully: And one to the left.

EM: And one to the left.

Gully: Then yuh come up to the top, yuh call that a ear-bang.

EM: A bang?

Gully: A ear-bang.

EM: That is what yuh call yuh shoulder or yuh head?

Gully: Here so to yuh face. That is two. Yuh understand, and then the punch. The punch is one so.

EM: Juck straight.

Gully: Yes. Right here so.

EM: That was three?

Gully: That is six. And the strollop.

EM: Right between yuh legs?

Gully: Yes, that is the most dangerous of all. But yuh could get away. If a man use a strollop at yuh, and yuh understand yuhself good, yuh could get away and yuh could destroy the man, because yuh could walk over that, yuh could brek it so, keep that stick down.

EM: Send it down?

Gully: Yes. And if yuh good enough, man, yuh step over dah lash and use licks and yuh got dah man down. Lick yuh right upside down! Yes, it is a very terrible lash.

EM: When did yuh start licking stick?

Gully: Man I start licking stick from all the way in the thirties.

EM: How old yuh are now by the way?

Gully: I am 94 years.

EM: That is a long run.

Gully: [I was] thirty years old when I start learning. I could remember, yuh know. I had a brother, he did name Edgar Walcott. He was a very terrible fellow. But when I say a terrible fellow, not a vagavun, yuh know. He did know the stick real, real good. Suppose he did know yuh and yuh go to St. Andrew, and he did see a crowd pon yuh, and he in bicycle, motor car or anything, he would jump out. He would represent yuh.

He did know de stick good but my brother never learn me. My brother learn my other brother name Herbert, a fellow name Golder Lovell, and a fellow name Charlie Elliott. All of them so dead. That is who my brother learn. When I started, there was this man Brooksie Byer, I learn then with Brooksie. Then from Brooksie, a fellow call Simmie Best, yuh hear about Doctor Best? He got a grandson is a Doctor. He was good. After he learn me, I could remember my father had a house down on Durant's Land and this house was dey so we used to go down there and practice.

I could remember when I went down there this man come down in a jacket wid a pipe in he mout. He was a Superintendent at Beulah. Elombe, that man come round and all the boys gone down. Let me tell yuh something. That man leh go some lashes at me first time. One time he come from out of de first to the third to the fourth and went back and he seh, "Get out dis corner now," and when he leh go, I was back behind he back and got de stick. "I gine kill yuh yeh." Yuh know what he do? Man he tek the stick outta yuh hand and go and tek up he blouse and put um on, tek up he pipe and go and sit down in de door. We had some great sport.

EM: Yuh used to have villages fighting other villages or communities fighting other communities or just one-off individual stick licking?

Gully: They used to get judge like stick playing just like Aberdeen. On festivals, he would got a big ting down above the house and got a platform and then all the fellows used to come. Yuh heard about Arnold Greenidge? He was a man who cud do anything. He used to brek licks. He used to walk over licks boy. He was good man.

EM: Where he was from?

Gully: From just up there in Lodge Road, but then he married a woman from New York and he and she disagree and he come back here to Lodge Road and was living just down below Aberdeen. He leave dey then and he went down to Deacons Road and he dead down there. All the boys went down to the funeral 'cause he bury at Westbury Cemetery. He was a hell of a stick licking man, and a quiet man, yuh know. Yuh hear bout a fellow call Small? Leon Small?

EM: He was from Lodge Hill too?

Gully: No. He was from Wilcox Hill. Yes, but he got a brother who lived down here up the Lodge Road, but he dead. He name Walter Small. He left hand. He was a good stick licker.

EM: Is it more difficult fighting a left-hander than a right-hander?

Gully: Yes. If yuh don't know, a left-hander could lick yuh, but if yuh know, he can't lick yuh and this is how yuh got to play him. Yuh got to play him square. Yuh understand? Square. He can't hit yuh. The main time that yuh set yuh foot pon a side, he licking yuh dey all the time, but when yuh play he square and stand in front he square, man, he can't hit yuh, but yuh got to know it.

I know me and a fellow, the fellow that get killed down by Oxnards. I gine tell yuh something. The caterpillar turned over with him. He was a good stick licker and me and he had a run down at a fellow name Gaskin used to live up the road there. He had to stop man. He left handed, yuh know. I leh go some licks at he, I change down pon he. The fellow know Queensberry. Yuh hear about dah?

EM: Queensberry and Johnson.

Gully: Well, them is 21 lashes, that rain down pon he. I leh go some licks at he. He had to done. I brek down all he hand, but he didn't touch me because yuh playing a man in this kind a ting, yuh can't go up wid de long seven.

EM: What is long seven?

Gully: Long seven is up in dey so. The seven lessons is only if yuh play friendly, yuh could—

EM: Well if yuh wet a man what happen?

Gully: When he wet yuh?

EM: Uh uh.

Gully: How yuh mean?

EM: If he hit yuh, sting yuh?

Gully: Yuh just can't get anxious, yuh got to wait pon he. Yuh wait till he mek he mistake, and then when he mek he mistake then yuh spring pon he. If a man go up in the long seven, yuh got to play pon he. Man, don't lick no where down heah. He out in long seven. This is the hand that he got the stick in.

EM: Knuckles?

Gully: He got to drop down dah hand. Yuh understand? He got to drop down dah hand. But the mean time yuh hit deah, he hand gine got to drop. Too much pain in dah hand. He was a very good fellow doah.

EM: So who is the best yuh ever fight?

Gully: Dey had a fellow name Audley Harewood, but they call he Audley Carter.

Audley Carter

EM: From where?

Gully: He arrived from Lodge Road, but then they moved from there and went just dey up above the Church at the corner like yuh gine to go down to Oistins, right away deah so, down below the corner. He did live deah. He was good. The two of we learn together, but what happen, I had the difference 'pon he and he had a lash that he couldn't get outah at all, at all, at all, and if yuh know, yuh could always hit him deah. The same fellow that I tell yuh 'bout, this man Robert that get killed he was from St. Philip, Cox Road.

EM: What was his name again?

Gully: Robert Nurse. I think that was his name, but he was from St. Philip.

EM: Yuh ever fight people away from Christ Church?

Gully: No. To be honest with yuh, I never fight nuhbody away from Christ Church. All I could tell yuh, I know that I went to Cox Road one Sunday night and, there was a big singing. I was working with the Wards at Adams Castle and that same Doctor Thomas father, he was the boss engineer at Adams Castle, so he get the job for me repairing the tank. They had a tank that couldn't hold water, so he come and ask me to come and go and see if I could do the tank. I went and do the tank. So after I do the tank, de engineer and all of them come and dey pass the tank yeh and ask me if it gine hold water, and I seh, 'Ef um don't hold water is ef um blow up."

But what happen, they had do this tank before, but they do it wrong. Yuh got cracks in the bottom of the tank and yuh only just gine cut out dem cracks, and yuh only gine put on an inch plaster, both sides, it can't work, and the foolish mason, who ever he is, not that yuh criticizing anybody, but when the white man cyah me and see if I could find out, by the minute time, I search, search the whole and I find out. I seh, "Yuh want to see something?" I seh, "Yuh hold down, take out yuh kerchief and put um unneat yuh knee" 'cause he had on white, yuh know. I seh, "Put yuh hand so." When he put he hand, man de air start coming. He seh, "Oh!" So I do the pond. So after I do the pond then, he gih me the job doin' the whole area too.

But at this singing, I remember, he change, he come up before me, I tending the furnace, and he come and seh, "Daddy, I done and I gine up. When yuh done and yuh come up, don't forget the singing." He gine to the singing. All the people who were working at the factory and ting, they had this singing out there.

Evening I come home and I forget. I bathe up and everything. I was home with muh mudda and muh fadda, and Lord yuh know Elombe, when I done eat and ting, that time they had some little flat chair that yuh cudda lay down and stretch out yuh foot in. I gone and I sit down in this chair and my bicycle outside. Yuh know when I open de eye I see the whole house dark. Dah time dey didn't no lights nor nothing so, bare kerosene oil lamps and such like and my murra turn and seh, "Brother D, yuh like yuh work hard enough today. Yuh had a good rest dey. I bring in de bicycle 'cause after I see yuh laying down in the chair I decide to bring in the bicycle."

And so said, I get up then and I went to the window. Now, Mr. John Nurse. Yuh know this fellow Will Nurse? Yuh should know Will Nurse, he got a brother name Bertie, school teacher, but he resigned, and we was to go out there by Mr. Nurse behind the place where all the girls and ting used to sell nuts and mangoes and all such like. I could remember like now those girls save me, a fellow wait for me, those rest of boys gone long and yuh know, the fellow wait for me and he seh, "Dudley, Carl and dem gone long and dey tell yuh must come and dey tell me wait for yuh and let me bring yuh across."

He turn up then and these girls seh, "Look, Dudley, he ent work no where. Yuh got tuh go tuh work in de morning, don't go out there now, that singing gine got a lot of people and dey gine fight bad enough out dey. If yuh go out deah and yuh get cut up, we ent coming to the horsepittal to look for yuh." Now, at that time it was the General Horsepittal. We didn't have no Queen Elizabeth then. It was the General Horsepittal. But after the fellow continue to beg me come, that he cudda gone long but he wait for me, I decide I would come, so I went back out home put on a pants and a shirt and ting, and bring cross me bicycle. And it is God mercy I didn't put on my watch. I forget muh watch pon the wagon. That time yuh used to cyah wagon, and I pump up the bicycle and the fellow get on and we gone up the Lodge Road, through market... out 'cross the grass pasture and up Norwoods Road, right out across below Small Ridge, way, way out and then swing down and gone down Cox Road.

Boy, when we gine 'cross, when we look down the fellow turn to me and seh, "Looka Charles and dem yonder," Yuh know wen we get dey now, he seh "Dudley, yuh stand very long." I seh, "I did forget." He seh, "Oh!" He seh, "Leh me go and put down yuh bicycle for yuh." I seh, "No, I gine and put down my bicycle myself, because if there is anyting I would know where to run and tek up my bicycle and I can brek all the back of the Church 'till I get out in the road, the Hope Road." Yuh know when we gone in, evah'body glad to see me, who dat working at de place, yuh know and who was tending mason with me. All uh dum!

When I gone in some fellows wid so much big sticks. Beresford Skeete, and yuh know a man bring a white rum and gih me. I seh I ent want no rum. I don't fancy dah. Well, dey gih me two bananas and some donkey, what yuh call russ. I take the russ and I put them in my pocket. I went on a long bench to the above part of the house. Nex' to this part of the house there was another house where yuh could shub in yuh hand to touch the other house. It appears that all is one family. Yuh can't run down the steps because if yuh run down the steps yuh liable to brek yuh foot because the ground did run high and low, so they had to bring up the front to suit the back, not to build a lot of steps running down the side running all way back down to the road.

I went and lay down pon the bench and drop asleep. Like in the middle of the night I could feel like something juckin me, juckin me. Get up, get up, like this thing telling me get up, danger ahead, danger ahead and all I go to get up, I so sleepy now, I can't get up, and all at one time I hear, get up, get up, I gine represent yuh. Like this body telling me I gine represent yuh. That was my brother, a dead brother.

Let me tell yuh something; I get up, I jump up and when I jump up, Elombe, I seh, "Lord haveth mercy." I can't run to the door, I can't jump through the door, because if I run down dey I liable to run down dey and brek muh foot, I can't jump through the window because that would brek muh foot too. I turn with a very uncomfortable mind. All the time dis ting juckin' me, I gine represent, I gine represent, but I get den to understand how this work out wid this juckin and ting. He turn and seh, "Yuh know what?" I seh, "What?" He seh, "Set up!"

I know some person that I can tek some lashes and gih some and lick out some of these people. When I shub me hand in me pocket and drag out me kerchief, I do so and I pull down my hand from my head. Man, I walk to the man that got this stick cutting and coming up, and I gine tek the stick from out of he hand. So I jump right in front he so and when he cut at me, I had de stick wid de kerchief out of he hand, the same way he had the stick come out he hand, I had the next man dey lick down. He down pon the floor, man, and I ent mind he dey. My man I lick the whole house. Everbody run down through Staplegrove and me one all tru' Staplegrove cane.

Let me tell yuh something. Yuh know about Roy Ward – Roy Ward from St. Lucy that kill he father? He was the under-manager at Adams Castle. So while he was up dey, and he had bring a fellow who was a groom from down St. Lucy up at Adams Castle because he cousin Eddie Ward did leave there and went down at Fairfield managing Fairfield Sugar Factory. So duh bring he up here and leh me tell yuh something, I lick the whole, whole house me one.

EM: Yuh beat all duh?

Gully: Man, wuh! I had to lick down some 'pon de ground. When yuh lick down a man, never yuh check pon he. When yuh lick down a man never yuh go down pon he. Yuh don't know if he got a knife. He could kill yuh. Yuh understand that way?

EM: Right.

Gully: We got a man outside now, me and the fellow one inside the house, a fellow call Colin.

EM: A fellow call who?

Gully: Colin King. He did from down by me, and he seh, "Dudley, Dudley, Dudley, Dudley, um is me, um is me, um is me." I seh, "Colin, Colin, jump behind me, and however I go yuh jump behind me all the time." Poor fellow, he ent able, and yuh know when we get the whole house clear, clear, clear, it was a big house, yuh know, dey had all the partition and ting tek down. Two big hip houses and we went out, standing at the door now and we hear a fellow outside and he snorting like a horse. Beckles had a horse from out Silver Sands used to go in town and he used to got that cart pack, and he sitting up top deh and that horse coming up and the sweat pouring off he and he hollerin like a mule or old horse and he gine. And this man outside snorting like a horse.

Yuh know who the man is? I turn and seh, "Colin, I hear dis fella outside snorting." He seh, "Yes, yuh know who dah body is? Dat is a fellow call Martin." I seh, "Yuh mean Martin Crawford, that got yuh aunt?" He seh, "Yes, dah is he? That is me to he." I seh, "Lord haveth mercy. Awright."

I seh, "Now listen, yuh don't go in the middle uh dat door. Yuh come to the corner uh the door and I want yuh to do what I tell yuh to do. I got the stick and when yuh get deh to the corner yuh stand up and yuh jump from off the platform down de side of the step and I gine jump behind yuh, because if he leh go either one uh de stones," I seh, "Look, he can't got no more than three stones in he hand, two in one hand and one to leh go and when he leh go, I gine pon he."

So said when he do so, I come from behind and I say leggo, leggo and I walking to he going all the time and I jump in front he wid de stick... leggo. When I get to he I seh, "Martin, drop those stones or I gine brek all two of yuh hands immediately, immediately!" And Elombe, this man tek de stones and do so an drop dem pun de ground and all he do is smile. I call he more vagavun than anything else. I seh, "Yuh is a real vagavun. When the night come, yuh come and yuh sit down wid we singing." Yuh know where Peanuts live? When the evening come, we used to go dey and sit down and sing and all such like.

EM: What sort of songs yuh used to sing?

Gully: We used to sing Church hymns.

EM: That used to be a singing?

Gully: No.

EM: Normally?

Gully: Yes. Ancient and Modern book, yuh know, and I seh, "Yuh should be shame of yuhself. When 12 o'clock and one o'clock yuh dey wid we and now yuh come out heah. I say if yuh had a stick, I would lambase yuh wid licks, but I ent gine hit yuh.

But yuh know why I ent gine hit yuh, I don't want nobody to say that I take advantage of yuh because yuh ent had a stick, but if yuh had a stick I would lambase yuh wid licks." He dropped de rockstones and put he hand in he pocket and left. Then myself and the boys left de singing.

I had to tek my bicycle and give a fellow yuh call Boy Blue King to cyah a fellow yuh call Johnny tuh horsepital. Johnny was a carpenter who worked in government. He dead now. He got some good children. The children got a lot of big houses. The children out in America and ting and some does teach. I had to put he 'pon me bicycle and let duh carry he to the horsepittal.

The Monday morning I had to go long to work, so good luck now I ent study dah no more, but this fellow Martin, he was working at Bannatyne and Adams Castle. He tell a fellow name Lovell how I went out deah, how I parade out dey, how he would do dis and do dat wid me. The fella seh, "Yuh, it would tek ten looking like yuh to run Dudley. Yuh tink I don't know who yuh talking bout?"

All two of we laugh and Elombe, yuh know wuh happen? Mr. Ward, a couple days after he carried one Albert wid he digging yams he send a message by Charles Thomas who is family to the Wards. Charles turn and he tell me, Dudley, I got a message fuh yuh. I seh, "Whuh de message?" "Mr. Ward tell yuh that Albert tell yuh he gun gih yuh flesh to the birds in the air and yuh bones to the dogs of the earth. He seh he ent gine forget to pour some licks in me."

I seh wait, I getting mad now. I seh, "Wuh I ent nuh tief. I don't tief nutten." I seh, "Ef I did a tief or I did want cement, my fadda does deal at Plantations Limited or at Mannings. I could go get a barrel of cement or anything." At that time cement used to come in barrels. Now this fellow was the watchman, he was the chauffeur, he was everything in Adams Castle yard. I seh, "Man if I gine out uh Adams Castle yard and he ever stop me. Yes, I gine stop, 'cause I en gine lick up my bicycle. But effing he ever come and hold back my bicycle an touch my bag that 'pon my bicycle, I gun put my bicycle oneside, an I gine gih he as much as anything else."

Archer did laughing, but he know that this fellow can't lick me or beat me. I ent know that he mean that this fellow say wuh Ward say. But Ward wen the evening come in seh, "Dudley, man I glad I get de chance to get to yuh to see how yuh gine, but yuh know, come in de yard from tomorrow and I gine start storing up yams, so I gine got all the time." I waiting now to hear wuh he gine tell me about this man, so after he ent tell me nutten, I put up my stuff an get pun muh bicycle.

And the day Mr. Ward come, he seh, "Dudley, man, Albert say he gine give yuh as much licks, as much blows that yuh could tek." I seh, "Whuh? Gih me blows?" I seh, "Leh muh tell yuh something, I ent needa tief. I don't carry out anyting outta Adams Castle yard. But let muh tell yuh, right so, any day, morning or evening I gine out or come in Adams Castle yard and he tell me to stop, I gine stop, but I am not going to lick up muh bicycle. Ef he ever hold back my bag, I gine gih he as much blows as yuh could ever think."

He laugh. He seh, "No, yuh can't beat that man, he is a Master Workman." I seh, "Master Workman? Who yuh mean is a Master Workman?" He seh, "Dat man when he down home [St. Lucy], yuh does can't get he 'pon uh Sarduh and Sundy. He does got uh whole room full uh fellas come up from all parts of St. Lucy learning stick licking. Dis man is a hell of a stick licker. He seh, "Look, I gine tell yuh wuh I gine do. He used tuh gine down Collymore Rock on a Sarduh. He does pay the money early. He gine pay the money early Sarduh."

De same fellow gine cyah he [Roy Ward] in de car, he gine use he motor car tuh carry de family down and dey gine spend the day down dey. He seh, "Look, I got about four sticks up deh. Yuh got some rum, corned beef, bread and sardines and all sort of ting up deh up in the room." Knight call and say they pay the money early dat evuh'body leave the yard 'cause we gine got a ramp down. I seh, "Awright, I in charge now." I did done know bout wuh gine happen. Elombe, I pour so much licks in this man, this poor man had to drop the stick out he hand. All I do is kill meself wid laugh. Mr. Ward seh, "Man, yuh mek me shame!" I seh, "Man, he ent mek yuh shame cause he ent know nutten." I tell he so. I tell he he now want learning man. So I had some real ting, but I never tell myself – not because yuh know a ting.

EM: Yuh ever was involved in many ramp downs?

Gully: I had many show downs, like a friendly something. But yuh see, even wid dis friendly something can be dangerous when we practicing. Now, yuh may be playing this fella wide-minded that yuh is not gine to damage this fella, but this fellow may be on the showing off. I know that me and uh fellow name Ossie Carter had a ramp uh Easter Bank Holiday

Now his brudda had a house; dah time dey were living in Halls Road [Christ Church] just in front where Peanuts Morrison live. He brudda Milton and all the big old men, the stick lickers, and all such like and men that is 50 and 60 years old, the Greenidges, all dem boys. And as I come down de road a girl by de name Manie Briggs seh, "Dudley, looka dem boys looking all de time fuh yuh wondering fuh know if yuh gone work or not. Evuhbody looking out fuh yuh." I seh, "Fuh tru? Wuh happen?"

So I gone tuh de house. Dey seh, "Man yuh come and sit down." And in dey did ram down, all the carpenters and masons and everybody at dat same 'Peanuts' uncle. He was uh hell of a carpenter. All uh duh, Crissie Perch and Isaac Dodson, a hell of a mason, a fussy man, all dum in dis house. Audley [Carter] now seh, "Well, Dudley, I gine gih yuh a ramp down." I say awright. Evuh'body now worry 'bout me. Den we start tuh lick stick. Leh me tell yuh, this man letting go—yuh could tell when a man finin' he playing rough. Every lash yuh had to brek, yuh could feel it in yuh hand ef he coming out wid too much weight.

EM: He putting a lotta power behind it?

Gully: He putting a lotta power behind it. Yuh understand what I talking. Every time I brek I feel this weight in the stick, rushing de stick. I seh, "Fuh trute? Awright bo!" Every time he fire at me I rush it down de ground, slide it down de ground. One time I seh, one, two, three and I had he do so. And the whole house jump up and holla for murder. I tek de stick and I trow um out of me hand and he shake me hand and that is the last time I play he, but he was a good stick licker.

EM: Who is the hardest man yuh ever play though?

Gully: The hardest man I play is the same Simmie Best and a fellow name Goldie Lovell.

EM: Duh beat yuh?

Gully: No man. Goldie was good but he couldn't beat me. Best was good.

EM: Simmie Best?

Gully: Simmie Best. He got a grandson. He is a Doctor [Wayne Welch].

EM: Yuh ever play Aberdeen?

Gully: He was rough and ting, yuh know, but I wouldn't consider him tuh be someone tuh tackle. Some person who din' know would. But he was strong. Yuh understand? If yuh ask me now if Jack Ashby cud play? Jack Ashby was good, I could tell yuh yes. He had a book, Jack had a book, but Arnold Greenidge is who learn Jack. He used to come just at the corner down deah. They had a big upstairs house down deah and duh had two house up top.

EM: Yuh never met any Trinidadian stick lickers?

Gully: No.

EM: Aberdeen went to Trinidad?

Gully: He went to Trinidad, but I don't know if it was to fight. Duh had immigrate fellas and ting from here and sometime the boys went to a show at the theatre and some of the Trinidadians must be interfere with duh and de boys went and brek down all sorta sticks 'bout de place and all de boys lick the whole a Trinidad. Yuh en hear 'bout dah?

EM: No.

Gully: Dah time Aberdeen den did a police down dey.

EM: Aberdeen was a policeman?

Gully: Aberdeen was a police in Trinidad. He come back from Trinidad and the first place he do business is down o'neat Oistins Hill and den after he move from deah and come just deah where the house is deah now and do business deah. Well, dah same place did concern some kind of family concern me, but he give it to a woman name Ms. Adams and Ms. Adams gih de spot that Aberdeen 'pon tuh Ann-Ruth sister which was the one involved wid Harold Greaves. She gih it tuh Aberdeen.

EM: Let me move from that slightly. Yuh know Archie Bumma [Potato Mout] father?

Gully: If I know Archie Bumma father? Yes.

EM: Wuh he name?

Gully: Edwy Taylor.

EM: Yuh used to play masquerade wid them?

Gully No man. Dah time I was small, but Edwy Taylor, yuh know Edwy Taylor and the same Aberdeen and the same Arnold Greenidge and them, Jeff Lovell, the School Master, my good friend.

EM: They used to play masquerade?

Gully Yes, Jeff Lovell and Aberdeen and Arnold and the same Edwy Taylor. They went down in Indian Ground. They like they had some kind uh someting up dey for them in the dancing house, man. They lick the whole of Indian Ground.

EM Edwy Taylor was a stick licker too?

Gully I wouldn't call he a stick licker. Aberdeen was a stick licker. They lick the whole of Indian Ground.

EM In St. Peter?

Gully In St. Peter. Yes. Aberdeen had an uncle that was a big shopkeeper down there. He was a big man down dey, so it was held down deah. Stick licking is a certain type of formal like stick meaning yuh got some fellas could get very hot-headed very, very, very quick.

I had tuh stop a couple of fellas well from taking advantage of people. That is true. I know there is a fella name Herbert Deane, he dead now. He did very cruel once he know dat he can tek advantage of yuh. He had a fella from Lodge Road pushing 'bout just down dey in Montrose. I seh, "Look man, leh me tell yuh something, yuh feel dat yuh own any way bout down in hey so dat yuh pushing 'bout dah man?" I seh, "Look, if he did any family to me I would lambaste yuh wid licks. Leh de man lone". I had to stop he man.

The way in learning exercise, two things yuh got to learn. If yuh know dat yuh could beat a man let a man hit yuh [laugh] but yuh know yuh could beat he, what yuh will do, if be brag. Yuh know some does do these things and den walk and brag. If he brag then yuh will know wuh yuh will do wid him, but if yuh meet a fella dat yuh know yuh could beat he, yuh sit down and talk and yuh keep yuhself from outta trouble.

EM: But yuh ever ramp with anybody outside Christ Church? Yuh ever went in St. George or St. Michael?

Gully: Nobody in St. Michael never challenge me. I know I had went in Jack Ashby drug store...

EM: In Swan Street?

Gully: Yeah. And duh had a man, I went in deah and find a man talking a lot about de stick and Ashby tell me, "Look, Dudley, I want yuh tuh gih he a play, I gine open out in de back and I got two sticks in deah. I will let de two a wunna go out in deah and have a show down." This man look at me and seh, "No dice!" That is the only chance that I had in town.

EM: What about St. George or St. Philip?

Gully: The onliest fella that I play from St. Philip is the same fella Nurse dat I tell yuh bout. He was a good boy. Nuh maybes. If I tell yuh dad he wasn't a good boy. I would be lying. He was a good boy. We had some good boys bout in Lodge Road.

EM: What about Silver Sands?

Gully: Silver Sands. The only body I know up in deah dat cud is a fella called Leon Small. He lived all the way up in Wilcox Hill but yuh know he use to still come down in Silver Sands 'cause he and dem had a showdown wid some de boys from here. Yuh hear 'bout a fella call Shamrock, a big strong man?

He from up here, but den he was living down town all de time. He was living dey in Collymore Rock and the whole bunch uh dem went on dey and duh open down wid some licks on de boys from down heah. Yuh know a fella called Jessie Yearwood, a mason? Well, he from up heah. He was a hellavuh mason. He left up here and he went town and was living somewhere just down below the hospital, but he dead now.

The whole bunch uh duh deah man, duh wonder to know weh dey boys gine run to come along down, 'cause yuh know dat duh ha' fuh run and come down de straight road. And the same Leon Small get down at the end waiting to cut off de boys and when duh get down to the end this man run out from outta de bush, man he leggo as much licks at Arnold and when Arnold lick he down to the ground, the man leggo as much licks with two sticks. He got two sticks and after Arnold lick de stick out he hand, he seh tuh Arnold, "I done, I done, I done. Um is me!" Arnold seh, "Who me?" He seh, "Um is me, Leon!" Arnold seh, "Leon, yuh get in heah fuh run we, yuh should be shame yuhself!"

Duh got a fella, he live in dah same Wilcox Hill. He was a hellavuh vagabond. He was a vagabond more than anything else. He name George. One day getting near to December month, my fadda use to work this land. I home and I went and had a cane outta me fadda ground and when I coming long he was digging dah well in Lodge Road just off in front where Peanuts Morrison live and he had two fellas digging this well. He was the boss. He ask me where I get this cane from. I seh, "How yuh mean where I get this cane from?" I seh, "Wuh yuh want?" He tell me he gine cyah me way. I seh, "Yuh gine cyah me way?"

So right there this lotta noise tumble down between muhself and he. I seh, "Man, get up from dey and come an put yuh hand pun me." But he din know me doh and then after Jeffrey Lovell mother, she is same Charles Thomas wife and all duh come and seh, "Look, don't put yuh hand pon he yuh.' So after de ting the fella Wood did working wid he, he ask the fella if he know me. He seh, "Yes." He seh, "Look, yuh know who he is?" "He is the fella who yuh call Edgar Walcott brudda." He seh, "Oh, I ent know." But I never go to interfere. What I would do is represent the family. If duh gine beat up my family when duh see me coming, look out down the road.

EM: When yuh stop fighting stick licking?

Gully: Well, I would hah fuh say years and ting now. I ent play de stick fuh long, but uh can still represent muhself. If I had muh sight and muh two foot did good, yuh understand?

EM: Let me ask yuh about being a mason. When yuh was cutting soft stone, yuh ever cut it in tandem with another man to a rhythm Pat pa pa pat pat pat, cutting soft stone?

Gully: Dah is wuh yuh call rolling the hammer.

EM: How yuh do it?

Gully: Yuh could do it but yuh got to do it by time. Yuh cutting, yuh gine down and this man coming down and he rolling he hammer all over y'own. He backing all the time and he singing this song

Ben gih de cow water
bup
Ben gih de cow ting

bup
Ben gih de cow ting
bup,
Ben gih de cow water
bup
Ben gih the cow ting
bup,

and yuh gine long so all de time.

EM: And just repeat that over and over?

Gully: Yes.

EM: And who sing? Both of wunna singing that?

Gully: Yes, and yuh rolling de hammer man, yuh rolling the hammer.

EM: That's the only song yuh used to sing?

Gully: Yes. Some fellas does play de music, some fellas does sing en say. 'doh ray me sol' and de hammer gine. Some fellas can't do it. When yuh meet de hard stone, boy I work for nutten boy, nexkin to nutten till muh nerves brek down.

EM: Yuh never fish for a living?

Gully: Fish? No man. Never work in dah.

EM: Where yuh learn yuh mason trade?

Gully: I learn my mason trade wid a man yuh call Isaac Dodson and I can remember now the first place dat we build going round Maxwell Coast belonging to Barnes, and I could tell yuh something.

EM: From Barnes and Company?

Gully: Yes, and I remember dat place build outta rubble stone. Yuh know wuh yuh call rubble stone? Rubble stone and mortar. Yuh gotta spread out de mortar and yuh tek the stones and pack it in. Yuh make yuh joints draw and then yuh tek a rod and yuh ketch a level and yuh cut and yuh lay all the time. That is the first place dat we went to work. We work there for about three or six months.

And yuh know then, I remember that Mr. Tyrol Barnes, Barnes son, one morning he came and seh, "Mr. Dodson, my aunt got a step down Worthing want doing very bad. I want yuh send Walcott and leh he do that step fuh me." Mr. Mottley, I so glad 'cause me boss din use to gih me no money. My poor sister use to dispatch shop and she got some flour and ting and use to mek me hard bake and ting pon a morning and put dis ting yuh call P.Y. butter and fold it up and a bottle of hot coffee tea and wrap it up and I had to cyah long dah fuh me lunch.

EM: How many brothers and sisters yuh had?

Gully: I had three sisters.

EM: Older or younger?

Gully: They older than me.

EM: Yuh are the youngest?

Gully: I am the last of all. One of my sisters died at ninety-nine. She only wanted two months to mek the hundred, but what happen she fall down coming from outta de bathroom and that was the end of she. Then I had another sister, she name Mrs. Campbell and she died at ninety-three. I had another sister, she died early. She died in child bed. She had a son did name Dennis Walcott. He died in America too. He was a hellavuh guy, a little fella, a disgusted man.

EM: What was yuh father name?

Gully: My father did name Charles Walcott.

EM: How old he was when he died?

Gully: He died at ninety-eight years.

EM: What about yuh mother?

Gully: My mother she died at eighty-five years. She died the year after hurricane Janet in 1955. I had a sister Mrs. Campbell and she had four children. One was in England and three was in the United States. But then the last one, she left England and she went down to America, so she down deah now.

EM: Any of yuh family was in the Landship?

Gully: No. I know dum had a Landship down here at Allamby house.

EM: Called what? Yuh know the name of it?

Gully: No. Straight down by Allamby near the Club Randall. They had a Landship first that I know and that Landship did had in some big boys. There had a woman did name Miss Welch; she was a Matron. Henry Forde uncle married she daughter. Had a next one name Ms. Barnett. She and de fella yuh call Bertie used to go to Water Street Boys' School, where Water Street Girls' School is. The mudda had a fella called Jimmy Perch who was the head Superintendent at the plantation.

EM: Tell me something. Yuh mother or father ever told yuh about their life in Barbados?

Gully: Well, I could tell yuh dis. I know my father had tell me dis. My father was a sugar boiler and he used to boil the sugar. They had a kinda sugar duh used to call de 'object' sugar. Yuh ever hear 'bout dat? A sugar something like a glass.

EM: Not muscavado?

Gully: A sugar, it was dark. He used to boil that sugar at Bridges and the Charles Webster father, he was the Manager at the same Bridges factory. And he, when the night come when evuhbody gone home, when twelve o'clock and ting he shutting evuhting to meet work next morning. When he done deah, he had den to come to Lodge Road. He had a donkey did name Sam and we could stand and hear dah donkey coming down the engine house hill. Yuh could hear he foot slamming pon de hill coming down.

Mr. & Mrs. King were the owners of Darrell's Hill plantation. My mother used to live next door to Mrs. King ground. They had a big pathway that the cars can go in and go out, change or something. Dah is my grandmother ground deah and dat is Mrs. King ground and Mr. King tell my father, "When the night come yuh one in dey. I gine come an get a load of sugar and I gine buy five acres of Pinder land fuh yuh." My father refused. Mr. King tell he, "An, nuh police en gine do me nutten."

He seh, "When three o'clock and ting I does open me door and dem police from Boarded Hall does come all de way and I does know wuh time dem coming so I does leave the light burning. Wen I hear de knock I does come and open de door. Wen four o'clock, five o'clock duh gine back down Wotton." Dah time police did use to run bout like dat. Duh use to come by horse. Wen seven o'clock or half past six they use to be trotting coming up heah. Dey use to go all up by the lighthouse [Christ Church up Enterprise]. They come down, duh go at Newton, duh go at Balls, duh go at Durant's checking.

EM: Your father never talked about growing up? Where he grew up? Where he born? Where your father was from originally?

Gully: He was from Lodge Road.

EM: He talked about growing up in Lodge Road when he was a boy?

Gully: Yes.

EM: Yuh remember anything he tell yuh?

Gully: He said things was hard and after he married, Mrs. King had to hold responsible for my mudda because at dat time yuh know yuh couldn't marry until yuh are twenty-one years and such like. So my mudda married before twenty-one so Mrs. King had to hold responsible for my mudda. Dah time he used to keep track and Mrs. King used to keep track.

EM: What yuh call track?

Gully: Mrs. King had a track with horse with rubber wheels.

EM: Like a buggy?

Gully: Yes. Yuh call it a track. A buggy is a buggy and a track is a track. He said he come along and he had about two or three more brothers. One named Francis Pounder, he live just going up Durants Road. That land deah got on 'bout four or five house 'pon it now. He said he lend his brother some money to bought that place and my mudda used to make this muffin and dis fish, all dis thing so to cyah out to the factory. Wen the evening come, my mudda go down Oistins and get this big lotta shark, dolphin, flying fish and prepare.

So a woman borrow a piece of change from ma and she lend this woman de change, so bad luck fuh my mudda, de woman tek de money and gih to my grandmudda and tell my grandmudda to give my mudda fuh she. She tell a woman she gine mek my mudda and fadda see hell. Duh got to sell everything duh have. My fadda had a big hip house with a big ground, two and three cows, and a donkey. My fadda sister Winifred Estwick dead. She was the Headmistress at Vauxhall. My father after she dead, den had to tek them children and raise them. Dey father Everton never left them up.

EM: He never worked in the cane fields?

Gully: Who?

EM: Your father.

Gully: No.

EM: Nor your mother?

Gully: No.

EM: Nor you?

Gully: No.

EM: What type of songs they used to sing when yuh were young growing up like yuh little grandchildren?

Gully: I used to sing 'Millie gone to Brazil, oh poor Millie, Millie gone to Brazil, oh poor Millie, a wire wrap 'round she waist and a razor tie to she throat'. Yuh hear 'bout dah song?

EM: Yes. What else? What other song?

Gully: I more believe in singing gospel songs.

EM: Yes. That was after. When yuh were their age, yuh were singing gospel too? Jane and Louisa?

Gully: I would sing 'Brown Girl come back and mind baby'. Yuh know that song?

EM: That was still late. That was a Trinidad calypso. 'Brown skin gal stay home and mind baby'. What about 'Brown girl in a ring, tra lah lah lah'.

Gully: Yes, that too. Brown girl in a ring, tra lah lah lah.

EM: Yuh used to do the Joe and Johnny dance?

Gully: No. I never like so much dancing. To be honest with yuh I never dance.

EM: Yuh had a lot of tuk band around yuh then?

Gully: Yes. Look, this month is the month of October. Today is the 13th of October if my memory serves me good. Now, the month of December that man Edwy Taylor – these people should be highly recommend. He used to got the whole of Christ Church pon he back. In the month of December two or three weeks before Christmas yuh would see he down dey in Water Street, yuh see Edward come up wid de band. He got a son yuh call Bumma – Archie Bumma [Potato Mout]. He died in the Almshouse. He is a cousin to these children by mother and Edwy gone right way up to the Engine House

Hill and Elombe, when Edwy tek up dat drum and kittle and coming back down the people running from all over the bridge and ting, yuh know where duh gine end up all the way down Maxwell Hill and gone down Top Rock and come up Maxwell long road to hit back through to Oistins. Dah is coming to Christmas.

EM: But yuh don't know anybody that used to participate in that? Anybody who used to join in masquerade?

Gully: Well, I think some de fellas. They had a fella named Johnny and he is one who used to go in dey to masquerade. But that masquerade ting is a great ting. Yuh got a kinda dance yuh call the Cent Dance. I had a brother he was a hell of a dancer. If yuh see he and dis fella yuh call Sammy King, uh next fella yuh call Timmy Brandon, a fella yuh call, he from up Pilgrim Road.

Errol Taylor and he come out dey and they strike up dah band and yuh see dem fellas dancing dis cent dance – man something dat yuh could stand up and enjoy. Dah was a dance. None uh dah ting don't happen so now. Yuh don't see cent dance or none uh dem tings so, so we had a great set up of various tings.

EM: Any of the stick fighters yuh know still alive?

Gully: Um don't look to me like duh got none 'bout here now 'cause Walter Maughan, he dead. I don't think I hear 'bout any uh he children was a stick licker. Well, Simmie Best son, he know de stick. He is still alive.

EM: Simmie Best son?

Gully: Dah is Welch who is Dr. Welch father.

EM: Where he live?

Gully: He live down underneath Scarborough [Oistins, Christ Church]. He name Boy. Welch is a boss mason. He is a good stick licker. We had a fella live in Pilgrim Road. Yuh call he Strong Man, a brown skin fella. He was an engineer at Kingsland factory. Yuh hear bout Mandeville? Mandeville learn he de stick and when he playing de stick he got he tongue licking out, the same foolish thing dat Mandeville used to do. He does do the same ting, longing out he tongue and all dat kind uh ting. The last time I see he is coming 'round by the Plaza up deah. Somebody tell me that dem think he dead. As far as I know, Archie and all dem boys so dead.

EM: What about the flute players?

Gully: Well, the flute player that we had was a fella yuh call Bow Lion.

EM: He was good?

Gully: Yes. He was the watchman at Wotton. When yuh see festival come and like Christmas and Easter and Whitsuntide bank, he ent watching nuh plantation. He out wid de flute wid Edwy. He used to go long wid Edwy. Duh had a fella called Richmond Rawlins wid dem. He dead too. He was a drum maker.

EM: Who Rawlins? What is his name?

Gully: He name Richmond Rawlins.

EM: He used to make the drums?

Gully: He used to make the drums and kittle and would play the flutes and everything. He had a band too, drum and kittle too.

EM: Where he live?

Gully: Well, he dead now, but he lived just like when yuh going down Thornbury Hill. He lived back pon dah side there so. There had a fella Milton Carter. He was a mason. That man could lick a kittle. Dey went fuh he to join the police band and he won't go. He said he din had sufficient education to join that band. The people seh, "Man, we gine learn yuh!" and he won't go at all, at all, at all. He dead too. He is Audley brother. The last place the two uh we work together, yuh see those two steps at the Drill Hall? Me and he build dem two steps.

EM: Just a couple more things before we go. When yuh look back pun yuh life, what is the most significant thing that yuh think happen in yuh life-time in Barbados? The first part of yuh life, let's say, before 1937. Between the time yuh born and the riot?

Gully: When the riot [tek place], I was home and my sister, (the one that died, she name Baby, but she married name is Mrs. Nurse. She died in child bed.). I remember at that time duh had to bring water, the pipe was down deah where Peanuts live and we did live just up above where Sonny Evelyn had the concrete product in Lodge Road. We did live just above there. I remember my sister come home and tell me, "Dudley, that is one of the worst things that I find myself in." She seh, "Dudley, yuh know wuh happen? Yuh know duh rioting in Bridgetown?" I en know bout wuh name rioting. I seh, "Wuh yuh mean rioting?" She seh, "Look, Charles tell yuh come round deah".

Dah time duh had from down Maxwell Hill right-a-way and come round up through the Lodge Road, nutten else but coral stone up to St. Patrick cover down with nutten else but coral stone against the road. I go down de road and Charles seh, "Man, yuh home sleeping and yuh en know dat duh rioting?" I seh, "Wuh is rioting?" and he up den and tell me. He said, "Man, duh doing bad uh nuff down town."

Now, I is the only man had bicycle. None de fellas din ha uh bicycle. He seh, "Man, Dudley, yuh got de bicycle, go and see wuh um look like". I like a fool running to me death. Mr. Mottley, I turn back home, I drink some tea. Yuh hear wuh I tell yuh? I eat a roast potato, what yuh call a six-weeks potato wid me tea.

EM: Why yuh call it six weeks?

Gully: A six-weeks potato is when yuh can start to dig potato. Yuh got potato and when yuh brek loose them potato inside white like silk, man, sweet, sweet for God sake. And I eat this potato, drink me tea, dah time I had a sweet bicycle yuh know, and I tek up the bicycle and I gone long down the road. Lord haveth mercy, and when I get gine down Collymore Rock, dey before I get to Banks, yuh know yuh pass de Y and coming down.

EM: Like canefields?

Gully: Yes. I see de Beatrice coming up. When de Beatrice do so and put on de light yuh know – now de Beatrice coming up pon de left side, I going down hey now, uh mean pon de right side.

EM: The police van?

Gully: No, dah din de police van.

EM: What was the Beatrice?

Gully: The bus did name so. That bus did belong to Codrington. A fella name Osford Powlett, he was driving dis bus and he put on de lights stopping me. He stop 'cause he know me, 'cause he wife from just below heah. He stop, he seh, "Dudley, man come and put dat bicycle in de back uh de seat and come and go back home. Man duh doing bad uh nuff in town. Evuh'body killing evuh'body in town." I seh, "Man, I want to see!" He seh, "Man, Dudley come back home." Yuh know I like a fool I still gone long down. I gone long down Collymore Rock and I gone 'cross de ole bridge and I swing gine 'cross High Street and I gine down Swan Street now. When I look I see two police gine cross wid de gun and I could only just run so to a store.

The woman dat duh shoot dat used to sell English apples down by de Advocate right at de corner in Broad Street. Mr. Mottley, boy when I hear de shooting I tek up de bicycle and I swing back up through Swan Street right-a-way out across and I gone long up through River Road and all I working a high and a low, high and a low, high and a low man and I fanning and gone up. Well, yuh know weh I go long. I en go round de road. When I hit by Kingsland I swing across Kingsland, I up through the avenue, up through the pasture and gone through Plumgrove and but right away by de pipe. When I get home all I could do is sit down and lay down. Duh ask me wuh happen. I up den and tell duh. I think dah was one de most of the funniest thing in my life.

EM: During the war years – World War II, after the riot between then and Independence, what yuh remember most?

Gully: World War II. I could remember the church. Yuh know Christ Church had burn down. The riot was in '37 and Christ Church was burn down in '35. Yuh know Christ Church burn down in '35?

EM: I know it burn down but I didn't know the year.

Gully: I could remember I was working at DaCosta, and the morning my fadda get up, my fadda seh, "Lord the whole a Pegwell burning down". I get up now and I gone to de shedroof window to de sea and when I open de window and I look, I seh, "No". I tell my fadda "no, dat en nuh Pegwell canes." I seh, "Dah is Christ Church." But what he didn't understand I cud mek out de pedestals pon top de roof. By doing masonry I exactly know. I seh, "Look dat is Christ Church". And he argue wid me. I seh, "Look, don't argue wid me, go outside and look and see da is Christ Church."

Good luck now when I did hear de shout a woman did name Alew who is my master workman sister, she pass across out by we, they going across by whey yuh call Coverley tenant that was a little plantation. Dey going cross right out by Durants right away down by the Church. She seh, "Dudley, Dudley, um is yuh master workman sister, wuh loss, muh brudda gine get burn up, muh brudda gine get burn up". But then anuddah woman run and come up by me and dis is wuh she seh: "Lord, look de moon gine down, de moon mek a bow, de moon look back at Christ Church burning." So dat was one of the biggest thing dat I see and den I get up and went long to work.

EM: What about after the war now?

Gully: Well, I did manage to get a call in de war. I would remember like dis here now. I could remember like dis here as duh tell yuh don't come to America if yuh got bad teeth in yuh head, yuh must get them fix before yuh come. So I remember then and I went to Mr. King – Dentist King. He had his office at Bert Ashby in Swan Street, and I remember that morning when I went in that office, it was so much people up in that office. When I get dey, I say to meself, wuh I in gine get dispatch, I in gine get tend to. Looka de people in here!

And when I speak, yuh know these fellows does always sit down where duh could sit down and see whoever is coming in through the door. He seh, "I know dat voice." I so glad when I hear dis man say he know dat voice, 'cause I seh if he seh he know dat voice, I gine get tend to. I seh, "No, yuh don't know this voice". He seh, "Don't tell me ah don't know this voice. I know yuh before yuh born". I so glad to hear the man saying so, but I know he know. I say yuh don't know. He seh, "Yuh don't tell me who yuh is, don't yuh tell me who yuh is." The fust thing he do was call my mudda name.

He seh, "Look, yuh mother raise up in Dayrells Hill long side me fadda ground. Yuh could step in yuh grandmudda and we could step in y'own. And look ah gine tell yuh now, she married a man name Charles Walcott, a quiet, quiet man." He seh, "Look, leh me tell yuh something – too honest too poor." I got me hand so. I ent saying one word. He seh, "Too honest, too poor". And all de people dey looking. He seh, "Look yuh fadda, a hell of a sugar boiler. He had all the opportunity at Bridges Factory and he won't mek chance of it." He seh, "My father, I ent shame to tell yuh, my father tell yuh fadda he gine tie up the truck wheel and he gine come fuh some sugar when the night come. Yuh know he keeping shop, so he gine mek de money wid dah. And all he do he won't come to and look if he had do it he would have five acres uh Pinder land, good land he would had and he won't do it." He seh, "Yuh mudda name Jane. We call she Jane, but she right name is Matilda. She got a sister name Gussie."

EM: So he knew yuh?

Gully: He did know me and I so glad I ent say one word. She got a sister name Gussie Brathwaite. She married to a boss fella, an engineer fella and had bought a little farm in Eastlyn [St. John]. She got a grandson now is the Postmaster.

He know me, but I know he. He had to come to Shop Hill yuh know. He turn and tell de people and he got a sister. She had a fella call Roberson – Roberson Goddard. She got a daughter name Mrs. Nurse. Well, she dead. She had some way around five or six acres of land. She went up to America. The one name Mrs. Yarde dead at a hundred.

He seh, "Look, I know if yuh din want something do, yuh din gine here, I would have to do it through respect of yuh fadda and yuh mudda. I will do it. Tell me wuh yuh want." He seh, "Now, yuh got money?" I seh, "Yes." He seh, "Well, left piece ah money." Well, everybody now start to say looka he now come in. He seh, "I know him, I know his parents, his parents is very good." Elombe, bad luck for me, he tell me, "Now when I going to fix these plates yuh have a piece of teeth I can't pull it not till I going to fix this plate. The same time I am going to put in the plate I am going to pull that teet."

Lord haveth mercy, the same time I had to go before the doctors. I turn and give him $22.00. He do the job for $22.00. He seh, "Look, I gine give yuh back $4.00. Take that $4.00 and help buy little things. I do the job for yuh reasonable, but I still going to give yuh that $4.00." I seh, "Look I gine fail now." He seh, "No, yuh are not going to fail." Yuh know, I gone up. When I get in de yard there was so much people up there, men, women, people enough. I heard this voice. I seh, "Who dah? Dah is Reifer up dey at de door?" But good luck for me, I know Reifer. Some the people say yes, dat is Reifer. I seh, "Lemme get near, lemme pass through here, so I went and I clap. I seh, "Mr Reifer, this is so and so down heah, I want to get up there." He seh, "Dudley?" I seh, "Yes". He seh, "Wen yuh hear I clap yuh come. Nuff people up heah. Uh gine get the rid of these first, but as yuh hear I clap yuh come."

Some people did vex and some people say, look, yuh see he is dat man friend. Me and he work side an' side together. The last place we work in Rockley on Rockley Golf Course. Mr. Hutson, Nurse and Jones, we did building a house there for Inniss who was Manager and Director of DaCosta. We were building a house there for he son-in-law and Reifer left there and went in de Police Force. So I gone in. The first ting I do, I say let me explain to yuh Doctor, 'cause they got the American Doctor there at the door. The American government say don't come down there with rotten teeth in yuh head. I went to Dentist King and had a piece of teet and he said he can't pull it not until he going put in the plate. I went this morning and he just pull it and he put in de plate. The man do back so and shout out, oh my God, this fella must be a top class dentist here in the country.

Well yuh know I gine make he good 'cause I is Barbadian. I seh: "Yes, he is a very, very one of the great, great dentist we have here". He seh, "He did a damn good job." The detective now running back the book, he seh, "Man, yuh can't find he name in there man." Time I tell yuh so he say go long in. Man, I did trembling and when ah get inside there the last Doctor I gine to get to did Dr. Ashby, so everything work good for me.

And Dr. Ashby seh, "Dudley, wuh yuh shaking so for?" All I could do is laugh. He seh, "Yuh go and sit down there." Dese is the words I could remember like now. Yuh would know how long dah is. He seh, "Look, if I find something 'pon yuh dat I feel yuh go up to the States and lose yuh life, I en gine leh yuh go, but if I find something that yuh can go up to the States and work and help work for yuh living and come back down here, man yuh going long and when yuh come back down here I gine get yuh better man."

I remember dem words like now and I sit down, he tend to a fellow and he seh, "Come now," and he tek de pressure and I asking he questions now. He seh the pressure very good. He test de heart, he seh, "Gully, the heart good too." He seh, "De only thing could turn yuh back is if yuh urine bad. I don't see no way where yuh urine could be bad because not from what I see here yuh urine can't be bad." I gone to the nurse. Good luck for me now, I see the Nurse had two or three fellas back down de stairs. The nurse seh, "Go down and go through the place and yuh would get dis thing." Good luck, when I get to de place a long line, and yuh know who was inside making out de place where yuh should go and where yuh should go, Miss Waterman [Montrose].

They taking down the fellas where they were going to various place, and Miss Talma, Miss Waterman know me because I worked for Mr. Waterman. And do yuh know Miss Waterman and Miss Talma trying to get me from there to get me to go to Campbell Soup Co. because de place duh did send me to is a cheap place. That is a place only paying fifty cents an hour. All duh do the American man there won't move at all. Yuh know how I know? When I got back home Miss Waterman seh, "Oh my goodness, we try all we best to get Walcott from outta dat line to go to Campbell Soup Co. and the American man won't move at all."

EM: Thanks.

Know de science good

Joseph Holder aka Youngster was a highly respected and admired sticklicker. He was also a Master Workman and can be considered one of the real Stick Gods. He was interviewed by EG and IK.

EG: Youngster, you can remember some of the people you sticklick with?

JYH: Man, how you mean! Dah is a question? People like Avery, Devonnes, Sonny Gamer, Leibert, Tee Campbell, Ward, Eagle, Joe Hoad, Butting Sardines. I know it good. I can call all them names. I spend three years and six months at two shillings a month to learn the science.

Let me tell you a story. In 1940, in Camp Murphy [USA farm] myself, Johnny Brown, Eustace Small, Sonny Brancker, Sylvan Chase, Clarence Lee, George Belle had to fight to get food to eat. They used to serve white rice and some sort of meat and the Jamaicans used to come with their collins and made sure that they got theirs first and by the time the Bajans got there, all the food would be gone. This went on for about three days, and the Bajans decided that they had enough of that foolishness. So the next morning, I went to the mess hall and broke a broomstick and tell the boys get behind me. I mean that I was getting food that day.

So when we went for the food, this Jamaican fellow rush me and I give him two water-lines (two lashes to the belly) and push him out de line, and using the stick we made our way up to the server and we got our food. You know that cause bare commotion in the camp. The gang super [supervisor] arrived and asked what happen and I tell he "from today, we will be getting our food or more licks going share bout here."

One Jamaican decided to attack me with a collins, and I used my sticklicking moves on him. And the fellows asked me to teach them to lick stick and I start then to teach them that didn't know it, and them that know it, I gave them more lessons. And we didn't have any problems after that.

I remember I went to Tee Chandler house drinking rum and playing stick, and I told them that I was going to cut Tee Chandler in the last round. I suh to Chandler, "Tee boy, put your best foot forward, I am going to cut you." And I cut he. I was at Smith Corner Club [Greens, St. George] talking to Sonny Smith, you know de undertaker man, I tell them, "Gentleman, this is the last round. Campbell if you break, you cut, and if you don't break, you cut." "What?" he answered a bit surprised. I suh, "Yes! Mark it." And I cut he.

EG: How long was a round?

JGH: A round was 3 minutes and the fight last fifteen rounds.

EG: Fifteen rounds at 3 minutes?

JYH: Yea. I tell he I was going to cut he and I did. Right in he head.

IK: You used to play for money?

JYH: You get a little money, not much but you get a little donation. Lady, I know de science good. Don't fool yuhself but remember I don't palaver against the road.

EG: A palaver is a person who pretends?

JYH: Yes, someone who pretends. I'm not a pretender. What I can't win, I'll draw.

EG: How can you guarantee at least a draw?

JYH: That is a tough thing, boy, when you see a fellow is going to KO you, you wait there for him. And if you see you can't win, stay home.

EG: What you are saying is that you are not coming out or going in?

JYH: That's it!

EG: There is Tom Johnson, Queensbury, Donnelly, Swab, Creole and Sword rules?

JYH: Yes. I am Tom Johnson. Queensbury is a trickster. He will trick you. He can use his left hand, he can use his right but chop him out of it. Queensbury have science too but he is a trickster. Hear.

EG: How many positions Queensbury got?

JYH: My man, Queensbury don't have many positions. You stand up, he can exchange his left hand for his right He fans, but be careful of he, he will cut yuh.

EG: Johnson is mostly holding the position and waiting?

JYH: Yes, hold the position.

Dr. Johnson wun got sufficient wire tuh stitch up yuh head!

Fitzherbert Maloney aka Buhbup was a sometime sticklicker but was really a fan of the science and a keen observer of the art form. He was interviewed by EM.

EM: Tell me your full name.

FM: My full name is Fitzherbert Maloney. As a nickname dey call me Buhbup.

EM: When were you born?

FM: 28 Sept 1919.

EM: I understand you are a sticklicker.

FM : I used to mek sport because my fadda tell learn me a couple cuts. He tell me to represent yuhself [and] not to go in de streets or go in nuh dance house and let nuhbody lick out yuh eye. He seh I giving you a couple cuts to represent yuhself.

EM: What was his name?

FM: His name was James Parris.

EM: Do you remember when he was born?

FM: No.

EM: How long ago he died?

FM: He dead some years, man.

EM: After he teach you a few cuts and ting, you learn de sport?

FM: Yes man I cud get it manage a certain way. But I neva go and play in nuh competition.

EM: You din' do uh satu or ramp?

FM: No no no no no no!

EM: Who you know did satus?

FM: Not 'bout heah, 'cause nuhbody 'bout heah ent kno' nutten. Duh is a fellow in St. George by the name of Joseph Holder... Youngster. He did the satu. He did a lot of that.

EM: You never do any ramps round heah?

FM: Not publicly.

EM: Duh had udda fellows dat play while you were around?

FM: Man all duh dead out. Not 'round me. Duh was fellows who come in.

EM: Who was the best wun you eva see?

FM: A fellow by the name of Yarde.

EM: Edwin Yarde or Rupert Yarde?

FM: He name wuh! Duh use tuh call he Stoway.

EM: From de Turning?

FM: No, he did come from someway up deah in Bourne Village (St. Michael).

EM: Stoway Trotman?

FM: Uh Yarde? No I tink Yarde learn him.

EM: Edwin Yarde?

FM: I tink Edwin Yarde learn him. But I cyan tell you if he was a Trotman.

EM: You saw him fight?

FM: Yes.

EM: Where?

FM: I see he fight in St. Joseph. I see he fight 'bout two places. In St. Joseph pun top Braggs Hill, and out at Todd Corner.

EM: Who did he fight?

FM: He fight a fellow from Hillaby call... I cyan remember he name. He was a good sticklicker.

EM: Dem is de only two places you see stick fights?

FM: Yes, I used to neva follow it up.

EM: So you seh your fadda learn you?

FM: Uh huh.

EM: Which method he teach you? Johnson or Broad Sword?

FM: He learn me de Single Stick first and den Double Deception. I din tek it very serious though. Although I cud do a few tings, I din tek it so very serious. In fact I din so like it.

EM: You frighten fuh de lashes?

FM: Man I very spiteful, I'll hit yuh hard too, yeh!

EM: You doan kno' nuh sticklickers 'round heah at all?

FM: No all ah dem dead out. Dese young boys is lick yuh down wid rockstones. I see Youngster fight Sonny Garner. Sonny Garner was de superintendent at Blackman's [Plantation, St. Joseph]. A very terrible man. And Joseph Holder put some licks 'pun him.

EM: Wuh job Joseph Holder did up deah?

FM: Joseph Holder use to drive bus and truck. He worked at Mount Wilton [St Joseph]. Dis fight tek place at Todd Corner. A bank holiday day. He lick him man.

EM: Wuh impress you 'bout de fight?

FM: Wuh impress me 'bout de fight [was] to know de type uh man Sonny Garner did and how Joseph manage him. Wuh I had see the very Sonny Garner fight a superintendent we had heah at Walkes Spring call Linward Edwards. Yuh neva hear bout him? Yes he was the superintendent at Walkes Spring and he and Sonny Garner fight a bank holiday. I think it was a Easter Bank Holiday, down Horse Hill, in a club. Dey had a dance house in the peak of Horse Hill coming up on de right hand side.

EM: Yuh remember de name?

FM: Wait, wuh dis club did name! Shirley West? I cyan remember. But it was in de peak of Horse Hill just as yuh pass the Risk Gap pun de right hand side coming up. Concern a man call Branch, one-hand Branch.

EM: A lot uh people was there at de fight?

FM: Yes man, especially all uh Blackman people dat he supervise. But my man was good though. My man put a fall pun he man he nearly kill he. Linward. Yuh cun get he beat dah easy. But dis man Linward was a strong man. Very strong. And he and a fellow call Sweetie Jackman, he dead. He left heah a bank holiday day and he went thru de gully up deah and we butt out at Mayers Corner and walk 'till we get in Coffee Gully. So Linward din went up dey really to play him, he went up dey to suh how de fellas dat he know play. So Sweetie Jackman was playing a fella dat went up deah wid we.

So the dancing house was a gable-top ting but dey had like a shedroof part off so. So Jackman had up some rum 'cause he drink all de way gine up and wen he get up deah Sonny was playing a man, I cyan remember he name now. So Sweetie send a fellow by the name of Thelbert and tell he [Sonny] dat he gine gih he a play. Sonny tell he wait until he done wid dis fella.

But wuh he was doing tuh de fellow he was playing was tuh shove he back down under de shed so dat wen de fellow stick guh up, it hook up. So he send back and tell Sweetie he gun play he, but wait till he done wid dis fellow. So dey mek de fellow stop playing because de Sonny cut he. Because he playing and back he back in de shed. Anyway he stop play and he and Jackman start playing. Well, he cun' get tru' wid Sweetie but Sweetie had in rum, and Sweetie din know wuh he doing, so Linward send de next fellow call Thelbert and tell Sonny he gun play he. So wen de two ah dem start playing, all two is two superintendents. But dis fella...

EM: Who are the two fighters?

FM: The two fighters now was de two superintendents, Edwards and Sonny Garner. Sonny Garner was from Blackman's and Edwards was from Walkes Spring. Anyway Sweetie Jackman now gone to de bench wen duh stop dem from fighting and he gone pun de bench and gone sleep. So Linward and Sonny Garner now ketch up. So ev'rytime he try tuh force Linward Edwards down u'neat dis shed, Edwards wun go. Edwards keep he from forcing he down inside deah. So one time he leggo a lash at he, a leg lash and 'stead uh Edwards brek it out, he brek it in, and de crowd bawl.

So ev'rytime duh play, somebody calling Garner and tell he something in he ears. Linward seh he gun find out wuh duh telling he. He seh he open up a guard pun Sonny and he seh he mek a lash so at he. He seh he ent mek nuh break. But he coming down wid a head cut. He seh he swing de black wood and pull it back in pun de break and he coming down wid a head cut. And he went on under and brek it and hook de stick round Sonny neck heah and tek he up and hold he leg and trow he flat tuh de groun'. Trow he flat pun he back. He tell he, "Ef yuh get up so, before I move off yuh, Dr. Johnson wun got sufficient wire tuh stitch up yuh head". He seh, "Ah cut yuh up!" Well it end so. So Sonny Garner lost.

EM: Dat was a good fight den.

FM: Yes. De onliest one dat interest me was said very Holder that I tell you 'bout, he and a fellow call Leibert from Proute Village had it at Todd Corner at Sonny Smith club and Joseph gih Leibert some licks. He went in de gully and cut a special stick fuh he of black sage. Dey call it rock sage, and he swinge it, and he play dat day a fellow call Edgar King from in Proute who had learn Leibert. [It was a] bank holiday day too. He and Joseph start fighting. Though Leibert brekking, he still getting de lashes. He had all he shoulder whale up and at de end of the whales was little specks uh blood.

Well Edgar King whilst de playing, yuh know wen dey stop, Edgar King tell he "ef yuh gine stan deah and tek dem, tek dem den." But wuh happen is, wen he brek de stick come over. He ent brek high enuff and he brek in de half uh he stick. Wen he find out dat he brekking and he still getting licks, he shud brek at de end. But den ef you square off tuh up me and I brek and you stick still hitting me wen I fire at you, you shun be able to brek me neither. Yuh unnerstand dat?

EM: Yuh used to get pay?

FM: Pay wuh! Nah just a couple cents! Dat was a game. If you stick wen you fire at me it go over and bend and still hit me, wen I fire at you, it shud bend de same way.

EM: You eva saw your fadda fight?

FM: No.

EM: Wuh job he had on de plantation?

FM: My fadda used to mind de mules at Mt. Wilton and drive de middle gang and guh town fuh de people groceries. He drive de middle gang at Mt. Wilton.

EM: None of the watchmen that used to work at Clifton and Mt. Wilton, and so play stick?

FM: Not all! A man call Berkley Smith was a watchman at Mt. Wilton and de same very Sweetie Jackman. I ent nuh mo'...

EM: But Joseph Holder was your man!

FM: Youngster, yes man from Braggs Hill.

EM: Proute village had some sticklickers too.

FM: De same very Leibert Lynch and Edgar King. The same Leibert Lynch I telling you 'bout from Proute and Edgar King.

Real sticklickers and mock sticklickers

Prince Albert Prescod was sticklicker. He was also a blacksmith and lived in Church Village, St. Phillip. He was interviewed by EG.

EG: Prince, you know a lot about old sticklickers, tell us a story we haven't heard before.

PAP: (Pausing for a moment, cocking his head to the side and smiling) There was a man who had a pig, and his pig ate down this sticklicker's crop. So the sticklicker seize the pig and tell the owner that he had to pay for the crop. The man said that he wasn't paying for no crop, that he going home and come back. The man left and come back with his stick.

Well, the man with the crop was a good sticklicker and it turn out that the man with the pig had a few lessons in sticklicking and didn't know a thing. The pig owner came back and start doing a lot of fancy things that he practice. But when the real sticklicker start to share licks, the next thing you know, the man eye out and he had to pay $1,400 to the doctor.

EG: Who pay the $1,400? The real sticklicker?

PAP: The real sticklicker had to pay the doctor the $1,400 for the eye that the mock sticklicker lost. He told me, "Prince, I thought the man know 'bout sticklicking."

EG: The real sticklicker was a friend of yours?

PAP: He used to work for Mannings. I used to shoe his donkey for him. He used to drive to work a donkey and cart. That was his car. There wasn't any cars like today. He was a big man at the lumber yard. He would go and check the load and put down the marks and then charge. When you want lumber he would go and put out the material and then tell you what to take out.

A stick lash is like a shot out of a gun!

DaCosta Alleyne was a sticklicker and a joiner. He lived in Sweet Bottom, St. George. He was interviewed by EG.

DA: I remember a lot of old sticklickers but most of them dead. All of them fellows so dead.

EG: You can't remember their names?

DA: Yes, I can remember some of them names. One was Arnold Greenidge from Christ Church, Bobby from Deane Village [Black Rock, St. Michael], another from Christ Church name Gifted, one from out Proute Village [St. Thomas], I can't remember his name.

EG: You mean Curds? Curds was a tall, dark, stocky fella who work at Transport Board.

DA: No, he was clear skin and short. I don't remember his name. I never used to linger around with them. I think his name was Herbert or something like that.

EG: There was Herbert and Curds. Curds was Herbert brother. Both of them used to work at Transport Board driving and both of them was good sticklickers from up there. Basically, dem used to do a lot of stick playing.

DA: Dey had a man name Stoway, he dead. Boysie Brathwaite was from Charles Rowe Bridge, [St. George], he dead. My father...

EG: What was your father's name?

DA: Gittens and I went down under all of them hands in sticklicking.

EG: That means that you know a little thing or two. The young people today don't want anything so.

DA: I went down under all dem hands. And we generally used to play sticklicking on Bank Holidays down there in Charles Rowe Bridge. There had a woman called Miss Brathwaite used to keep shop, used to carry on Service-o-song and dance. And we used to generally play on Bank Holidays or any time at all during the week. And let me tell you something. I went through so much with sticklicking. And all you learn whenever you done, the Master Workman still keep one from you. Don't give you all.

One day I was coming up Black Rock, a Saturday evening and I saw some fellows playing and I stand up and watch them. And when the fellow pass the lash 'pun the fellow and I see the fellow block, I suh, "Whuh! my Master Workman didn't learn me that one at all. Dah is one he keep from me."

And there had a thing in Charles Rowe Bridge, a Service-o-song and dey also had sticklicking. And the same fellow Boysie Brathwaite, he learn he, my father learn me, my uncle learn me and all of them had that key lash and keep it from me. And I come up and saw a man with it.

Boysie went and play his man and Boysie didn't get it. But I went there, and I play he. And when I play I change pun he and pelt de lash. He jump back, "Hold it! Who you get that from? I didn't learn you that." I suh, "Dat is the one that you keep back, but I got it."

EG: Dem men was smart.

DA: When I mek de change pon he and I wrap up on him, and I come back and say, "Ah!... and put the lash pon he, he say "Where you get that from? I didn't learn you that." I replied, "But I get it." He said, "That was one that I was keeping from you. You don't give away everything."

EG: Out of all de fellows that train you, who it is that you put the move on?

DA: Pun my Master Workman.

EG: Which one this was?

DA: Clarke. That was one he had on me. And my father had on me. All of them had dah one on me, one dat they didn't learn me. Let me tell you how serious sticklicking is then. I had a family and she and I had a noise and I put a lash pon she and she tek me to Court. The magistrate warned me, telling me, "Look I have five minds to take you from the bar and lock yuh up. A stick lash is like a shot out of a gun. I have five minds to lock you up." My cousin carry me to court and had to turn around and beg for me.

EG: You know anybody that play stick now?

DA: All of them fellas dead out now. I don't know anybody that knows sticklicking now. But I would still use my stick if anybody attack me. I don't worry with sticklicking anymore. I is just keep my stick to walk with.

Sardines

"I was playing a man on Lazaretto pasture and he keep putting his foot in my face, and I couldn't get him cut out. He would have his stick up in the air between the sixth and seventh position and he would say, 'Come Danby, come Danby.' And I playing between the first and second position couldn't do anything.

Man I came home that night and went to my brother. I said, 'Boysie, you know a man called Sardine? He do something today to me, and I can't get it manage'

Boysie replied, 'Show me, show me.'

I started to demonstrate. He was playing upright in the air and I was playing between the first and second. Boysie asks me, 'And you couldn't get he touch, right?'

I replied, 'Man, no.' So I went back down by the Lazaretto Pasture and told Bob and the boys that I was going to put some lashes in his backside. This man Sardines name was Richard Richardson and he was the overseer on Lazaretto Pasture and he brought a young boy with him.

I told him, 'Don't bring the boy. I want to play you.'

So we started playing, and he went through with his moves again. This time when he cut, he put up his hand and I was hitting him on his knee. You see, when he cut with the stick, I put my hand on his stick and block. And the stick drop out of his hand and I hit him quick so on his knee.

So from then, if I play anybody and couldn't get through, I would come home and ask my brother and they couldn't do that again."

Man, I would lick you stiff!

Colvin Sargeant was one of the few woman stick lickers around. She was one of the hawkers who carried fruits and vegetables on their heads. Herbert Parris came from Proute Village St. Thomas. Curds was his bother and Pin was their father. Herbert and Curds were bus drivers with the Transport Board. Herbert was interviewed by EC and IK.

EG: There are stories of a woman sticklicker, but I can't remember her name....

HP: Yuh mean Colvin Sargeant?

EG: So you know she story?

HP: Colvin Sargeant was a black woman sticklicker. Yuh cun interfere with she. Man, she used to beat men. She'll pull she stick out and share licks for days. She wud tek out a cigarette, put it in she mout and dare anyone to tek de cigarette out she mout. She used to walk from Clifton Hill [St. John] to town with a tray of bananas and apples pun she head, sell dum and walk back home. She never tek a bus an' all midnight, dat woman walk with a tray pun she head. She wud wear a cap an' she used to walk with a stick under she arm. Yuh see, wen she pull out dah stick, she cud hit yuh whey eva she want.

Moonie tell dis story that she did someting to he one night going up Marshall Gap dat he din expect. She was walking a night and he did gine up de road. He did watchman at Walkes Spring, [St Thomas]. He see dis woman and he attack she.

IK: You mean he made a pass?

HP: Yes. And she prop he up. He suh dat she tek de stick and prop he up. Yuh know wuh prop he mean?

EG: No! Yuh got me there!

HP: Wen he tek de break, she tek de break de udder way, then she shot for he stomach and lower she height, and put de end of de stick in he stomach and prop he up pun de stick.

EG: Now that you talk about she, I know she.

HP: One time she was in front Joseph [Youngster] and he like he had up some liquor and he start parrying. And she tek up she stick and put it behind she head holding it in she hands and suh "Wen you ready Youngster! Wen eva you ready!" Youngster just mek a couple moves, but won't bring he stick up. She suh, "Man, I would lick you stiff."

By dah time, ev'rybody start gathering round as they thought that real licks was gine share. Youngster din do nutten as he had up a couple of drinks. Youngster step back and told Colvin, "Girlie, you is my girl, I won't hurt you." She boldly replied, "It ent a matter of hurting, we wudda find out who wudda hurt who!"

De crowd looked at Colvin for a moment and den start to move way. Colvin Sargeant was a tall woman and had a huge voice. Yuh cud stand all the way down de road and hear she. She din nuh sweet bread. Wen she back up in a corner, yuh cun get close to she. Wen ever yuh come, she wud trap yuh. If yuh go to the right, she trap yuh. Ef yuh guh to de left, she wud trap yuh. Yuh cun get 'round she.

Colvin Sargeant's husband did name Theophilus. Man, she put some good licks in he back-side. He din like it, but he had to move out de house. She din frighten for nobody.

Ione Knight is also a
sticklicker in her own right.

I was gine empty he bread basket!

Trevor "Bay" Brown was 83 years old. He was raised by and knew the notorious Elliot Haynes. He also knew and saw Eagle Blackman, Snotty Man Bispham, Tee Downes, Ajax, 98, and Mice-in-a-tot lick stick. He was interviewed by EG and IK.

Bay: I din like it. I used to watch it. Um is a dangerous thing. I learn enough to protect muhself.

EG: Can you remember the names of some of the people who you watched play?

Bay: Yes, but all of them dead now. There was a fella called Eagle Blackman, Snotty Man Bispham, Mice-in-the-tot, and Elliot Haynes. The fellas used to play in grades. They had masons, carpenters, agricultural workers, etc.

EG: So they used to play according to their jobs?

Bay: Yes, agricultural workers cun play de masons or carpenters as de masons etc. felt that de agricultural workers was below them.

IK: I hear the name Eagle Blackman before, he seem to be very popular.

Bay: Yes, he did like to show off and he was very good at sticklicking, so he and de fellows would play. Elliot Haynes was good too, but he was notorious. He was notorious with he stick and notorious with he knife. He was known for both. He did like gambling too. I used to live at Elliot Haynes and he wife as a youngster and he would tek me wid he wen he went gambling. As a matter of fact, I would say that I used to take him. What happen was I did tek out a bicycle pun credit and wasn't able to pay fuh um and he decide dat he would pay for um. So wherever he had to go, I would tek he.

One time he cyah me with he to Ellerton to a spot called De Mingo. Dah was de place where de Bulkeley Plantation workers used to stop to drink and gamble. At dah time, when yuh wuk at Bulkeley you got money. Dey had three bad men dat used to play the game. One was called Tee Downes. De other two were Ajax, and 98.

EG: 98?

Bay: Yes, he was called so because that was he number when he was in Glendairy prison. Dey seh that de warden came one morning and seh, "98, 98 take up yuh bucket and face de door."

[Anyhow] Elliot came to me and seh, "Boy, dis look like a long night." Now later in the night when dey was gambling and playing for a while, Elliot look up at me and seh "Boy, you sleepy?" I seh, "Yes!" He seh, "Alright, I gun mek dis muh last game and come and tek you home." He used to talk wid a drone. So he play de last game and seh, "Man, gentlemen, dis boy sleepy so I'm gine cyah he home, hear."

Ajax seh, “Wuh! We doan gamble so. I does gamble to a finish. You brek me or I brek you.” Elliot replied, “dah is yuh law, you play. Dat is not de law I play by. Man, wen I lose and time up, I guh long and when I win and time up I guh long.” Wen he swing round to go, 98 seh, “Man, hold he and shake he out.” Back den, men used to hold yuh and shake yuh up and down.

Wen Ajax mek de move toward Elliot, Elliot pull he stick and hit he behind he head. Elliot gi’ he three good lashes. Wen he ketch heself, Elliot had a knife in he hand and Elliot drive the knife towards he side and it hit he belt and bend back. Ajax got up and tremble, Elliot got up and cried. When he start straightening the knife, he start to cry. He seh, “Be Christ, Bishop is gine ha’ to gi’ me back my money ’cause he fool me. I thought I had this man bread basket empty on de groun’ and de blasted knife bend.”

And ev’rybody looking to see wuh um is dat save Ajax. Ajax tek up he dices and tell 98 to come and dey left. Elliot seh, “I was gine empty he bread basket and de blasted knife let me down, man.” De knife did mek out uh piece of sickle wid a wooden handle. De next Sarduh evening, he call me and tell me dat he gine back again. Dere I was with a look of surprise pun muh face. I seh, “Wuh, [after] that knife let you down man?” But I still tek he back up deah. Now when Ajax saw he coming he put de dice in he pocket and seh, “We done. Nuhbody ent gambling here. At least not wid you.”

Elliot reply wid, “Well ef wunna ent gambling wid me, wunna ent gambling at all.” Ev’rybody had to go on their way.

Ajax seh, "Man, if it wasn't for my belt you woulda kill me." Ajax had a piece of belt mek from centrifuge belt. Yuh know de centrifuge belt? You know dat dum have a piece of canvas material line wid strands of wire woven into the canvas. Um was used like de fan belt of a car.

EG: Yes. That works the machines.

Bay: Yes. At dat time all of dem man dat did handy work used to wear an inside belt. Fellows that dig cane holes, lift things, all uh dem used to wear an inside belt. So dat inside belt save Ajax life dah night. I doan know how true, but I understand dat Elliot died dat same way. I understand that he and some boys was gambling and dem attack he and hide he 'cause dey neva' find he body till days after. He used to live pun he own.

IK: He wife died?

Bay: No, you know. She run 'way and left he and he was out deah pun he own. And wen dey find he, de dogs had pieces of he. De ting is, he did a kind man. He did a very kind person and suddenly so by the drop of a hat, he would be very dangerous. You heard about Eagle?

EG: Yes. We heard about Eagle. You seh that there was Eagle Blackman, Mice-in-the- tot?

Bay: Yes, there was Eagle Blackman, Mice-in-the-tot, Elliot Haynes, Snotty Man. He was Bispham. The same Elliot Haynes nickname was Nicky.

EG: So who teach you?

Bay: De little bit dat I know I learn from de same man Elliot Haynes. He always told me that he was gine to teach me enough to stop anybody from tekking advantage of me. I never did like um. Dem men used to cut yuh up, give you trollops and tings like that.

IK: So you was a bit frighten?

Bay: I don't know. Um was a very nice game, but too cruel a ting. Too cruel a ting! De few men that knew um used to do all sort of tings with their sticks. Prop dis man on his navel, prop dis man belly and prop de next man. Snotty Man was about de best dat I knew in all. Snotty Man was so good dat he used to keep he stick under he arm and tell you to touch he. All yuh do yuh couldn't touch he. He move here, he move there, he move under. We used to wonder if he was disguise.

EG: Disguise?

Bay: Yes. One minute yuh will think yuh see he here, de next minute yuh will see he some place different. De last time dat he get trick was by some lil' children dat trick he one night. He was a yard watchman.

De children dig a hole in de bagasse and put some sticks in de hole and wen he run them dey mek sure dat he run in dat direction and he drop down in de hole. So wen he get out uh de hole, he seh, "Well, look wuh de children do to dis old snotty man. Look wuh dese naughty children do to dis snotty old man."

De one ting dat I like bout Bispham was dat even wen he was getting down in age he used to mek sport with de children.

Dat was why I did like he. He was a scientific man, very scientific. De cruel things dat de udder fellas used to do, he never do.

EG: You have given us good food for thought.

IK: Well, we heard some more names that we didn't hear before. What was Eagle's real name?

Bay: Ah, I don't know. He surname was Blackman.

IK: Well, we heard about a man called Butting Sardines and we found out what his name was Joseph Blade.

Bay: He was from St. Philip?

IK: I ent sure whey he from. We were talking to a man called Knocka White and he tell us he real name.

Bay: Oh! Knocka White! He send you out here?

EG: No. I researching sticklicking. I teach sticklicking and I am researching it as much as possible.

Bay: I entirely forget 'bout Knocka White. Knocka White used to be a sticklicker. Both he and he brother Pauper used to like sticklicking. He still alive?

IK: Yes. He just got an operation on he eyes and he tell us dat he will be 84 years on 28th June 2000. We got some of de people dat used to sticklick real name from he.

Bay: He would know. He and he brother had like sticklicking.

EG: We talk to Joseph Holder, the Youngster from St. Joseph, Herbert from Proute Village, and Babutts.

Bay: I know Babutts. Curds was Herbert brudda and he and Herbert use to work at Clifton Plantation. All two of dem used to drive lorry and den dey went and drive bus.

Dum had dis agricultural fellow call Hinkson who seh that he was a sticklicker. I don't know. But de fellow he was dealing with was definitely a sticklicker, a man call Archie Wall. He used to live in Green's, St. George. Dis fellow Hinkson was playing the fool with he stick and ting after he drink up and feel merry. Wall tell he to wait until he go home and come back. So Wall went home for he stick and come back. Hinkson pelt a few lashes at Wall and Wall move away. While he was looking around at Wall, you know these fellows was just like the Kung Fu fellows, when dey attack you, dey make this funny noise. As he open he mouth, Wall had he stick down he mouth.

Dere was another fellow who used to play stick. He learn Elliot Haynes and quite a few of de fellows. He name Lawrence Moore. He was the Task Master down here.

Dere was anudder fellow dat was very good at it and he learn it because he got a job at de Mental Hospital dealing wid de mad people. Wen he get de job, he was a small fellow in stature. He come down and Moore teach he the science and he was very good at it. A fellow called Cobham.

EG: So basically Cobham learn because he was too small to deal with those people.

Bay: Mostly de people in dat time who learn de science was small men, you know. You get very few big strong fellows dat learn de art. It was de small man dat had to defend heself from de bigger fellow.

Don Norville[71] was a good boxer. He learn to box because as a little boy at school he was very small and the fellows used to beat he up. So he uncle learn he to box so as to take care of heself.

71. Don Norville was a well known sportsman who played football for Empire. He was also a prominent sports writer with the Barbados Advocate.

De Mingo

There is a mythical place in St. George called De Mingo. That is the name given to me by the old people who lived around Ellerton. To reach this place called De Mingo, you had to turn left at Ellerton cross roads, opposite the playing field by Barrow (the son) Shop where they used to hold all the political meetings from the 40's through to the 70's. This road came to a major road which when you turned right at the junction would take you to the Farm. Most of this land has subsequently developed.

De Mingo was at this junction. In the middle of the junction was a water well. It is covered by the manhole cover in the accompanying pictures. It was a deep deep well, maybe 100 ft or more deep. I don't know if it was part of Ellerton Plantation or the Farm or the nigger

yard of one or the other of these plantation, but my encounter with De Mingo came about in my search for legendary sticklickers. All the old people tell me I should go down to De Mingo and ask around there. Most of them were repeated stories from their youth in the late 19th Century.

The mystique about De Mingo is that it was named after a man called Mingo who controlled or dictated who or when anyone could draw water from the well. Mingo used to enforce his rules by the mere fact that he was a superb sticklicker. Because of his skill, he was also a watchman at one of the plantations mentioned above. The history of plantation development in Barbados is quite peculiar and there is the possibility that a much smaller plantation existed at this spot. Many small plantations failed and were amalgamated into nearby larger plantations.

So it is possible that this well was abandoned and in the early part of the 20th Century became the source of water for the small settlement that developed in the area. Whatever the reason, Mingo controlled the water supply in the area and it became known to all as De Mingo. Mingo was also the organizer of several social events in De Mingo near the water well. People told me of sticklicking battles, wrestling bouts, service-o-songs, and other forms of entertainment.

Mingo, according to many informants, was a formidable sticklicker who took on all corners. He apparently never travelled much, but would invite several sticklickers from St. Thomas, St. Michael and St. John to ramp at De Mingo. Many of the sticklickers from the Hothersal Turning/Lears Gap area used to be involved in these battles. These battles used to be attended mostly by the workers on the adjacent plantations, but the white managers and overseers also used to attend.

None of my informants could give me details about Mingo's appearance as they were very small when he was an old man, but they knew from their parents and other people in the area that Mingo was the baddest of the bad and none would mess with him on his turf.

Stick chanting de Psalms like a church bell!

Clyde Cephus Carter was a former active sticklicker until glaucoma curtailed his activity. He vividly describes some fights and sticklickers that he saw and knew. He was interviewed at his home in Market Hill, St. George by EM.

EM: What is your name?

CCC: I name Carter, man. Clyde Carter.

EM: What was your nickname?

CCC: Cephus.

EM: Wuh year you was born?

CCC: 1926.

EM: Where you worked?

CCC: At the factory. It was an all day job plus....

EM: Which factory?

CCC: Uplands, St. John. I used to work on de hoist liffing up de canes.

EM: Scrambler?

CCC: No dah was a crane! No no! Not a crane, a hoist, a cane hoist that liff de cane off de lorry and tractors and so forth and pack de heap or wen de table want a cane dey load. De money din so bad but dah is wuh gi' me glaucoma and cause my sight to cut down right now. 'Causing I din know ah had it and it grew worst and worst. So wen I did check de doctor, de eyes cun cut on account of de glaucomas. De doctor heah seh dat ef he cut dem I wudda go blind entirely. So he ask me ef I wanna go blind. I seh no. I wud neva like to guh blind. I wud like tuh see eva so slight. So I had tuh use drops and so forth.

EM: Whey did you learn tuh lick stick?

CCC: Well I learn all about it 'cause I went wid about three men and all of dem know. Dem dead and gone long.

EM: What were their names?

CCC: Tell yuh de honest trute, the names beat me. One was uh Blenman, but I din' know he first name. He was fairly good and anudder one from down Applewaite side. He dead too. All uh dem men dead! I were a youngster at de time but ah did like de sport, learning dis science. So I went into it wid de two uh dem, one after de next.

EM: Which science you played?

CCC: Well I mostly used to play de stick.

EM: Single stick!

CCC: Yeah! I did like dah one. But wuh cause me did to stop afta de eyes start getting nil, I had to stop entirely. Yuh wud go round watch some of de fellows dat I know, de operations.

EM: Like who?

CCC: A man name Edwin Nichols, one name Edgar King. Edwin Nichols was as hot as fire man. And he din used to drink out broad but sometimes he wud tek a drink and wen he in action man fellows does ha' tuh keep duh eyes on him otherwise duh get cut up. Yeah man.

EM: He's de best fighter you eva see?

CCC: Uh Uh.

EM: He was from where?

CCC: St. George. He live gine down deah tuh guh tuh Applewaite, on de left, whey dem houses on de left hand deah before yuh get down tuh Locust Hall.

EM: Wuh udder fights you saw dat impress you?

CCC: Well de fight I saw wuh did impress me a lot is a time dey had a satu at Braggs Hill between Edgar King and Eagle Blackman. Blackman was a fellow from St. John who did challenge King. Dat time Applewaite factory used to work so Blackman did get on tuh King tru' deah.

EM: It was a good fight?

CCC: Oh God man, terrible, man dah did looking like murder.

EM: Why you say dat? Describe de fight fuh muh.

CCC: Well de fight was hot. Well Blackman was a bragger. He did know de wood good though, de stick good. I remember in de third round Blackman had King in a corner and ef King din know wuh gine on he wudda cut he up man like souse, man. I did hear de stick chanting de Psalms man like a church bell, man. I hear "ring ding ding, ring ding ding, ring ding ding, ring ding, ring ding, ring ding, ring ding," and all Blackman, duh used tuh call he Eagle, all yuh can hear is "whum whum, whum whum", with de stick chanting man. People holla fuh murder, man. Afta a time, dey stop de fight because um did look too dangerous.

EM: Who won or was it a draw?

CCC: Well according to rules a draw becausing Blackman leggo nuff nuff nuff licks. Nuff nuff nuff. So he wudda had de benefit of de fight. But de man he did fighting was uh older man dan he at de time but de man was a master workman also but he did know de wood good.

EM: What work he do?

CCC: Edgar King was uh agricultural worker. But he was a master sticklicker. Eagle Blackman, he did from St. John.

EM: Did you see any other classic fights?

CCC: Well dah time I din ha' nuh time tuh run about tell yuh de trut. But dah one in particular being knowing Blackman and King, I seh well I ha' tuh go, had tuh mek some time tuh guh tuh see dah deah. Dah was in Braggs Hill, St. Joseph, dah tek place deah.

EM: You used to make your sticks?

CCC: Well wen yuh seh mek dem like anybody, duh had a wood call de bay wood. Dah was strong strong. Yuh cut dum a Sarduh a certain time and yuh swinge dum.

EM: Wuh time, wen de moon high or wen?

CCC: Ah, we din had nuh time pick out. As um get to be like a certain age we cut dum and swinge dum wid some fire and put dum up leh duh cure, yuh know.

EM: How long yuh put dum fuh?

CCC: Well duh put up sometime fuh bout two months or more. Sometimes less.

EM: Somebody tell me dey used tuh have men used tuh go tuh obeah men tuh put obeah pun duh sticks.

CCC: Man dah is bare shit, man. All I gun 'put pun a stick is put some lashes in a man behind ef he cyan brek de lashes yuh pelt to he. But putting obeah pun a stick is bare... I ent know wuh yuh does call dah!

EM: You ent know nuhbody who did do dah?

CCC: No no no no.

EM: Dey used tuh fight in a ring?

CCC: Yeah.

EM: Fight fuh money or fuh rum?

CCC: Nuh rum man. Dem satu din used tuh tek place fuh nuh rum. Men wud buy rum awright, but it was fuh money and reputation. Dem satu yuh had tuh pay tuh enter tru de door, yuh know. So de winner wud get a certain amount and de loser wud still get something too.

EM: So dey used guh round in a circle in de ring? How de fight used to start in a satu? De sticks had tuh be pun de groun' crossed or what or dey start wid de sticks in duh hand?

CCC: Dey start wid de sticks in duh hand in de late day. But one time dey used tuh put sticks pun de groun' crossway and you were tuh snatch up yours. But late days yuh start wid yuh stick in yuh hand 'cause wen de man tell yuh march, yuh got tuh march. Well ef de man is better dan you and he ketch you in de quarter march, yuh got a cut right deh up front. Um was nice enjoying watching dose kinda tings but ah tell yuh it was a dangerous set up. It was very dangerous.

EM: You used to play, you din' tink it was dangerous?

CCC: Yes but how yuh mean but ah tell yuh dah time ah had good eyes, yuh know, the sight was perfectly good. So....

EM: You used tuh live up here all de time?

CCC: No, I live in St. George but higher up.

EM: Dey never used tuh have sticklickers whey you was in de village?

CCC: Yeah duh had a fellow name Nicholls. He did live up dah side dah time wid he grandmudda who did raise him. He die now a few years back. Nicholls did good. He was a boxer and a sticklicker. Wen yuh see dah man in action, man he fast so help my god pun he two feet. Dey ent ha nuhbody to match he wid speed. Ah telling yuh man. He went tuh de Virgin Islands and spend a few years down deah. Afterwards he come back home wen he did done work. Wen he come back home he neva work nuh more. And he had a nice house down deah.

EM: Wen you were a lil' boy, you born in 1926, wuh is de first stickfight you remember seeing?

CCC: Well I neva see nuh stickfight till I did mature wen I cudda tell me ole lady I gine such and such a place. She seh, "Awright boy be careful." But I used tuh practice in a tenant call Cottage [St. George]. I used tuh practice up deah den ah lef deah and went tuh Workmans. Duh had a fellow name Blenman who teach me. We had two good stickfighters in Drakes Hall – Beresford and William White. Beresford come off de best afta' a time 'cause he was a patient man. Had patience but William din ha nuh patience. Ef he ketch yuh outside loose, yuh cut.

EM: Is it tru dat a lot of de watchmen on plantations used to be sticklickers?

CCC: I really doan know. Dey used to cyah a stick really but ah doan' know. In dah day dem men din use tuh tink about nutten so. Dem use tuh tink 'bout watching de master tings, yuh unna stand? In dem days. But we had some good sticklickers wen I come up deah as a youngster and some brilliant men, man. Dey had a man name Leon Small, dey used to call he Gifted, from Fair Valley, Christ Church.

EM: He was a good fighter? You neva saw him fight?

CCC: I see he one time. He and a son did skylarking wen de two uh dem march and snatch stick and open the first fight. Small tell he son, boy, I din learn you so. De son get vex.

Yuh doan know de son leggo some lashes at he in the third fight dat ef he cun brek dem he wudda get cut up like souse, man! The son was a young man and yuh know de fadda cun get around like de son, yuh know. It was enjoyable watching those things and yuh shud learn something dat will help yuh in de later date. Yuh unnastand?

EM: Was there music around dese satus and ting, tuk band music or anyting so?

CCC: No. Duh din' ha' nutten so.

EM: Nuh singing or service-o-song?

CCC: I was invited tuh one cause a fella was asking me some questions, dah is down in Airy Hill, down inside deah. But de Sunday I had tuh work. De factory did close down but I did doing a job painting and I had tuh gi' de people satisfaction 'cause I was leader uh de work, so I neva had chances tuh go. Since den I outta date now so I doan worry muh head wid dah. I doan tink about um now at all.

EM: Thank you, I certainly appreciate your contribution.

Rough as the sea in full rage!

Clyde Cephus Carter describes a stickfight between the legendary Joe Eagle Blackman and Edgar King. He was interviewed by EG and IK.

EG: I just come from up the road by the old sticklicker man.

CC: You mean DaCosta Alleyne?

EG: Yes, we had a little talk bout sticklicking and ting.

CC: He know it good; but he don't play it no more.

EG: DaCosta call some names and he tell me that all uh those players dead now. And there is only 'bout three people he know who still alive that know bout sticklicking, but they don't play anymore.

CC: I got family that used to play stick, and them dead too. The Bryans. Herbie Bryan.

I hear the fellows used to go to church in their collar and tie and their jackets and with their stick too. Oh boy, you should have seen them, they used to look so good! I like to see it play but it look so hard to me.

EG: So you used to watch it?

CC: Yes, I used to watch them play.

EG: I was trying to find out from DaCosta if he know about any women that used to play stick. But he said no.

CC: I had uh aunt that used to play name Dorcas Bryan from St. Philip. She dead too. But she could play real good. I was trying to remember about the third position for you since I last see you, but I ent get through fully yet. I was trying to remember what you do in the third position and all I can remember is that in the third, you ask the man to march, that is, round in a circle.

But in the quarter march, if you catch the man offside, there is about seven lashes there for him. And if he break, well, he good. But if he can't break them, the licks going in to his stomach. To be honest with you, I stop with that so long that I can't remember the rest of the lessons. I stop so long ago that I can't retain what I learn. I had to stop because of poor eye sight.

EG: But is there anything you can remember that stands out? Like the way some fellows would play or two women playing?

CC: Women used to play stick 'cause women used to go round and peep through the paling to see what was going on. I know women enough learn cuts that way, and they would play enough to get out. But two women playing one another? I never see that or hear anything about that.

About two years ago in Braggs Hill, there was two masters playing though. These were two men who could have given anybody lessons. But the youngest man was rough, rough as the sea in full rage. One was a man from St. John, but he lived somewhere in South District [St. George]. The other man used to work as an agricultural worker. He did know the stick real bad. He used to give men lessons. His name was King. Edgar King. This other fellow, he was a Blackman.

EG: You don't mean Joe Blackman?

CC: Yes, Joe Blackman. He dead now. I din know you hear he name call. But you did know he?

EG: No!

CC: Man, that Saturday was a human cry. Men enough start to holler. And how that did come about was, Blackman played with a stick nearly as big as a hoe stick. And one time he hold King in a corner. He put so much licks on King down in there. King break them though. All you hear was pix, pix, pix.

EG: What was the matter with the stick?

CC: The weight of the stick that Blackman had was too heavy and King had to hold a strong one to break them. But you should know a round should last three minutes with a minute for the break. Man, them men play with intensity for more than nine minutes with no breaks. Blackman din give King nuh quarter, nuh quarter at all. That was the most dangerous fight that I watch, and I din like it. It was too rough, man. It was rough, rough.

EG: So Blackman stick was too big?

CC: Too big and heavy! Men holler for murder and criticize Blackman and he had to come off. And when Blackman come off, King hand drop down like when you cut down a weak tree. That was the only fight I had time to watch 'cause it was crop season and I was working in the crop at that time.

Sundays, sticklicking, service of song and dancing

Colvin Burnett a.k.a. Mudsoup was a sticklicker. He was taught by Rupert Yarde. He was interviewed by EG and IK.

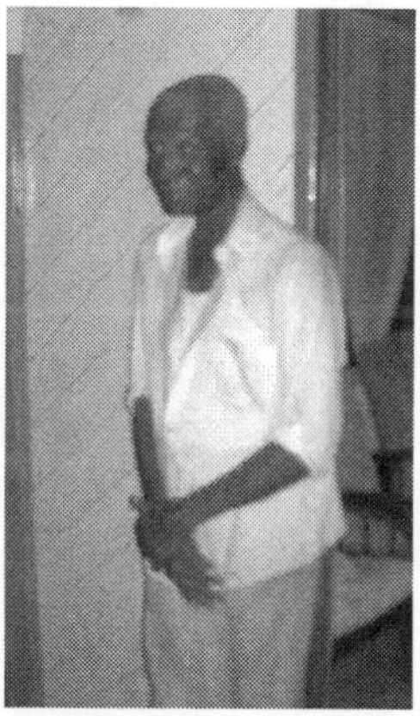

MS: Sticklicking, I like it bad. On Sundays we used to leave home to go and see sticklicking. There used to have it at Cheryl Corner Club, belonging to [Lloyd] Smith. You know where the Corner club was?

EG: I ent sure.

MS: Man look! As you come to the major road, when you cross Sugar Hill [St Joseph] and come to Todds [St. John] corner, round there where they have Greens [St. George]? The Corner Club was there in them bushes... at the corner of them. There used to have dances down there every Saturday night and Sunday night. We would go there and dance and watch so much sticklicking.

Sticklicking and service of song, they used to have on Sundays. Dance Saturday, service of song and sticklicking on Sundays. The service of song at that time used to carry pork chops and pudding and souse. Dem days we used to lef

Sunday night and we used to go straight to work on Monday mornings. We'd go down to Mount Wilton, and back out the trucks and load them with sugar and molasses and we gone to town and back.

Leh me tell you bout dese days. CB Brown was the top band. Clevie Gittens was the second. Sidney Niles? No... Happy Jordan was the third band and Sidney Niles was the last band. When you see Sidney Niles down at Todds comer, he ent got nuhbody because everybody where Clevie gone. Then they would leave there in the midnight and go over to Braggs Hill [St. Joseph]. If Sidney Niles down Braggs Hill and Happy Jordan at Todds Corner, he ent have anybody. Ev'rybody where Happy Jordan is.

IK: We were told that men used to play stick for a bottle of rum?

MS: Yes, I sit down and see that. They used to put a bottle in the ring, in the middle of the ring. You walk 'round, right a way round with the bottle of rum in the middle of the ring. Only so you tack back and attack me. The bottle of rum is yours. I shouldn't let you touch me, I should be able to cut out the lash.

IK: How long the fight would last?

MS: Sometimes about four of them. I take on you, you take on me, and so on.

IK: For a bottle of rum?

MS: No, that bottle of rum is mine. But we will still play one another for a little time to see who is the best out of the two of we. That is the way we used to play. That is how I come along and find it. Sticklicking is a good sport. We used to make money out of it.

IK: How?

MS: You had to pay to go in there and see the sticklicking you know.

Pin Parris - Herbert father

"My father used to sticklick. He show me what I know. Dixie told me one day, 'Herbert boy, you would never be the man your father was.' When you see my father going out to play stick, you would think he going to a wedding. He got on his chain, his pocket watch—you know in these days the men used to carry a pocket watch—kerchief 'round his neck. And wherever a bad man is, they would say, 'Come for him.'

And the men would bring a car and carry him. He would go and rough them up and come back home until the next time."

If you brek my pipe, I will buy you three gills!

Manning used to go to the theatre and watch stick playing and decided that he would begin to teach people to play stick. He had a few fellows as students: Chrissy, Sam Ifill and... I can't remember the other fellow name.

So Boysie carry us out there one night. Boysie had me and Samuel with him. Manning introduced us to the boys and told Boysie that these was his best students.

Boysie said, "Play and let me see." So we playing and from the time you hear pix, pix (sticks hitting together), the man on you.

Boysie tell Manning that, "Man, you fooling these people."

Manning replied, "I fooling them! I gine to fool you too."

"Alright, I alright with that," Boysie replied.

Manning then told Boysie that he was going to play him the best of three for a three-gill [bottle of rum]. He told Boysie that he was going to put some lashes on him.

Now Manning had a white pipe and he had it in his mouth. Boysie told Manning, "You see that pipe, I am going to break it in three."

Manning replied, "If you break it, I will buy you three gills."

Making an irritating sound between his teeth, Samuel egged on Boysie, "Man, brek the foolish man pipe."

So they start to play and Manning played between the fourth and fifth Tom Johnson position, and Boysie stayed in first position

Queensbury. Then Manning start prancing 'bout, and Boysie just turn away and send a lash and hit the pipe. When you look, one piece of the pipe in Manning's mouth, two pieces on the ground, and a look of surprise on Manning's face. And Samuel down 'pon the ground rolling up laughing.

Ione Knight

Sticklicking under the tamarind tree

Joseph Harewood was a sticklicker. He was interviewed by Elvis Gill and Ione Knight.

EG: We come to ole talk bout sticklicking.

JH: Sticklicking?

EG: We want to know who you see play, if you play, who you played and names of people that you see play.

JH: That last part I really don't know if I remember anybody now. There is one single fellow that I know that was a sticklicker, they used to called him Two Moons. I don't know if he still alive cause I haven't seen him for 'bout two years. Then there had a fellow called Mr. Clarke and a fellow called Boysie Brathwaite. I don't know if his brother William could lick stick too. I never saw him in any action. All of those fellows like Israel and Moonie. Also had a fellow called Willie.

IK: Willie Scott?

JH: No, Willie Weekes. He was what you call a real sticklicker. He was something else. An old man called Mr. Green, a short old man name Mr. Green. They used to play under a tamarind tree like Bank holiday days. Fellows would come from St. Thomas, St. John, different locations and play under the tamarind tree.

IK: How did you get involved in sticklicking?

JH: Boy, I saw a fellow name Seibert Rock and he said come and learn to play stick. I couldn't afford to stay in it 'cause I had to walk to work and in those days you had to walk half of Barbados to get to work. You work here this morning and they tell you don't come back tomorrow, go somewhere else... you have to take up your tools. So I wasn't too involve in it, but I would go and see when I got time. If there are going to have Mr. Clarke and Mr. Blackman and them going to play on Saturday nights at a place called Rogers. You paid a penny, 4 cents, 6 cents according to the amount of people that they play.

EG: So where they used to play? You said a place called Rogers?

JH: A place called Rogers in Workmans [St. George]. Them old men! They were full ripe men. One had name Jessamy, short man call Jessamy. Man, regardless of how he come around Jessamy had a...

EG: ....counter to touch him.

JH: And that time rum was cheap. Rum was cheap. The fellas would drink rum and a lady would sell pudding and souse. That was that day. It was a decent day unlike today. A decent day dan today because everybody had respect for each other but not now.

A man called Willie Jude had lived above we, he used to play stick real good. The first body that I saw play stick was Willie, old Willie Jude and the same fellow Willie from over 'pun the hill. You know them is the first two people I saw play stick. I remember a big man name Small used to play with a big stick. At that time there was no violence. The entertainment was a drum and kettle, a wood horse that was just that day. But now there have this and that and still they have no value for it. In those days those things had value and you would see big people, you will hear that a fellow from such a place will play such a place; you will see big people go and sit down or stand up and watch.

EG: None of the fights you watch or see didn't look interesting or sport come out of it?

JH: How you mean! When you go to see the man Clarke! People used to go down in the Turning or out Flat Rock [St. George] to see Clarke and a fellow name Gilbert, a left-hand fellow name Gilbert. See the two of them play you just enjoy it, if you had time to do it. But really and truly I didn't put in any time. That was because my mother was a member at the Christian Mission and she was very strict, you understand. I would get away and if I get out I would go and see this thing and then I start to learn. Start. You would go and play all night until you sleepy and you still have to jump up real early in the morning to go to various places to work.

IK: What kind of work you used to do?

JH: Mason. You work one day here, next morning a different place, and you had to walk. The bus used to be going in the opposite direction to where you going. Barbados got eleven parishes, and I can tell anybody that I work in all eleven. I work at the [Bridgetown] Harbour when they built the place for the containers. I work at Ellerslie School, too.

There had a man name Mr. Fields used to have sticklicking on bank holidays. He had a son that was a police and they used to have sticklicking down in the back. At that time there had certain a little thing that was promotion for Barbados, not like now. Now that Barbados get to a certain standard it has vagabondism, not promotion. Common decency was the pattern of the poorest fellow behavior.

IK: So you had known Elliot Haynes?

JH: He came from Middleton [St. George]?

IK: Some place in St. George.

JH: Yes, Elliot Haynes had come from Middleton. Now that you ask about Elliot Haynes, there had a fellow called Phono, he had come from up by the lion [Gun Hill, St. George]. His real name was Alphonso but we used to call him Phono. Boy, he could play some sticklicking. He used to play on Saturday nights when dey had the little shops. Dey had a little shop in Workmans and all the old men would come out and drink and play drum and thing. Some playing stick and dice gambling.

EG: Dey still have dice gambling?

JH: I hear there still have dice gambling but I don't follow it up. I like my money but I don't like to lose it. I don't mind losing but not my money.

IK: So you never saw any women playing?

JH: Playing stick? Yes, there had a woman name Phyllis Lorde. Her husband learn she to play stick. They had lived by the shop, where the same fellow name Seibert and Two Moon and a fellow name Llewellyn that dead, all of them so dead and gone, but them had sticklicking as their hobby. You know that everybody have a hobby? Sticklicking was their hobby.

IK: You didn't know a woman name Colvin Sargeant? She was from St. Joseph.

JH: No, I wasn't acquainted with her. But dey had a fellow that work at Andrews factory called Daryl, he was the watchman at Andrews. Man, he would stop selling potatoes and play stick.

EG: What you mean stop sell potatoes and play stick?

JH: He was watchman and when people come to buy potatoes and the old fellows would have their sticks, some have umbrellas, some have swords 'cause collins only recent come in. They used to have the long sword and those sort of things on their carts. Man, them fellows start and play and he would stop selling and play stick. Another fellow that have lived above us, Mr. Duke used to live in the corner, and a tall fellow had live on the other side they call Leopard, Cyril, a tall fellow name Cyril.

On Saturday nights we would go up the road to the shop. The shop had belonged to a man called Danner. They had different bread sellers selling. There would be a little square for the fellows to play. And the fellows playing and licking stick, people drinking and eating black pudding and souse. Barbados then had a beauty to it. Although people was not working for any large amount of money and people didn't have this excess of homes, they had common decency. But now they have all this and more, but they don't have any common decency. I'm am talking about 50 to 60 years ago.

Conclusion

Until the advent of World War II and the subsequent expansion of technology (airplanes, radio, television, the telephone and later computers and the internet) to narrow the world, Barbados had the luxury of time to evolve its own cultural expressions. Some of these cultural expressions were very distinctive and were unique to Barbados, even though some of them were similar to other practices in the Caribbean and further afield.

Sticklicking joins the Barbados Landship, marble cricket, cricket firms, road tennis, Tuk Bands, cork sticking, and licking cork in defining the unique nature of the Bajan character. There is also the chattel house, the tenantry, the Landship, the donkey cart, and carts in general that are very definitive of being Bajan.

The influence of the outside world has led to massive changes, in that many of these practices have been abandoned for more international pursuits. But in this fast-changing world and the creation of one global village that gives greater emphasis to American values and practices, it is imperative that we are able redefine ourselves for our own survival.

The cultural context for much of what I have outlined has disappeared, but with imagination we can create new situations in which we can revive these practices for the benefit of future generations. It is not that what we have is archaic, but that we place a higher value on foreign things without recognizing the uniqueness of our own expressions.

Towards this end, Elvis Gill, a lowly sanitation worker who loves the art of sticklicking, established in 1987 an organization to perpetuate the art of sticklicking. He created the DBSS Sticklicking Martial Arts School in Bibby's Lane, St. Michael, Barbados. Bibby's Lane produced many sticklickers who were Master Workmen and who can be considered Stick Gods. Elvis named the school after two of his Master Workman teachers, McDonald "Deaf Donald" Tull and Leonard Oscar Brown, thus the Donald Brown Sticklicking Science (DBSS).

McDonald Tull

In Appendix C, I have included the rules and regulations of the organization.

Interestingly, Elvis has been given the run-around by the Ministry of Culture, the National Cultural Foundation, the Ministry of Sports, and the National Sports Council about getting official recognition and other support. Since 1987, he has been trying to get recognition for the sport of sticklicking. What is so ironic and ridiculous is that they do not recognize the art of sticklicking and its possibilities because of its association in the past with ordinary Bajans like themselves. But of course, someone introduced fencing in 2000 and its association, The Barbados Fencing Federation is now a member of the Olympic Association, and according to the Barbados Advocate of Wednesday, March 16, 2005, "The BFF became the 114th member of the Federation International d'Escrime (FIE), the world governing body of competitive fencing, in Paris, France, on December 4, 2004, at the FIE Annual Congress."

To add insult to injury, the Barbados Olympic Association

recognizes the following martial arts organizations: Amateur Boxing Association of Barbados, Barbados Judo Association, Barbados Karate Federation, Taekwondo Association of Barbados, and such groups as the Barbados Water Ski and Wakeboarding Association, the Barbados Federation of Island Triathletes, Barbados Surfing Association, and Barbados Archery Association. I am not attacking these groups, but broadcasting the contempt for ourselves and what we do to ourselves.

It may be that we are ignorant about who we are and what exists in our heritage that we should be proud of. In the marketing of Barbados as a visitor's paradise, we clearly have failed to determine what constitutes that paradise. What is special about us is our people and their achievements. Sticklicking is one of these achievements, and should have a prominent place in our consciousness.

Appendices

Appendix A

STICKLICKERS

First Name	Last Name	Occupation	District	Parish
DaCosta	Alleyne	Joiner	Sweet Bottom	St George
Jack	Ashby	Jeweller	Oistins	Christ Church
Simmie	Best	Watchman		Christ Church
Simmie	Best		Lodge Road	Christ Church
Snotty Man	Bispham	Watchman		
Eagle	Blackman	Superintendent		St John
Joe	Blackman			
Joseph Battling Sardines	Blades			St Michael
Boysie	Brathwaite		Charles Rowe Bridge	St George
Colvin Mud Soup	Brathwaite	Bus Driver	Lears	St Michael
William	Brathwaite			
Trevor Bay	Browne			
Herbie	Bryan			
Dorcas	Bryan (W)			

First Name	Last Name	Occupation	District	Parish
Colvin Mud Soup	Burnett	Bus driver	Lears	St Michael
Brooksie	Byer		Lodge Road	Christ Church
Brad	Cadogan		Garden	St James
Gifterd	Callender		Searles	Christ Church
Ten Pound	Callender		New Orleans	Bridgetown
Tee	Campbell		Belleplane	St Andrew
Audley Harewood		Carter	Lodge Road	Christ Church
Clyde Cephus	Carter	Cane Lift Operator	Market Hill	St George
Ossie	Carter			
Tee	Chandler			
	Clarke		Proute Village	St Thomas
	Cobham	Orderly (mental)		
Herbert	Deane		Montrose	Christ Church
Tee	Downes			
	Duke		Airy Hill	St George
Linward	Edwards	Superintendent	Walke Spring	St Thomas
Charlie	Elliott		Lodge Road	Christ Church
Sonny	Garner	Superintendent	Blackmans	St Joseph
	Gaskin	Mason	Lodge Road	Christ Church
Elvis	Gill	Mechanic		St Michael
	Gittens			
Harold	Greaves (Drakes)			
	Green			

First Name	Last Name	Occupation	District	Parish
Arnold	Greenidge		Lodge Road	Christ Church
	Greenidge			
Audley	Harewood			
Bomey	Harewood	Watchman	Hothersal Turning	St Michael
Joseph	Harewood		Airy Hill	St George
Elliott Nicky	Haynes		Middleton	St George
Bomey	Hill			
Joe	Hoad	Athlete	Vaucluse	St Thomas
Joseph Youngster	Holder		Braggs Hill	St Joseph
Sam	Ifill			
Sweetie	Jackman	Watchman	Mount Wilton	St Joseph
	Jessamy		Workmans	St George
Aberdeen	Jones	Shop keeper	Gall Hill	Christ Church
Curry	Jones		Speightstown	St Peter
Colin	King			
Edgar	King	Agri-worker		
Jerome	King			St Michael
Ione	Knight (W)	Food	Westbury Road	St Michael
Elwin	Lampitt			St John
Vernon Hopper	Lashley			
Cyril	Leopold			
Phyliss	Lorde (W)			

First Name	Last Name	Occupation	District	Parish
Goldie	Lovell			
Jeff	Lovell	Headmaster	Lodge Road	Christ Church
Leibert	Lynch		Proute Village	St Thomas
Fitzherbert Buhbup	Maloney		Clifton Hill	St Thomas
	Manning			
Rupert	Mapp		Roebuck St	Bridgetown
	Marshall			
Pa	Massiah		Hothersal Turning	St Michael
Walter	Maughan			
Lawrence Task Master	Moore			
George	Newton		Lodge Road	Christ Church
George	Newton		Lodge Road	Christ Church
Inspector	Nicholls	Policeman		St Andrew
Robert	Nurse	Mason	Cox Road	St Phillip
Curds	Parris	Bus Driver	Proute Village	St Thomas
Herbert	Parris	Bus Driver	Proute Village	St Thomas
James	Parris	Third Gang Leader	Clifton Hill	St Thomas
Pin	Parris		Proute Village	St Thomas
Chrissie	Perch			
Sorry Boy	Pilgrim			St Lucy
James	Prescod		Hothersal Turning	St Michael

First Name	Last Name	Occupation	District	Parish
Prince Albert	Prescod		Church Village	St Phillip
Edward	Prescott		Jackson	St Michael
Richard Sardines	Richardson			
Son	Richardson			
Abraham Dynamite	Rock			St Thomas
Seibert	Rock			
Colvin	Sargeant (W)	Hawker	Clifton Hill	St John
Willie	Scott			
Fitz	Simmons		Garden	St James
Beresford	Skeete			
Leon	Small		Wilcox Hill	Christ Church
Leon	Small		Lodge Road	Christ Church
Walter	Small		Lodge Road	Christ Church
	Small			
Berkley	Smith	Watchman	Mount Wilton	St Joseph
Dandy	St Hill	Watchman (Road)	Fitts Village	St James
Harold	Trotman			
Stoway	Trotman			
Stoway	Trotman		George V Parlk	St Phillip
Lightning	Vaughan			St Thomas
Dudley Gullyboar	Walcott	Mason	Gall Hill	Christ Church
Edgar	Walcott			

First Name	Last Name	Occupation	District	Parish
Herbert	Walcott		Gall Hill	Christ Church
Archie	Wall			
Patsy	Ward			
	Ward			
Willie	Weekes			
Boy	Welch			
Knocka	White			
Pauper	White			
Sonny	Wilkinson		Hothersal Turning	St Michael
Edwin	Yarde			
Edwin	Yarde		Bibby's Lane	St Michael
Rupert	Yarde	Mason	Hothersal Turning	St Michael
Jessie	Yearwood			
Ajax				
Albert				St Lucy
Alphonso			Gun Hill	St George
Avery				
Babutts				
Barlow Woodruff			Porey Spring	St Thomas
Big Syrup				
Bobby			Deane Village, Black Rock	St Michael
Butting Sardines				
Chrissey				

First Name	Last Name	Occupation	District	Parish
Cyril				
Cyril				
Danby				
Daryl		Watchman		
Devonnes				
Dixie				
Gifted				Christ Church
Gilbert				
Gilly			Hothersal Turning	St Michael
Israel				
Leopard				
Leopard				
Llewelyn				
Mandeville				
Mice-in-de-tot				
Moonie				
Ninety-eight				
Seibert				
Shamrock				
St Judes Joe			St Judes	St George
St Simon Shadow		Watchman	St Simons	St Andrew
Strong Man				
Tauties		Lighterman		St James

First Name	Last Name	Occupation	District	Parish
Two Moons				
Willie Jude				

Appendix B

They use stick to beat the grave!

Dr. Trevor Hamilton is a consultant whose roots go deep in the countryside of Jamaica. He was interviewed by Elobme on June 23, 2005.

EM: Trevor, just give me some background to this sticklicking thing or stick fighting. First, where were you born?

TH: I was born in St. Elizabeth up in the hills in a little community called Woodlands. I then moved to another little one called New Market. It is still to this day very very rural. Much of the traditions remain in those little pockets.

EM: How many people?

TH: In those communities they were maybe less than 100 households and a household maybe four, so less than 500 people. Small community. They were traditionally farmers, subsistence farmers.

EM: How did stickfighting come to your attention?

TH: First of all, people 'round there use sticks for everything. When I was growing up some people use sticks for yam, they use it for even picking a breadfruit, or picking a mango.

They use it for houses, what you call wattle house. So it is the same type of twisted stick they used for wattle housing, dey use it for roofing. The stick we are talking about is less than a half an inch in diameter. It was a typical stick. We call them stick.

EM: What type of wood?

TH: The wood we used was the most flexible type of wood – wild guava and packy which is like the calabash tree, some of us call it packy. They are very flexible. You can bend them into circles and all sort of shape. We used those sticks for all sorts of things, everything, whether it is cricket, whether it's beating a donkey or a mule, whether it's a horse, even unfortunately children. For fighting and even in the schools, it was part of that institution.

EM: Was there any fighting in the community?

TH: Yeah! Any dispute you have with somebody, the first thing you'll go for is to pull a stick. And there is an art in doing it. People defend themselves and there was an art in how you use the stick. The length of the stick was important and the curing of it. The guys who really did it were professional, but the guys who would do it with a little more finesse were the guys who would actually treat the stick. The guys would tell you that the fresh stick is not as penetrating whether you beat a horse or a man. You would normally cure the stick so you would cut the stick and you would cure it, cure it.

So you can use the sun or hang it up in the smoke in the outdoor kitchen where you have wood-fire smoke going up like how we used to dry the tobacco. So you would normally dry the stick for 14 to 21 days before it is used for whatever it is supposed to be used for. And it's cured. It is a way to bringing out all the moisture.

EM: Did they ever use oil on it?

TH: Yes, they used linseed oil the same way we used to use linseed oil, mostly, to give the stick some flexibility. In fact when I was growing up we use the linseed oil for the stick, for the bat. It was something we used which gives some kick. I don't know how to explain that. But we used on the stick

EM: Were their any obeah practices?

TH: Yeah! People would use obeah. I recall growing up seeing older folks. They would use two types of stick that they use to associate with evil works. One was the packy, the same one I mentioned before, the calabash, and the other one was something they called the cotton stick, because they usually believe that once a cotton tree grows in your place that's where the dead used to be buried.

EM: This is the silk cotton or wild cotton tree?

TH: The wild cotton tree. So they say that... apparently the cotton is symbolic with slavery and so they say the slave master used to hang the slaves on the cotton tree. But they grow into big trees these days. So they usually use the cotton and the packy. They would use that and they cure the packy as they would cure the stick. Again the curing is done in a scientific way. The number of days and nights that it has to be cured for, I understand it cannot be even days for example, it has to be odd days. And they cure it and it had to be a certain size (diameter) and a certain length.

They would then use it to beat the grave and send whatever message they send when they beating the grave.

EM What do you mean beat the grave?

TH Well they use the stick to beat the grave and hope that it would empower the dead to go out and do what they have to do. So they give the dead instructions. But they have to use the stick to empower them. If they don't use the stick, the dead won't listen or won't move. So it was used a lot as a symbol for the obeah.

EM Were there many fights between the men using sticks?

TH Yeah, but it wasn't really scientific. It was natural that they would use the stick to fight but I wasn't impressed with the art of it, how they did it. They would go for the stick and they were a lot of fights and people use to use sticks.

EM This was in St. Elizabeth?

TH Yes. A lot of fights and they would use sticks. But it was not a sport like you go and watch sword fighters and so on. We did not do it as a sort of exhibition. I did not see any people exhibiting the skill of stickfighting. They do it out of a case of sheer survival or aggression. Stickfighting would not be a coastal thing. It was more of an interior activity. It was near cockpit country

Appendix C

The History

Stickfighting is an art of self-defense which was brought to Barbados from Africa. Slaves first took up stickfighting imitating the plantation owners who practiced the art of fencing.

Stickfighting integrated the art of fencing to beat the sword and was then known as sticklicking. Stickfighting became popular as a game among many men folk.

Sticklicking was most prevalent during the post-emancipation period when it was used a self-defense mechanism.

Sticklicking showed a decline during the 1940s in Barbados with the introduction of boxing and firearms. However, the art of Bajan Sticklicking continues to be practiced today as a form of self-defence.

Mission Statement

The Mission of the DBSS Sticklicking Arts School is to preserve the art of Bajan Sticklicking by passing on the skill to interested individuals and at the same time, to build up an interest among Barbadians in keeping this part of our cultural heritage alive.

Doctrine

- Loyalty
- Honesty
- Courage
- Obedience
- Motivation
- Pride
- Dedication
- Adherence
- Commitment
- Self respect/control

Objectives

The objectives of DBSS Sticklicking Martial Arts School are:

1. To organize, encourage and spread stick science as a form of physical education and self-defense;
2. To ensure the preservation of stick science as part of our cultural heritage;
3. To heighten the awareness of stick science among Barbadians from all walks of life; and
4. To share the art.

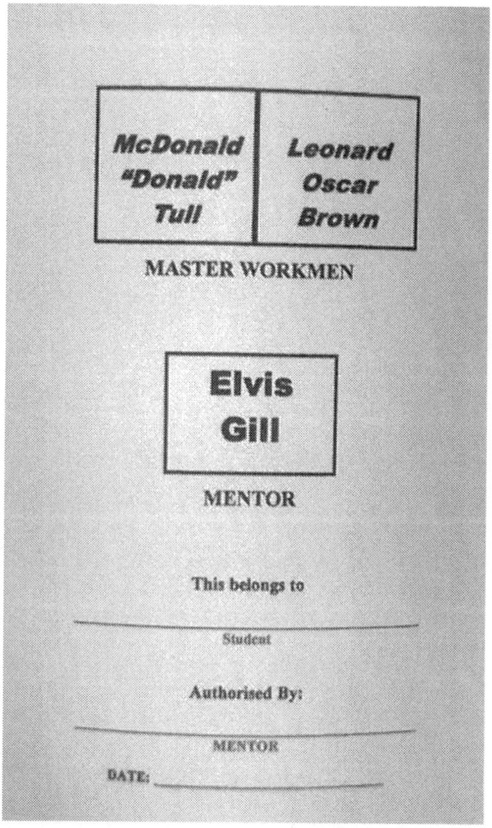

The Badge and Colours

The colours of DBSS Sticklicking Martial Arts School were selected to represent the tenets which the Martial Arts School upholds. Green represents growth and development of our heritage through the art of stick science. Black ________________ Red ______________

Membership

Any individual of good character, irrespective of race or creed, may apply to the Mentor for membership. An application form for membership is available and the rules and regulations are explained to any prospective member. Fees paid for membership are nonrefundable whether in part or as a whole.

Uniform

All students in classes must be dressed in full uniform to be admitted to the class. The casual format is the green T-shirt and black pants, the rank of sash and soft wear. All men must wear protection boxes during training.

Students participating in official exhibition or functions must wear the DBSS polo shirt along with the black pants, black soft wear and protective boxes (for men). The sash of rank must be worn.

Etiquette

The student must bow to the instructor when entering and leaving the training place. A class commences and finishes with a group bowing to the instructor.

An attitude of sportsmanship is emphasized. A student should try to create a friendly and happy atmosphere and train with the spirit of comradeship.

Only official DBSS uniform may be worn in class and should be kept clean and in good condition.

No smoking or use of alcohol or non-prescribed drugs is allowed in class or when wearing the DBSS uniform.

Grading vs. Competition

Grading is not an actual competition or real combat. In competition, each contestant must try to knock out the opponent as quickly and as best as he or she can. In grading, each candidate must try to show good and effective technique without hurting the opponent and very often, the superior candidate has to protect the opponent if he or she is much smaller, weaker, or younger, or his/her technique is not as good.

Grading

Grading is held every 4 months according to the syllabus. Only the chief instructor or the grading panel has the authority and competence to grade students.

For first grading, the student membership should have attended at least 36 hours of training.

A successful candidate will be issued with a certificate, which is valid only if the chief instructor's signature and the official stamp are affixed.

Grading System

Students will be graded in the areas of

- Science and technique
- Response and accuracy
- Flair
- Control
- Speed
- Dominance
- Subduing
- Disarming

The System

Beginners will all wear green and will train to reach the first position. On reaching the first position, beginners will wear green with the distinguishing marks to signify the level reached. Green will also be worn for the second and third positions and various distinguishing marks will also signify the rank.

Black will be worn for the fourth, fifth and sixth positions with distinguishing marks to signify the level reached.

Only persons reaching the seventh position will wear red. The seventh position is the highest level of the Johnson science.

Dismissal and Nullification of Awarded Position

A member will be dismissed if he or she fails to conduct himself or herself in a manner consistent with maintaining the honour and aims DBSS.

The dismissal will result in the nullification of his or her grade.

No abuse of the DBSS uniform will be tolerated. Members found using abusive language or mis-conducting themselves are liable to a fine or in the extreme case, immediate dismissal after investigation.

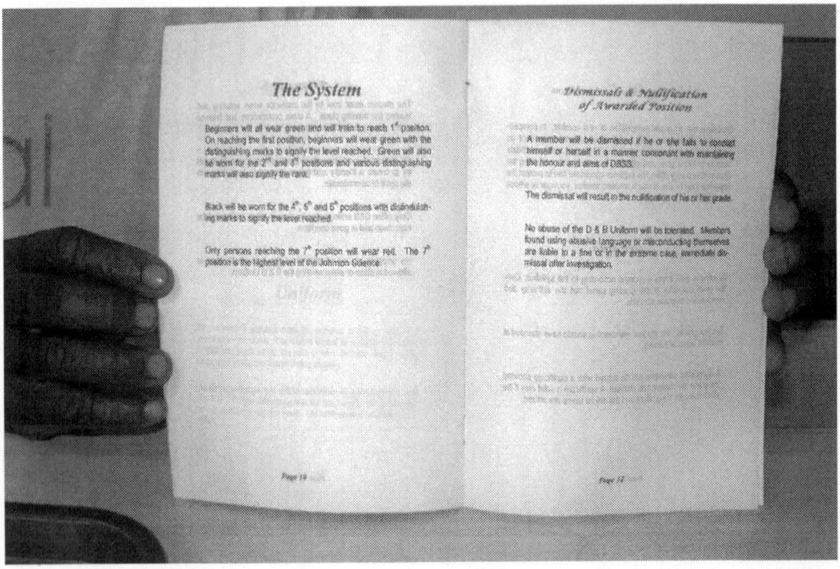

Appendix D

Tom Johnson Rules

PUGILISTIC PROSECUTIONS: PRIZE FIGHTING AND THE COURTS IN NINETEENTH CENTURY BRITAIN (Extract)

Jack Anderson School of Law, University of Limerick, Ireland

The paper aims to demonstrate that the illegality of prize fighting was based initially on charges of unlawful assembly, riot and tumult and not on the question of physical risk. Therein, fundamental and relevant legal issues such as the mutual consent of the parties, assault, manslaughter, even murder were not of immediate concern to the common law courts of the nineteenth century. It wasn't until the end of the century that the courts felt the need to elaborate on the reasons why prize fighting should be declared illegal and dangerous, as opposed to an initial desire to simply keep the lower classes, and their disruptive activities, in their place. Finally, it will be demonstrated that in attempting to reconcile prize fighting with basic principles of criminal law, the courts of the nineteenth century may have sown the seeds for the eventual prohibition of the sport of boxing.

Prize fighting and the Presumption of Corruption

Tom Johnson was the bare-knuckle champion of England from 1784 to 1791. Not since the founders of the sport—Figg and Broughton—

did a fighter so completely capture the sporting public's imagination; for Johnson was a courageous and skilful fighter and was regarded by his contemporaries as having plenty of `bottom' i.e., ability to take punishment.[1] Crowds flocked to see him fight and amongst these masses were royalty, notably the Prince of Wales, later King George IV, who became a key patron of the sport. A "golden age" of prize fighting began and between the reign of Johnson and the implementation of the London Prize Ring Rules in 1838 some of the most celebrated boxers of the bare fisted era fought for the title of English champion.[2]

http://www2.umist.ac.uk/sport/SPORTS%20HISTORY/BSSH/The%20 Sports%20Historian/TSH%2021-2/Art3-Anderson.htm

Appendix E

Queensberry Rules

The first prize fight under Marquess of Queensberry rules took place in Cincinnati, Ohio August 29th 1885. John L. Sullivan defeated his opponent, Dominick McCaffery in the sixth round.

The Marquess of Queensberry Rules:

1. To be a fair stand-up boxing match in a 24-foot ring, or as near that size as practicable.
2. No wrestling or hugging allowed.
3. The rounds to be of three minutes' duration, and one minute's time between rounds.
4. If either man falls through weakness or otherwise, he must get up unassisted, 10 seconds to be allowed him to do so, the other man meanwhile to return to his corner, and when the fallen man is on his legs the round is to be resumed and continued until the three minutes have expired. If one man fails to come to the scratch in the 10 seconds allowed, it shall be in the power of the referee to give his award in favour of the other man.
5. A man hanging on the ropes in a helpless state, with his toes off the ground, shall be considered down.
6. No seconds or any other person to be allowed in the ring

during the rounds.

7. Should the contest be stopped by any unavoidable interference, the referee to name the time and place as soon as possible for finishing the contest; so that the match must be won and lost, unless the backers of both men agree to draw the stakes.
8. The gloves to be fair-sized boxing gloves of the best quality and new.
9. Should a glove burst, or come off, it must be replaced to the referee's satisfaction.
10. A man on one knee is considered down and if struck is entitled to the stakes.
11. No shoes or boots with springs allowed.
12. The contest in all other respects to be governed by revised rules of the London Prize Ring.

http://www.answerbag.com/a_view.php/13242

Appendix F

Queensberry rules

PUGILISTIC PROSECUTIONS: PRIZE FIGHTING AND THE COURTS IN NINETEENTH CENTURY BRITAIN (Extract)
Jack Anderson School of Law, University of Limerick, Ireland

In this, the courts distinguished between the (indoor, regulated, exhibitionist and amateur) sparring match and the (outdoor, unregulated, antagonistic and professional) prizefight, on the grounds that the likelihood of one of the combatants becoming seriously injured was reduced in the former. Sparring matches were taken to be regulated by variations of Broughton's Rules (1743), the London Prize Ring Rules (1838) or the Queensberry Rules (1865), hence less dangerous. Upper and middle class supporters of boxing realised that the greater codification of sparring matches would lead to greater respectability for the sport and ultimately its legitimisation. In fact, it could be argued that the Queensberry rules were specifically framed with the object of making boxing a sufficiently safe spectacle to be accounted legal...

Yet, it can be argued that the changes introduced by the Queensberry rules were superficial only and may even have intensified the physicality of the sport. Under the old rules, if a boxer was tired he could go down on one knee and recover for up to a minute, but now the fighter was required by the rules, and the referee, to fight for a full three minutes. Furthermore, the ten-second knock out rule encouraged vicious, intense attacks, usually centred on the opponent's head...

First, the Queensberry rules, outwardly at least, sanitised the rougher edges of the sport and subjected the sport to greater uniformity, hence popularity. Second, the new regulations permitted the ring to be built indoors on a stage or plinth, thus superseding the long held tradition that it be staked on turf only. For the middle classes, this meant that boxing events could now be held in exclusive gentlemen's clubs and for the urbanised working classes it meant that boxing could be easily facilitated in various local halls. Moreover, for the promoters of these events, an indoor arena meant that they could exert greater control and collection over the admission price, though in turn it would be easier for the local constabulary to patrol. Third and finally, the marketing of boxing, legitimate or otherwise, was an `easy sell' among the working class of Britain. In Britain there had always been a sub-culture of `the fight' and the working classes needed little encouragement to support the officially sanctioned version of the sport. In short, amateur boxing was extremely popular in the second half of the nineteenth century particularly in Britain, as evidenced by the foundation of the Amateur Boxing Association in 1880, which in the following year held its first official amateur championship, from a feeder of local competitions. In fact, the 1890s was a golden period for the sport as a new era of legal clubs flourished in all areas and among all classes of British society.

http://www2.umist.ac.uk/sport/SPORTS%20HISTORY/BSSH/The%20Sports%20Historian/TSH%2021-2/Art3-Anderson.htm

Appendix G

The Agreeable Recreation Of Fighting (Extract)

by Carolyn Conley
Journal of Social History, Fall, 1999 University of Alabama at Birmingham
http://www.findarticles.com/p/articles/mi_m2005/is_1_33/ai_56027317

Studies of the history of violence, especially homicide, have focused on a number of explanations: economic, political, demographic and cultural. An overabundance of young men, a culture of honor and the absence of other means of achieving status have been among the factors demonstrated to influence violence in a society. However, a study of violent crimes in nineteenth century Ireland suggests another factor – that of violence as recreation.

This study is based primarily on the records of 1,932 homicides reported by the Irish police between 1866 to 1892. The government compiled a Return of Outrages which included a brief description of homicides reported by police outside metropolitan Dublin. The figures in this paper are based on these returns, supplemented when possible by newspaper and court records. A fire at the Irish Public Record Office destroyed a large portion of nineteenth century criminal records. However some criminal records survive for seventeen counties. The British Library has extensive holdings of Irish provincial newspapers.

The recreational aspect of Irish violence does not mean that other causes are not involved. However, the Irish evidence includes cases in which other explanations do not suffice. The thesis here is that while violence at times serves as a substitute for something else or as a reaction to negative stimulus, it is also sometimes deliberately chosen as a pastime. Anthropologists have used the term "agonistic" to refer to violence which is "playful, symbolic or ritualistic." While the symbolic and ritualistic elements have often been the subject of scholarly analysis, relatively little work has been done on the playful aspects. More often the recreational aspects of violence are overlooked in the search for deeper meanings. Perhaps the idea that humans find pleasure in violence is simply unpalatable, though, as Gwynn Nettler has pointed out, "It is not at all clear that human beings prefer lives without some violence." In his classic study, Homo Ludens, Johan Huizinga argued that fighting "is the most energetic form of play and at the same time the most palpable and primitive. Young dogs and small boys fight 'for fun;' with rules limiting the degree of violence nevertheless the limits of licit violence do not necessarily stop at the spilling of blood or even killing."

The Irish evidence is particularly colorful and in some ways distinctive, though recreational violence is not unique to nineteenth century Ireland. Much of the violence of late nineteenth century Ireland resembles the patterns Norbert Elias and Eric Dunning characterized as typical of pre-industrial societies. Dunning describes the distinction between instrumental violence which is rational and goal oriented and expressive violence which is emotional and "more closely associated with the arousal of pleasurable feelings." The idea of pleasurable violence may be jarring to modern sensibilities. However in addition to evidence for pre-industrial Europe, similar actions have also been documented in the American West and South, Australia, the Mediterranean and parts of Central and South America.

Further, while the amount of recreational violence has declined in the past century, I would argue that it still exists in milder forms. Recreational violence is distinguished by clearly defined rules, willing participants, a sense of pleasure in the activity and an absence of any malicious intent. Under these conditions, fighting can be seen as the far end of a spectrum of play or sport. Though seldom acknowledged, violence is an integral part of most team sports. As Don Atyeo point outs: "The thing about sports is it legitimizes violence, thereby laundering it acceptably clean. Incidents routinely occur in the name of sport which if they were perpetrated under any other banner short of open warfare would be roundly condemned as crimes... The pain inflicted in sport is somehow not really pain at all; it is Tom and Jerry pain, cartoon agony which doesn't hurt." Anyone who has played pick-up basketball or touch football or has childhood memories of sharing the backseat with a sibling on a long car trip probably has had some first-hand experience of a mild form of recreational violence. Obviously the consequences in these recent examples are far less severe, but the basic concept of physical conflict as a form of pleasant entertainment is the same.

Many scholars have suggested that violence provides a means of attaining status for those who are barred from economic or political achievement. For example, Kenneth Polk has suggested that physical violence is the means of competition for status only among groups where economic or political avenues to dominance are denied...

But while violence was not always motivated by economic or political concerns, it could be a response to other needs. In his study of the American West, Roger McGrath points out that even though men went to the frontier in the pursuit of material gains their fights were over the non-material values of honor, pride and courage...

Scholars have also identified honor cultures, in the American south and along the Mediterranean among other places, in which masculine honor requires a willingness to answer insult or challenge with physical violence. Violence in defense of honor and recreational violence are not synonymous though they may and frequently do coexist. Societies marked by an honor culture have a very high level of violence...

The goal of recreational violence was not to injure or kill, but rather to participate in a mutual display of skill and strength. Consequently, Irish perceptions of criminal liability for physical violence were distinctive...

The clearest examples of recreational violence in Ireland are the faction fights. These huge ritualized brawls have been compared to football and other sports as a form of community entertainment. A formal faction fight, which might involve hundreds of men on each side, usually began with the ritual of wheeling which included chants, stylized gestures and insults...

The rules of Irish brawls were not those of the Marquis of Queensberry. Two and a half percent of homicide victims died from kicks and five from infected bites. Both tactics were apparently standard in brawls, though parity of results was a factor.

Though the openness about the pleasure to be found in violence may have been more prominent in Ireland than elsewhere, the concept of violence as sport (as opposed to violence in sports), is important in understanding interpersonal violence. This is not to discount economic, social and psychological factors, but violence as an outlet for other frustrations or as misdirected rebellion cannot account for all such acts...

Historians of sport frequently study the problem of violence in sport (e.g. soccer hooliganism) but not as sport. However, the Irish evidence indicates that violence can be perceived as a mutually pleasurable form of recreation. Historians would do well to consider the seeming oxymoron of the "good fight" and the very mixed reactions violence as pastime has received.

Appendix H

The Science of Defense Exemplified
In Short and Easy Lessons for the Practice of the Broad Sword and Single Stick

by a Highland Officer
http://www.geocities.com/cinaet/anti-pugilism.html

Whereby Gentlemen may become Proficients in the Use of those Weapons, without the help of a Master, and be enabled to Chastise the Insolence and Temerity so frequently met with, from those fashionable Gentlemen, the Johnsonians, Big Bennians, and Mondozians of the present Day, a Work, perhaps, better calculated to extirpate this reigning and brutal Folly, than a whole Volume of Sermons,

LONDON. Printed for J. Aitkin, NO 14, Castle-street, corner of Bear Street, Leicester Fields 1790. Entered at Stationery Hall.

Preface

The author humbly submits the following work to the public; not only as it may tend towards the refinement of a very troublesome set of gentry, (delineated in the title page,) but also presumes it may in some measure be worthy the attention of the Officers, both of army and navy, equally, or more so than the use of the small sword: the attitudes are graceful, and the exercise as conducive to health; besides, the Broad Sword, or Cut and Thrust, is a necessary appendage to their profession, therefore it would be superflous to dwell on the propriety of their making themselves perfect masters thereof.

To those who are not professional men, it must also be a most useful and desirable accomplishment, as, now a days, scarce any person walks the streets without a stick; and, when attacked by robbers, or fool-hardy Lyceumites, anxious to put in practice their last lesson on the peacable and inoffensive, naturally have recourse to it.

A moment of reflection will imprint on the imagination of the candid reader, the awkward figure they cut, and the danger they run in this situation, provided they are unacquainted with the rudiments of defence. On the other hand, a person skilled in the use of a stick, may defend himself, with ease, from the attack of three or four at a time. It is likewise a very necessary and indespensible qualification for both soldiers and sailors; more particularly the latter. It enables them to board the enemy with a confidence and success, unknown to those ignorant of the science, who rashly rush on the points of weapons, that the least judgement would have enabled them to put aside.

My countrymen, the Highlanders, have, from time immemorial, evinced the utility of the Broad Sword; and, by their skillful management of it in the day of battle, have gained immortal honour. Such has been the effect of their dexterity and knowledge of this weapon, that undisciplined crowds have made a stand against, nay, and have defeated a regular army.

An attentive perusal of the following lessons will qualify the Reader to handle the sword, or stick, in his own defence, and enable him to repel, and secure himself from unprovoked insult

Contents

LESSON 1 - Of Holding the Sword, or Stick

It is requisite, in order to hold a sword well, that the hilt be flat in your hand, observing that it be directly perpendicular with the right knee; and, when you lunge, your thumb stretched at about an inch distance from the shell: when you do not intend to lunge, lay it across the knuckles as in doubling the fist. The pummel close to, and under the wrist. Keep it flexible, and loose in the hand; but when you mean to parry, thrust, or cut, it must be gripped with strength, in order to throw your adversary out of the line, or conduct your blow with force and precision. By continually having the hand fast clenched you will soon tire, as the muscle of the thumb will grow stiff, and subject you to the cramp.

LESSON II - The Inside Guard

Always, when you join your adversary's sword, do it on the inside guard; for which purpose, in the first place, turn your hand that the nails be upward, and the knuckles perpendicular with the ground; your wrist on a level with the flank, the arm a little bent. Secondly, keep your point directly in a line with your adversary's right eye, holding it just fast enough to prevent tottering. Thirdly, narrow your body so that your shoulders, right arm, and sword, form a straight line. Raise the left arm as high as the forehead, forming a half circle; the hand open. Fourthly, bend the left knee so that the body be sustained upon that hip, and rest thereupon. Place the right leg at a foot and a half distance; or, according to your size, that you stand easy. The knee perpendicular with the buckle; the heel in a line, that you may flip it behind the left.

LESSON III - The Outside Guard

This guard does not differ with the inside, respecting the position of the body. The hand is to be reversed; the nails downward, and the arm a little more stretched to guard the outside. The recover is generally on this guard, in which case the elbow is drawn in to the side; the wrist bent; your point a little inclining to the left, forming an angle, through which you must always take especial care to look your adversary full in the face.

LESSON IV - The Medium Guard

Is between the inside and the outside; the thumb nail upward, so that the flat of the swords meet, both being on that guard. It is made use of when you oppose yourself in a posture of defense, before your antagonist, not knowing on what guard he means to join you. If he joins you on the outside, take care to oppose the outside; and vice versa, if he engages on the inside, oppose the inside.

LESSON V - The Hanging Guard

Is formed by raising the hand as high as the head, keeping the wrist firm; the thumb pointing to the ground; the arm bent, so as to form an angle, through which you must always see your adversary. Keep your point sloping so as to cover the left knee. Place the left hand under the sword arm; the palm flat and close to the body, in order to parry your adversary's thrust, should he attempt it on the recover. If he attempts a cut at your arm, or head, you have only to straighten the arm.

LESSON VI - St. George's Guard

Is seldom used but in order to prevent being broke in upon by common cudgel players, or for show. It is performed in the following manner: being on the hanging guard, draw back the right foot obliquely until it be parallel with the left, and about the same distance as when upon the former guards; the body fronting your adversary, sinking well upon both knees; the left hand placed upon the thigh to support the body firm and upright—draw the right elbow a little back, so that you just cover the left shoulder.-Should your antagonist persist in pressing upon you, parry his stroke as from the hanging guard; and, in the action of parrying, pass the left foot behind the right, and swiftly deliver your thrust, direcctions for which will be given in a subsequent lesson

LESSON VII - Of the Salute with the Five Guards

The salute has long been established in the schools as a piece of politeness, and an indication that the parties are friendly, and profess not the least rancour towards each other. It is most essentially necessary for the scholar frequently to practice the salute; it gives him a graceful and easy carriage, and enables him to manage his sword, and change to the different guards with facility, ease, and safety.

The swords being laid across on the ground, the inside of the hilt towards the right hand, place yourself two paces from your sword. Fix your eyes on your adversary's; your hands a kimbo; heels joined, turning out well your toes. Advance the left foot, and then the right, which will bring you near enough to take up the sword; to do which, keep the left knee straight. Sink as you advance, joining the backs of the hands together; separate them slowly, making a figure nearly resembling that of an 8, thus: timing the action so as when you bring down the right hand, you may join in to the sword. When you have taken up the sword, sink well upon both knees, forming the above figure with it; the left hand as when upon guard. Draw back the right foot to the left heel, lowering the left hand to receive the hilt of the sword from the right, which is to rest on the left arm; the point upward; the inside of the hilt inclined to the right. Step forward and salute your adversary by shaking hands, regarding him steadfastly, in recovering: join the right hand to the hilt; draw back the left foot, making the aforelaid figure, and come to the inside guard; then raise the right foot a little, shifting your sword to the outside of your adversary's change to the outside guard. Now let your fooot fall as you join blades; repeat the foregoing figure; change sides, and come to the medium guard. Again, change sides, falling back as before: come to the hanging guard, upon which take great care you always see your adversary well under the arm; then draw back the right foot obliquely, parallel with the left, forming the figure aforementioned, come to St. George's Guard. Lastly, pass the left foot behind the right, and return to the inside guard. In the performance of the foregoing, observe that each attitude and change, must be executed with ease and without precipitation. N.B. Scholars should accustom themselves to make this figure, as it is not only graceful, but absolutely necessary, for every cut that is made forms a part of it: they must also observe, that, the motion of the sword is to proceed from the wrist only.

LESSON VIII - The First Position

Being on the inside guard, your adversary changes to cut on the outside of your left—flip back the right foot to the left heel—

your point parallel with the left shoulder, seeing your adversary through the angle, beneath your sword: bring your left hand to support the sword-arm, in which attitude you are ready to riposte upon him, and are perfectly secure from his attack.

LESSON IX - The Second Position

Is the same as the first, with only this variation: instead of drawing in the arm, extend it, and let fall your point direct in the line, which will then hit the inside of your adversary's. The reason of not making a return from the first position is, supposing your adversary had only made a feint at the leg, and you extend to deliver the return, he parries with the outside guard, and most probably cuts you in the recover.

LESSON X - The Third Position

Is but a small deviation from the two proceeding ones. Your adversary making a cut at the outside of the leg, reserve the wrist; the nails downward, and meet him, your edge will then most probably catch the outside of his arm; drawing in yours, and step back with your left foot; recover, and receive his return on the outside guard

LESSON XI

Your adversary making a cut at the inside the leg, flip the foot as before, and forming a half circle, with your point rather low, meet him on the inside the arm; or, should he attempt the knee, flip the foot, and drop the point as in the second position.

LESSON XII - Engaging and Disengaging

To engage, is to oppose your adversary's sword, either on the inside, outside, or medium guard. If you perceive any opening, (which is frequently the case, by his negligently coming to the guard), through which you may probably hit him, immediately throw in the cut, without waiting his attack. To disengage, is to shift your point from side to side; to do which, with dexterity and neatness, you most hold your sword loosely and with ease, pass the point quickly under your adversary's blade, turning the wrist as you pass his edge, that your hilt may receive it, should he attempt to cut on your passing; but take care that the motion proceeds from the wrist, and that you keep perfectly in the line. When he presses with force against your blade, I would advise you nimbly to disengage, and make the cut on the contrary side, as most probably, your disengaging will throw him out of the line and give you an opening.

LESSON XIII -
The Cut on the Outside of the Leg or Thigh

This cut is dangerous to attempt, you being thereby exposed to your adversary's throwing in the cuts mentioned in the second and third position. It is performed, on your adversary's recover, by reversing the hand, with the nails downward, extend the left knee, and raising the right foot at the same time; lunge about a foot forward, and make the cut; draw in the arm, and recover on the hanging guard, springing back so far that the right foot may fall lin the place of the left. Riposte on the outside guard.

LESSON XIV - The Cut on the Inside of the Leg, or Thigh

The attempting this is likewise attended with the risk of receiving either of the cuts described in the first and fourth position: it is executed by lowering the point, forming a half circle; making the extention and lunge as in the preceeding lesson; deliver the cut, to avoid which, see the fourth position. On recovering, should you not choose to make a return, come to the inside guard; if he reposts, your return is on the outside, and come to that guard. I would never advise the young practitioner to attempt this or the proceeding cut, till he has by use acquired a thorough management of his weapon; and when he perceives his adversary stands wider than common.

LESSON XV - The Cut under the Wrist

Your adversary being on a high inside guard, form a small half circle, turning the wrist on passing his blade, so that your hilt will be upward, and your swords edge to edge. Place your left hand on the swordarm to steady it, and drawing in your arm, bending the wrist, and raising your point, you will most likely hit the under part of his arm, and wrist; his parry will be the outside guard, to which you instantly recover, observing to turn the wrist the moment you have made the cut, or felt his parry.

LESSON XVI - The Cut on the Wrist

Is performed by disengaging under the wrist, as in the foregoing; but, having passed your adversary's blade, you reverse the wrist, the nails downward, and make the cut. In this movement your wrist exactly performs this figure 8 (turned sideways), which I strongly recommend to beginners the frequent practice of, as not only the success of these two cuts entirely depend on its being neatly executed, but all the cuts and disengagements are a part of it; and it will render the wrist pliant and flexible, which is an indispensible requisite in order to become a master of your weapon. Parry and recover the same as the preceding.

LESSON XVII - The Circular Cut

Being on the inside guard, quickly disengage, forming a whole circle; riposte on the inside. To parry which, follow your adversary's sword, and oppose the same guard; if made from the outside, oppose the outside.

LESSON XVIII - The Single Feint

Consists of two motions with the wrist, either from the outside guard to the inside guard, or vice versa, from the inside to the out, without turning the hand. You disengage over the point, making the first offer not more than three of four inches down his blade;—he not perceiving the feint, and supposing the cut will come home, parries your first motion; you quickly disengage, and riposte on that side on which you were on guard. In performing this, make an appel* with the foot on each disengage. Make the extension on your first disengage. Parry as in the preceding.

LESSON XIX - Of the Double Feint

The double feint consists of three motions or disengages. Example: from the inside guard, I disengage to cut on the outside; you parry; I proceed to the inside, and perceiving you again disposed to parry it likewise, I nimbly disengage a third time, and deliver the cut on the outside the arm, and vice versa, from the outside guard; but would not advise its being made from the outside, as it is both difficult, and likewise dangerous to attempt to cut on the inside: observe to make the extension with the left leg, as if you meant to deliver the cut on the first disengage.

LESSON XX - Of Forcing the Blade

If your adversary comes to the parade before you, on the medium guard, and does not appear frm, raise your hand on the outside guard, making the extension of the left leg as you raise the hand; beat his sword out of the line by striking on the feeble of his blade, and cut home in the line. You may parry this cut by dropping your point, and come to the outside guard; by a quick change you may cut under your antagonist's arm, but as you may receive an interchanged thrust, I would not advise you to make the attempt, but rather draw back the body and right hand, so that you gain his feeble, bring him round, forcing him in the line.

LESSON XXI - Of Springing the Blade

Your adversary having come to the parade as before described, raise your hand, and make the extension; seize your adversary's feeble, and bear your stroke home in the line, sliding along his blade you will hit the inside of his arm; recover the outside guard. The parry is the inside guard. These are very good attacks, as they determine, and necessarily oblige your adversary to alter his position which you are narrowly to observe, in order, if possible, to throw in a cut in the change.

LESSON XXII - Of the Advance Cut across the Breast

Your antagonist being on the medium guard, raise your hand, and seizing his feeble, make a lunge, holding your body upright, bearing down his sword; and draw yours across the breast, to oppose which he will drop his point, turning the wrist, the nails downward; break the measure of the body by drawing a little back, and drawing his arm till he gains your feeble, then brings you round and ripostes on the outside. Observe the moment he moves his arm for that purpose, before he gains your feeble: riposte on the outside, and you will most probably hit him, or, flipping back the foot, draw it across the body, and you will cut the inside of the arm.

LESSON XXIII - Of the Disarms Incidental to the Above

Upon attempting the cut above mentioned, if your adversary lunges forward at the same time with you, he means to disarm you in the following manner: having parried the thrust as above described, he quickly seizes the wrist of your sword arm, under his, and pulls you forward with force; the least struggle on your part after he has possession of your wrist; must be fatal, as his sword is at liberty; to prevent which, disarm when you find he has parried, bear your wrist down as low as possible, (bending his sword) so that he cannot get his left hand beneath to seize your wrist; and, should he attempt it over his wrist, bring forward your left foot behind his right; seize the sword arm, and draw it close down to your left thigh; snatch your sword from the hold, and place the point to his breast; he cannot keep his hold on your sword, as on the least resistance, if you bend your knee against his, you may with ease throw him down, should he persue in opposing you.

LESSON XXIV - Observations on the foregoing

Your adversary having attempted the cut, and you have parried it, both weapons being bound, his leg seems to invite your stroke, but beware of trying that experiment, as he will easily slip it, and effect the cut across the body, and will be in readiness to enforce it with a most powerful thrust, so that, on the whole, it is better to endeavor, by breaking the measure, to bring him round, and riposte on the outside.

LESSON XXV - Of seizing the Time, to cut under the Arm, on your Adversary's changing to the Hanging Guard, before he comes into the Line

Both being either of the in, or outside guard, you perceiving your adversary going to change to the hanging guard, change quickly, meeting with your edge, his blade before he comes to the line. Turn the wrist, the nails up, and cut within the arm, gliding along his weapon; to parry which, he will turn his hand at the same instant with you, and most likely cut you under the wrist; which, if he makes good, you will naturally drop it a little, and make an opening above, which he immediately seizes, so that this cut is not the most safe to be practiced when you play with an artist, as you have two to one against you.

LESSON XXVI - Forcing the Blade on the Hanging Guard

Your adversary being on this guard, and you have not joined him, force him out of the line as in the preceding lesson. Turn the wrist, and make the cut as in the foregoing: this being parried as the preceding, you likewise run the risque of the two cuts in return as aforesaid.

LESSON XXVII - Of the Thrust from the Hanging Guard

If your adversary makes the thrust, either put it by with the left hand, which is ready for that purpose, when on that guard, and cut immediately right down the forehead; or parry with your weapon, and bring your left foot forward behind his knee, seizing his wrist, and keep it down to your thigh: place your point to his breast, this is the safest method of disarming, as it exposes the least, and is certain.

LESSON XXVIII - Of the thrust when your Adversary holds a Crooked Wrist

If your adversary holds a crooked wrist, on the inside guard, there will be a small opening, through which you will see his body uncovered; disengage nimbly under the hilt, and lunge with your nails up; if you feel him parry, turn the wrist instantly, and recover: if you make the thrust nimbly, he will hardly parry it; but, if you are not used to thrusting, I would not advise you to attempt it, but make the cut over the wrist, as if he parries, which is only turning the wrist to the outside guard; he will most likely force you out of the line, and cut you in return.

N.B. If you keep the pummet of the sword close to the wrist, there will be no opening for the thrust.

LESSON XXIX - Of lowering your Point, to Invite your Adversary to Cut over the Wrist

Both being on the outside guard, your adversary covers his point, by which his wrist is quite uncovered; you make the cut, he meets your stroke with the true edge, and forcing home in the line, will, most probably, hit you; if not, it will oblige you to alter your position, and bring you to action. Should you continue on the inside, and take no notice of his lowering his point, but lower yours likewise, he will cut you above the wrist, where there will be an opening, or he will lunge forward, and make a thrust over the arm, which you are to parry with the outside guard with force, to drive him out of the line, and return on the outside.

LESSON XXX - Of the Distance, or Measure

Nothing is so material, and at the same time so difficult, as to know with precision, the distance you are to keep from your adversary, as almost on every motion the measure is broken. There are no certain rules, whereby to determine it; frequent practice and attention to the size, and agility of your adversary, will give you an idea of it; it is by not paying proper attention to the measure that most hits are given in an assault, than any other defect in play. For example: if you are within your adversary's reach, upon the extention of the left leg only, he will throw in a thrust, or cut, with such force and velocity, that most probably will be out of your power to parry. If upon your lunge you can reach the leg, you will be sufficiently near, at which distance, with the extension of the left leg only, you will reach the forepart of your adversary's arm; and, as you riposte on his recover, a swift motion will reach him before he regains his position.

LESSON XXXI - The Spadroon Guard

You generally have recourse to this guard when you are pressed hard, and have little room to act in: it is performed with the greatest safety from the inside guard; lower your point, and form a half circle, you bring your edge, or hilt, directly under your adversary's blade, where you stop. Sink well upon both knees and bring the left hand to steady the sword arm, which is to be a little bent, the body perfectly upright: in this position, you are secure from either cut or thrust of your adversary. Should he attempt the outside, flip the foot, and turning the wrist, you receive his arm on that edge of your sword, as mentioned in the third position; if on the inside, flip back, and form the half circle, you meet him as in the fourth. If he attempts the head, raise the hilt as high as your face, in a line with your eyes, the other hand covering the left side of your forehead, in order to put by his sword after he has delivered his blow, and instantly make the extension and lunge. Being come to this guard, you must be particularly careful not to suffer your adversary to beat upon the feeble of your sword, which will most probably force it out of your hand, therefore narrowly watch his motions, and you will easily perceive if he is acquainted with the disarm, or the guard; should he make the attempt, nimbly elude him, and cut outside the arm. If he comes to the spadroon guard, you must, by a quick and rapid beat, endeavor to disarm him, if not, it will oblige you to alter your position, and bring you to action. Should you continue on the inside, and take no notice of his lowerng his point, but lower yours likewise, he will cut you above the wrist where there will be an opening; or, he will lunge forward and make a thrust over the arm, which you are to parry with the outside guard, with force, to drive him out of the line, and return on the outside.

LESSON XXXII - Of the Distance or Measure

Nothing is so material, and at the same time so difficult, as to know with precision, the distance you are to keep from your adversary, as almost on every motion the measure is broken. There are no certain rules, whereby to determine it; frequent practice and attention to the size, and agility of your adversary, will give you an idea of it; it is by not paying proper attention to the measure that most hits are given in an assault, than any other defect in play. For example: if you are within your adversary's reach, upon the extention of the left leg only, he will throw in a thrust, or cut, with such force and velocity that most probably will be out of your power to parry. If upon your lunge you can reach the leg, you will be sufficiently near, at which distance, with the extension of the left leg only, you will reach the forepart of your adversary's arm; and, as you riposte on his recover, a quick return will reach him before he is firmly planted in the position; if you are too late, do not attempt it, but rather wait his attack. This is a most excellent guard, and well calculated for chance encounters in the street, as there is no show or preparation in it, and our adversary probably supposing you are totally unacquainted with the stick, will heedlessly attack you, when in all human probability you will settle the difference with the point of your stick, without any trouble, or receiving a single blow.

The Scholar, having attentively gone through the preceding lessons, will now be able to play loose, which is a representation of a single combat, when he must perform all the cuts, thrusts, and parries before described, endeavouring to deceive and discompose his adversary, by appels, false attacks, beatings, disengagements, and extensions; that by his parrying a judgement may be formed in what manner to attack, with a probability of success. When two gentlemen are going to play loose, or in the terms of the fencing schools, to make an assault, they must (having made the salute) take care to preserve a proper distance, and to oppose each others cuts or thrusts, lest they touch each other at the same time. At the beginning of an assault, you must observe whether your adversary means to commence the attack, which you will quickly see by his gripping his sword; force a little upon his blade, and invite him to cut on the outside, by giving him an opening, which, if he does, parry, and make a quick return over his wrist; if he attempts the single feint, parry, forming a circle with the inside guard, keeping your body somewhat backward, and throw in a strait return.

Never lean over to your adversary, but keep upright and firm: let not your eyes be fixed on any one part more than another, which will mask your intentions in what you are going to perform, and baffle his parrades. Look boldly, and with confidence in his face, and reflect on the probable consequence on every motion before you make it. Appear undetermined in your mind, and aim in all your attacks, that he may be at a loss what you are about to do. Make your attack cooly and with prudence, and when your blow has succeeded, recover quickly, lowering your point, but so that you may act defensively. Should you be more skillful than your antagonist, never attack him; to be sure you may not hit him so often, but then he will not have the satisfaction of touching you.

There are many good players that are hit by very bad ones, but it is their own fault; they probably may give fix hits to one, but, however, they seldom or never come off untouched, which proceeds from their impatience and imprudence: in making frequent attacks they are hit by chance rather than by the skill of their adversary, therefore always keep on the defensive, taking care to parry well, and then you will be almost certain of throwing in a hit on the return, unless you perceive a palpable opening. When you engage, be careful of not remaining on the medium guard; if it is on the inside, turn your wrist well up, if on the outside, reverse the wrist, and secure well the outside, so that you have but one side to defend. When you advance to give your measure, never disengage, but make sure of your antagonist's blade, for should you quit if you expose yourself, to be forced from the line, and consequently to his return. In parrying, keep the sword fast in your hand, on the contrary when you propose a feint; your arm must be flexible, and the sword easy, so that you may perform your intentions with more celerity, disregarding the disengages and false attacks of your opponent, but follow him cooly, and you will soon find an opportunity of throwing in a cut, or lunge, with effect. When you come to the guard, and have a mind to attack in your turn, change quickly from the in to the outside guard, and observe narrowly by the motion of his wrist, what parry he puts in practice, and then determine on your stroke. If you perceive him languid in his motions, force his blade, and make the cut across the breast, or strait home in the line. Should you perceive any irrefolution on the part of your adversary, in making his attack, force him out of the line, and attack him with vivacity; if you perceive him changing to the hanging guard, change with him, and cut under the arm, taking care not to lay too much stress on the cut, lest he parry it, and make good the two cuts described in lesson xxvi, but a thorough attention to the foregoing, will, with practice, enable a person to sustain an assault in all the various changes that occur in loose playing, and which to expatiate further upon, would be tiresome to the learner, and would unnecessarily swell these few pages to a volume, as they are all described, with little variation, in the preceeding sheets.

Appendix I

Journal of Manly Arts: Nov 2001

SINGLE-STICK

by C. Phillipps-Wolley

(Originally published as chapter IV of "Broadsword and Single-stick, with Chapters on Quarter-Staff, Bayonet, Cudgel, Shillalah, Walking-Stick, and Other Weapons of Self-Defence", by R.G. Allanson-Winn and C. Phillipps-Wolley; George Bell and Sons, York Street, Covent Garden and New York, 1898)

SINGLE-STICK is to the sabre what the foil is to the rapier, and while foil-play is the science of using the point only, sabre-play is the science of using a weapon, which has both point and edge, to the best advantage. In almost every treatise on fencing my subject has been treated with scant ceremony. "Fencing" is assumed to mean the use of the point only, or perhaps it would not be too much to say, the use of the foils; whereas fencing means simply (in English) the art of of-fending another and de-fending yourself with any weapons, but perhaps especially with all manner of swords.

In France or Spain, from which countries the use of the thrusting-sword was introduced into England, it would be natural enough to consider fencing as the science of using the point of the sword only, but here the thrusting-sword is a comparatively modern importation, and is still only a naturalised foreigner, whereas broad-sword and sabre are older than, and were once as popular as, boxing. On the other hand, the rapier was in old days a foreigner of particularly shady reputation on these shores, the introducer being always alluded to in the current literature of that day, with anathemas, as "that desperate traitour, Rowland Yorke."

"L'Escrime" is, no doubt, the national sword-play of France, and, for Frenchmen, fencing may mean the use of the foil, but broad-sword and sabre play are indigenous here, and if fencing is to mean only one kind of sword-pay or sword-exercise, it should mean single-stick.

Like the swordsmen of India, our gallant fore-fathers (according to Fuller, in his "Worthies of England") accounted it unmanly to strike below the knee or with the point. But necessity has no laws, still less has it any sense of honour, so that before long English swordsmen realised that the point was much more deadly than the edge, and that, unless they were prepared to be "spitted like cats or rabbits," it was necessary for them either to give up fighting or condescend to learn the new fashion of fence.

As in boxing, it was found that the straight hit from the shoulder came in quicker than the round-arm blow, so in fencing it was found that the thrust got home sooner than the cut, and hence it came that the more deadly style of fighting with the rapier supplanted the old broad-sword play.

Single-stick really combines both styles of fencing. In it the player is taught to use the point whenever he can do so most effectively; but he is also reminded that his sword has an edge, which may on occasion do him good service. It seems then, to me, that the single-stick is the most thoroughly practical form of fencing for use in those "tight places" where men care nothing for rules, but only want to make the most out of that weapon which the chance of the moment has put into their hands. It may further be said that the sabre is still supplied to our soldiers, though rarely used for anything more dangerous than a military salute, whereas no one except a French journalist has ever seen, what I may be allowed to call, a foil for active service, the science of single-stick has some claim to practical utility even in the nineteenth century, the only sound objection to single-stick being that the sticks used are so light as to not properly represent the sabre.

This is a grave objection to the game, when the game is regarded as representing the real business; but for all that, the lessons learnt with the stick are invaluable to the swordsman. The true way to meet the difficulty would be to supplement stick-play by a course with broad-swords, such as are in use in different London gymnasiums, with blunt edges and rounded points.

But gunpowder has taken the place of "cold steel," and arms of precision at a thousand yards have ousted the "white arm" of the chivalrous ages, so that it is really only of single-stick as a sport that men think, if they think of it at all, today. As a sport it is second to none of those which can be indulged in the gymnasium, unless it be boxing; and even boxing has its disadvantages. What the ordinary Englishman wants is a game with which he may fill up the hours during which he cannot play cricket and need not work; a game in which he may exercise those muscles with which good mother Nature meant him to earn his living, but which custom has condemned to rust, while his brain wears out; a game in which he may hurt some one else, is extremely likely to be hurt himself, and is certain to earn an appetite for dinner. If any one tells me that my views of amusement are barbaric or brutal, that no reasonable man ever wants to hurt any one else or to risk his own precious carcass, I accept the charge of brutality, merely remarking that it was the national love of hard knocks which made this little island famous, and I for one do not wish to be thought any better than the old folk of England's fighting days.

There is just enough pain in the use of the sticks to make self-control during the use of them a necessity; just enough danger to a sensitive hide to make the game thoroughly English, for no game which puts a strain upon the player's strength and agility only, and none on his nerve, endurance, and temper, should take rank with the best of our national pastimes.

Gallant Lindsey Gordon knew the people he was writing for when he wrote:-

"No game was ever worth a rap,
For a rational man to play,
Into which no accident, no mishap,
Could possibly find its way."

Still, there comes a time, alas! In the lives of all of us, when, though the hand is still ready to smite, the over-worked brain resents the infliction of too many "merry cross-counters," and we cannot afford to go about with black eyes, except as the occasional indulgence. Then it is that the single-stick comes in. Boxing is the game of youth, and fencing with foils, we have been assured, improves as men fall into the sere and yellow leaf. Single-stick, then, may be looked upon as a gentle exercise, suitable for early middle age.

There is just enough sting in the ash-plant's kiss, when it catches you on the softer parts of your thigh, your funny bone, or your wrist, to keep you wide awake and remind you of the good old rule of "grin and bear it;" but the ash-plant leaves no marks which are likely to offend the eye of squeamish clients or female relations.

Another advantage which single-stick possesses is that you may learn to play fairly well even if you take it up as late in life as five and twenty; whereas I understand that, though many of my friends were introduced to the foil almost as soon as to the corrective birch, and though their heads are now growing grey, they consider themselves mere tyros in their art.

That single-stick is a national game of very considerable antiquity, and at one time in great repute on our country greens, no one is likely to deny, nor have I time to argue with them even if I would in this little brochure. Those who are interested in spadroon, back-sword, and broad-sword will find the subjects very exhaustively treated in such admirable works as Mr. Egerton Castle's "Schools and Masters of Fence." (EN5) These pages are merely intended for the tyro – they are at best a compilation of those notes written during the last ten years in black and white upon my epidermis by the ash-plants of Serjeants Waite and Ottaway, and Corporal-Major Blackburn. Two of them, unfortunately, will never handle a stick again, but the last-named is still left, and to him, especially, I am indebted for anything which may prove worth remembering in these pages. A book may teach you the rudiments of any game, but it is only face to face with a better player than yourself that you will ever make any real advance in any of the sciences of self-defence.

And here, then, is my first hint, taught by years of experience: If you want to learn to play quickly, if you want to get the most out of your lessons, whether in boxing or stick-play, never encourage your teacher to spare you too much. If you get a stinging cross-counter early in your career as a boxer, which lays you out senseless for thirty seconds, you will find that future antagonists have the greatest possible difficulty in getting home on that spot again. It is the same in single-stick. If you are not spared too much, and are not too securely padded, you will, once the ash-plant has curled once or twice round your thighs, acquire a guard so instinctively accurate, so marvellously quick, that you will yourself be delighted at your cheaply-bought dexterity. The old English players used no pads and no masks, but, instead, took off their coats, and put up their elbows to shield one side of their heads.

There are today in England several distinct schools of single-stick, the English Navy having, I believe, a school of its own; but all these different schools are separated from one another merely by sets of rules, directing, for the most part, where you may and where you may not hit your adversary.

The best school appears to be that in which all hits are allowed, such as might be given by a rough in a street row, or by a Soudanese running a-muck. The old trial for teachers of fencing was not a bad test of real excellence in the mastery of their weapons – a fight with three skilled masters of fence (one at a time, of course), then three bouts with valiant unskilled men, then three bouts against three half-drunken men. A man who could pass this test was a man whose sword could be relied upon to keep his head, and that is what is wanted. All rules, then, which provide artificial protection, as it were – protection other than that afforded by the swordsman's guard – to any part of the body are wrong, and should be avoided.

Let me illustrate my position. I remember well, at Waite's rooms, in Brewer Street, seeing a big Belgian engaged with a gentleman who at that time occupied the honourable position of chopping-block to the rooms. The Belgian had come over to take part in some competition, and was an incomparably better player than the Englishman, but then the Belgian wished to play according to the rules of his own school. It was arranged at last that each should do his worst in his own way, and it was hoped that Providence would take care of the better man.

Unfortunately the worse man of the two had been very much in the habit of taking care of himself when subjected to the attacks of such punishing players as Ottaway and Mr. Jack Angle.

The Belgian's legs had been protected by a rule of fence, which made it illegal to hit below the waist, or some such point, and now naturally they fell an easy prey to the Englishman's ash-plant. The result was, of course, that in a very short time the Belgian's thigh was so wealed that at every feint in that direction he was ready to be drawn, and to uncover head or arm or any well-padded spot, not already sore, to the other man's attack.

Let me touch lightly on one or two little points before plunging in in medias res. In spite of what I have said about hard hitting, please remember that I have recommended my pupil only to suffer it gladly for his own sake. It will improve his temper and his play. On the other hand, hard, indiscriminate hitting is to be discountenanced for many reasons, and principally because, as a rule, a hard hit means a slow one. Always remember that the time taken to draw your hand back for a blow is time given to the enemy to get his point in, and that a blow delivered from wrist and arm (bent only as much as it should be when you "engage") would suffice to disable your adversary if the sticks were what they pretend to be, "sharp swords." Again, in ordinary loose play, remember that you are playing, or are supposed to be playing, with the weapons of gentlemen, and should show the fine old-fashioned courtesy to one another which is due to a foeman worthy of your steel. If there is a question as to a hit, acknowledge it as against yourself, as in the cut below, by springing up to attention and bringing the hilt up to the level of the mouth, blade upright, and knuckles turned to your front.

Again, should you get an awkward cut, do all you can not to return savagely. If you make any difference at all, play more lightly for the next five minutes, otherwise you may drift into a clumsy slogging match, ending in bad blood. Finally, if you do get hold of a vicious opponent, do not, whatever you do, show that you mind his blows. If he sees that a cut at a particular place makes you flinch, he will keep on feinting at it until he hits you wherever he pleases; but if, on the contrary, you take no notice of punishment, you are apt to dishearten the adversary, who feels that your blows hurt him, and is uncertain whether his tell upon you in like manner. I may as well say here that throughout this paper, I have, as far as possible, used English words to explain my meaning, abstaining from the French terms of the fencing school, as being likely to confuse a beginner, who may not want to learn French as an introduction to fencing.

OUTFIT

The accessories necessary for single-stick are much more numerous now than in the old days on the village green. Then two stout ash-plants and the old North Country prayer (beautifully terse) "God, spare our eyes!" were considered all that was necessary. Now a complete equipment costs rather more than a five-pound note.

First, then, there is the helmet, constructed more solidly than that used for foil-play, although the wire mesh of which it is made is generally a good deal wider than the mesh of a fencing mask. The best helmet is made out of stout wire, with a top of buffalo hide, completely covering the head, with padded ear-pieces to take off the effect of a slashing cut. These are better than those made of cane, which are apt to give way before a stout thrust and let in the enemy's point to the detriment of eyes and complexion. Be careful, in choosing your helmet, to see that it fits you exactly, for a nodding helm may, in a close thing, so interfere with your sight as to give your adversary a very considerable advantage. The jacket generally used for this play is made like a pea-jacket, with two sleeves, and should be of stout leather. If this is loose fitting, it will afford ample protection, and is not so hot as the padded coat sometimes seen. Besides being too hot, the handsome white-kid padded jackets soon get holes made in them by the ash-plant, whereas the brown leather is seldom torn.

In addition to the jacket, an apron of leather, extending from the waist almost to the knee, should be worn, covering both thighs, and saving the wearer from dangerously low hits.

Some men wear a cricket pad on the right leg. This, I think, makes a man slow on his feet, and is besides un-necessary. The calf of any one in condition should be able to despise ash-plants; and, as I said before, a bare leg makes you wonderfully quick with your low guard.

Stick play is a fine test of a man's condition. At first every hit leaves an ugly mark, but as soon as the player gets really "fit," it takes a very heavy blow indeed to bruise him. The sticks themselves should be ash-plants, about forty inches in length and as thick as a man's thumb, without knots and unpeeled.

If you want them to last any time it is as well to keep a trough of water in your gymnasium, and leave your ash-plants to soak in it until they are wanted. If you omit to do this, two eager players, in half an hour's loose play, will destroy half a dozen sticks, which adds considerably to the cost of the amusement.

The old English sword hilt was a mere cross-piece; but in play it has always been customary to protect the fingers with a basket. This may be either if wicker or buffalo-hide. The latter is infinitely the best, as wearing much longer, affording a better protection to the fingers, and not scraping the skin off the knuckles as the wicker baskets too often do. The basket has a hole on either side; one close to the rim, and the other about a couple of inches from the edge. In putting your basket on, put your stick through the former first, as otherwise you will not be able to get a grip of your stick or any room for the play of your wrist.

There is only one other thing necessary, and then you may consider yourself as safe as a schoolboy with the seat of his trousers full of dormitory towels: and that is either a stout elastic ring round your wrist—a ring as thick as your thumb—or a good long gauntlet. I rather recommend the ring as interfering less with the freedom of your hand, and as protecting more effectually that weak spot in your wrist where the big veins are. If a blow catches you squarely across this spot, when it is unprotected, you may expect your right hand to lose its cunning for a good many minutes. By the way, it is as well to see that the collar of your jacket is sufficiently high and well-supplied with buttons, otherwise there is apt to be a dangerous gap between the shoulder and the bottom of the helmet.

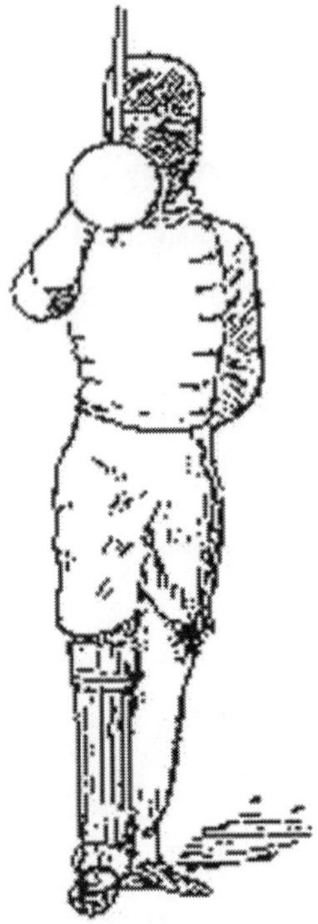

Figure 1. The Outfit, also the position of acknowledgement

One last word: if you see that the point of your stick is broken, don't go on playing; stop at once. A split ash-plant is as dangerous as a buttonless foil, and just as likely to go through the meshes of a mask, and blind where you only meant to score. As the chief fault of single-stick as training for the use of the sabre is that the stick does not properly represent the weight of the weapon which it simulates, it is not a bad thing to accustom yourself to using the heaviest sticks in the gymnasium. This will strengthen your wrist, and when in a competition you get hold of a light ash-plant, you will be all the quicker for your practice with the heavier stick.

Figure 1 by Mr. Graham Simpson represents the way to acknowledge a hit, and this cut by the same artist (Fig. 2) illustrates, as far as we know it, the less careful method of our forefathers.

The use of the elbow to shield the head, though common in contests on the village greens, was in its way no doubt more foolish than our pads; for though a sturdy yokel might take a severe blow from a cudgel on his bare arm, without wincing, the toughest arm in England would have no chance against a sabre.

Figure 2. A guard-stance from an earlier form of single-stick fighting

POSITION

Having now secured the necessary implements, let us begin to learn how to use them. First, as to the stick, which, you will remember, represents for the present a sabre, and consequently a weapon of which one edge only is sharpened. In order that every blow dealt with the stick should be dealt with what represents the sharp or "true" edge of the sword, it is only necessary to see that you get a proper grip of your weapon in the first instance. To do this shut your fingers round the hilt, and straighten your thumb along the back of the hilt, thus bringing your middle knuckles (or second joints of your fingers) and the true edge into the same line. If you keep this grip you may be assured that every blow you deal will be with the edge.

And now as to position – the first position from which every attack, feint, or guard, begins. Ned Donnelly, the great boxer, used

Figure 3. The engaging (hanging) guard

to tell his pupils that if a man knew how to use his feet, his hands would take care of themselves.

And what is undoubtedly true in boxing is equally true in fencing. "Look that your foundations are sure" should be every fighting man's motto. Take trouble, then, about the position of the feet from the first. To come on to the engaging guard, as shown in Fig. 3, stand upright, your heels together, your feet at right angles to one another, your right foot pointing to your front, your left foot to your left, your stick in your right hand, loosely grasped and sloped over your right shoulder, your right elbow against your side, and your right hand about on a level with it, your left hand behind your back, out of harm's way.

It is not a bad plan to put the fingers of the left hand through the belt at the back of the waist. If this is done, it counteracts, to a certain extent, that tendency to bring the left hand in front, which a good many beginners display, and for which they get punished by many an unpleasant rap on the knuckles.

Now take a short pace to the front with the right foot, and, in the words of the instructor, "sit down," i.e. bend both legs at the knee, so that the calves are almost at right angles to the thighs. This position will be found a severe strain upon the muscles at first, but they will soon get used to it. The object of the position is twofold. First, the muscles are thus coiled, as it were, ready for a spring at the shortest notice; and in the second place, the surface which your stick has to guard is thus considerably reduced. Be careful to keep the right heel in a line with the left heel, a space equal to about twice the length of your own foot intervening between them, and see that your right toe points squarely to the front and your left toe to the left. If your right toe is turned in, you will never advance straight to the front; and if your left toe is turned in, you contact the base upon which your body rests, and very soon will begin to roll and lose your balance altogether. As far as the legs and feet are concerned you are now in your proper position, which you will only leave when you lunge, or when you straighten yourself to acknowledge a hit, and to which you will invariably return as soon as you engage.

If you wish to advance, advance the right foot a short pace, bringing the left after it at once, so that the two resume their relative positions to one another, half a pace nearer your enemy. If you wish to retire, reverse this movement, retiring with the left foot and following it with the right. In both cases keep your eyes to the front, your feet at right angles, and your knees bent.

Now as to the stick. There are two forms of guard in common use among players, the hanging and the upright guard, of which both illustrations will be found in these pages. In Rowland Yorke's time men sought for what I think they called "the universal parry" almost as they did for the alchemist's stone which should turn all things to gold. Of course such a thing has never been found, but either of these guards, if truly taken and kept, will stop the attacks of most men so long as you keep them at their proper distance.

In passing, let me say that if a man will try to overwhelm you with rushes, the best thing you can do is to straighten your stick, thrust, and don't let the stick run through the basket. This has a wonderfully soothing effect upon an excitable player.

In Fig. 4 the upright guard (or high tierce) is shown, in which the right elbow should be close in to the side, the forearm at right angles to the body, wrist bent, so as to turn the knuckles outwards, and the stick pointed upwards, at an angle of about 45 degrees. In Fig. 3, the hanging guard, the point of the stick should be inclined slightly downwards, the knuckles turned upwards, the forearm should be slightly bent, the hilt a little outside the right knee, the point of the stick a little low and in the direction of the left front.

If the point of the stick be kept up, the adversary finds a way in by cutting upwards under the point; if the hilt is not outside the right knee, the back of the sword arm will be unprotected; and if the sword-arm itself is not kept slightly bent, no effective blow can be delivered by it without first drawing back the hand.

This, of course, is a fatal fault. The moment your adversary sees your hand go back, he will come out. As you retire for the spring, he will spring. Time is the very essence of single-stick, and the chief object of every player should be to make his attack in the fewest possible motions. For this reason a slightly bent arm is necessary when on guard. Of course if the arm is unduly bent the elbow will be exposed, but a little practice will soon enable any moderately

Figure 4. Upright guard, or high tierce

supple man to so hold his arm as to be ready to cut direct from his guard and yet keep his elbow out of peril. And this brings me to a question often discussed amongst players, viz. which is the better guard, the upright or the hanging guard, for general purposes.

Although I have been taught to use the hanging guard myself ever since I began to play, I unhesitatingly say that the upright guard is the better one, as enabling a player to save time in the attack. In the hanging guard the knuckles (i.e. the edge) are up and away from the enemy; the wrist must be turned before the edge can be brought into contact with his body, and this takes time, however little. In the upright guard the knuckles (i.e. the edge) are towards your opponent, the arm is ready flexed, everything is in readiness for the blow. If, then, as I believe, the advantages of the two guards, as guards, are equal, the advantage of the upright guard as a position of attack seems to me undeniable.

In all guards remember that it is not sufficient to oppose some part of your weapon to your adversary's. You must meet him, if possible, with what the old masters called the "forte" of your blade, that is, the part from the hilt to the middle of the sword, with which you have naturally more power of resistance than with the lower half of the blade. Of course all guards must be made with the edge of the sword outwards, and make sure that you really feel your enemy's blade (i.e. make a good clean guard) before attempting to return his attack.

There is another matter to which many teachers pay too little attention, but which is as important as any point in the fencer's art. It is obvious that the player should try, if possible, to hit without being hit. To do this effectively it is necessary to maintain in attacking what fencers call a good "opposition", that is to say, to so carry your stick in cutting or thrusting at him as to protect yourself in the line in which you are attacking.

This is easier to explain in practice than on paper, but it may perhaps be sufficiently explained by examples. If, for instance, you are cutting at the left side of your opponent's head, you must, to stop a possible counter from him, keep your hilt almost as high as the top of your own head and carry your hand well across to your own left. If you do this correctly you will, in case he should cut at your left cheek as you cut at his, stop his cut with the upper part of your stick.

Again, in thrusting at him, if you keep your hand as high as your shoulder, and in a line with your right shoulder, you will protect the upper half of your own body from a counter, so that, even if your thrust fails and does not get home, the upper part of your blade will stop his cut.

It is necessary to study so to attack your opponent that, in the very act of delivering a cut of thrust, you may stop him in as many lines or directions of attack as possible.

If you find your man will counter in spite of all that you can do, take advantage of this habit of his by feinting a cut to draw his counter, stop this, and return.

This will have the effect of making him do all the leading, which will be all in your favour.

HITS, GUARDS, FEINTS, ETC.

For the purposes of instruction and description, the principal hits in single-stick have been numbered and described according to the parts of the body at which they are aimed.

There are four principal hits: (1) a cut at your opponent's left cheek; (2) a cut at his right cheek; (3) a cut at his left ribs; (4) a cut at his right ribs. Cuts 5 and 6 are mere repetitions of 3 and 4 at a lower level, being aimed at the inside and outside of the right leg instead of at the ribs.

In the accompanying figures numbered 5, 6, 7 and 8 the four principal attacks and the stops for them have been illustrated, and with their help and a long looking-glass in front of him the young player ought to be able to put himself into a fairly good position.

In addition to the cuts there is the point, which, as our forefathers discovered, is far more deadly than the edge. Of this more later on.

Almost every cut is executed upon the lunge. As you and your adversary engage, you are practically outside each other's range unless you lunge.

Standing in the first position the heels are two feet apart. On the lunge, I have seen Corporal-Major Blackburn, a man, it is true, over six feet in height, measure, from his left heel to a point on the floor level with his sword point, a distance of nearly ten feet. This gives some idea of what is expected from a man who can lunge properly. To do this, throw out the right foot as far as it will go to the front, keeping the heels still in line and the right foot straight.

Keep the outside edge of the left foot firmly down upon the floor, and keep it still at right angles to the right foot. If your left foot begins to leave the ground you have over-reached yourself; you will find it impossible to get back, and you will be at you opponent's mercy. See that your right knee is exactly over your right ankle, your left leg straight, your chest square to the front, and your head well up. If you can get yourself into this position, you will have no difficulty in recovering yourself if your lunge fails, and you will gain nothing by bending your body forward from the waist. On the contrary, you will spoil your balance.

This lunge will do for every cut and every point.

To recover after a lunge, throw your weight well back upon your left leg, and use the muscles of the right thigh and calf to shoot yourself back into position. If the knee of the right leg has been kept exactly over the ankle, the impetus necessary to regain your original position will be easily obtained. If, however, the right foot has been protruded too far, and the caution as to the knee and ankle disregarded, you will find yourself unable to return quickly from the lunging position, and will consequently be at your opponent's mercy. It is in the operation of returning from the lunge that the player realises to the full the advantage of keeping the shoulders well back and the head erect.

The illustrations should speak for themselves, but perhaps I had better explain them.

(To perform cut 1 as shown in Fig. 5,) lunge out and cut at the left cheek of your opponent, straightening the arm and turning the knuckles down.

To stop this cut, raise the engaging guard (hanging guard, Fig. 4) slightly, and bring the hand somewhat nearer the head, as shown in the illustration, or stop it with the upright guard, with the elbow kept well in and the right hand about on a level with the left shoulder.

(To perform cut 2 as shown in Fig. 6,) lunge out and cut at your opponent's right cheek, with your arm straight and knuckles up. The natural guard for this is the high upright guard, with the elbow well in to the right side, the arm bent and turned slightly outwards, and wrist and knuckles turned well to the right.

(To perform cut 3 as shown in Fig. 7,) make free use of the wrist, bringing your blade round in the smallest space possible, and come in on your man's ribs with your arm straight and knuckles turned downwards.

Figure 5. Cut 1 and defence with the hanging guard

Figure 6. Cut 2 and defence with high upright guard

To stop this cut you may either use a low hanging guard, brought across to the left side, the right hand level with the left shoulder, or a low upright guard, with the hilt just outside the left thigh.

The hanging guard is the safer one of these two, as it is difficult in practice to get low enough with the hilt in the upright guard to stop a low cut of this kind.

Figure 7. Cut 3 and defence with low inside hanging guard

Figure 8. Cut 4, and defence with low outside hanging guard

(To perform cut 4, as shown in Fig. 8,) cut at your adversary's right ribs, and keep your knuckles up, and when he attacks you on this line, stop him with the hanging guard held low on your right side, or with the upright guard, with the arm, wrist and knuckles turned outwards.

Cuts 5 and 6 are made with like cuts 3 and 4 respectively, and must be met in all cases by a low hanging guard. It is well to practise these low hanging guards continually, as a man's legs are perhaps the most exposed part of his body.

The point when used is given by a simple straightening of the arm on the lunge, the knuckles being kept upwards, and, in ordinary play, the grip on the stick loosened, in order that it may run freely through the hilt, and thus save your opponent from an ugly bruise, a torn jacket, or possibly a broken rib.

When the knuckles are kept up in giving the point, the sword hand should be opposite the right shoulder. But the point may also be delivered with the knuckles down, in which case the hand should be opposite the left shoulder.

The point may be parried with any of the guards previously described.

Figure 9. The point

It is well to remember that one of the most effective returns which can be made from any guard is a point, and that a point can be made certainly from every hanging guard merely by straightening the arm from the guard, lunging, and coming in under your opponent's weapon. But perhaps this is a thing to be learned rather from experience than from a book.

Now, it is obvious that if any of the foregoing guards are as good as they have been described, it is necessary to induce your adversary to abandon them if you are ever going to score a point.

This may be done in a variety of ways, when you have assured yourself that he is invulnerable to direct attack, not to be flurried by a fierce onslaught, or slow enough to let you score a "remise" – that is, a second hit – the first having been parried, but not returned.

The first ruse to adopt, of course, is a feint – a feint being a false attack, or rather a move as if to attack in a line which you threaten, but in which you do not intend to attack. All feints should be strongly pronounced or clearly shown. A half-hearted feint is worse than useless; it is dangerous. If you have a foeman worthy of your steel facing you, he will detect the fraud at once, and use the time wasted by you over a feeble feint to put in a time thrust.

The ordinary feint is made by an extension of the arm as if to cut without moving the foot to lunge, the lunge being made the moment you have drawn off your enemy's guard and laid bare the real object of your attack.

Sometimes, however, if you cannot succeed otherwise, a half or short lunge for your feint, to be turned into a full lunge as you see your opening, may be found a very useful variation of the ordinary feint. If you find feints useless, you may try to compass your adversary's downfall by "a draw." All the time that you are playing you should try to be using your head, to be thinking out your plans and trying to discover his. In nine cases out of ten he has some favourite form of attack. If you discover what it is, and know how to stop it, indulge him, and invite him even to make it, having previously formed some little scheme of your own upon this opening. Let me illustrate my meaning by examples. If you notice a hungry eye fixed yearningly on your tender calf, let your calf stray ever so little from under the protection of the hanging guard. If this bait takes your

Figure 10. A ruse

friend in, and he comes with a reckless lunge at it, throwing all his heart into the cut, spring up to your full height, heels together, and leg well out of danger, and gently let your avenging rod fall along his spine. This, by the way, is the only occasion, except when you are acknowledging a hit, on which you may be allowed to desert the first position for legs and feet.

But this is a very old ruse, and most players know it: a much better one may be founded upon it. If, for instance, you think you detect any coquettish symptoms in the right leg of your adversary, you may know at once what he is meditating. Oblige him at once. Lunge freely out at his leg, which will of course be at once withdrawn. This, however, you were expecting, and as his leg goes back your hand goes up to the high hanging guard, covering your head from his cut. This cut stopped, he is at your mercy, and you may cut him in halves or crimp his thigh at your leisure. This position is illustrated in Fig. 10.

Once again; some men set their whole hearts on your sleeve, and you may, if yours is the hanging guard, lure them to their destruction through this lust of theirs. Gradually, as the play goes on, your arm tires, your hand sinks, your arm at last is bare, and the enemy comes in with a cut that would almost lay open the gauntlet, were it not that at that moment you come in with a low upright guard and return at his left cheek.

These are what is known as draws, and their number is unlimited.

Another thing sometimes heard of in single-stick play is "a gain." This is a ruse for deceiving your opponent as to distance, and is achieved by bringing your left heel up to the right, in the course of play, without abandoning the normal crouching position. This, of course, makes your lunge two feet longer than your victim has any reason for believing it to be.

A false beat is another very common form of attack, consisting of a cut aimed at the hilt or at the forte of your stick, the object being to make you raise your point, if possible, so that the attacker may come in under with cut 3.

This is very well met by a thrust, the arm being merely straightened from the guard, and the lunge delivered directly the "beat" is made.

A pretty feint having the same effect as the "beat," as opening up cut 3, is a long feint with the point at the chest, cut 3 being given as the sword rises to parry the point.

But probably I have transgressed the limits of my paper. What remains to be taught, and I know full well that it is everything except the merest rudiments, must be learned stick in hand. I can only wish the beginner luck, and envy him every hour which he is able to devote to acquiring a knowledge of sword-play.

THE SALUTE

Although the salute is a mere piece of sword drill, of no use for practical purposes, it is still worth learning, as being the preliminary flourish common at all assaults-of-arms, and valuable in itself as reminding the players that they are engaged in a knightly game, and one which insists on the display of the greatest courtesy by one opponent to the other. Even if you are playing with bare steel, it is expected of you that you should kill your enemy like a knight, not like a butcher; much more then, when you are only playing a friendly bout with him, should you show him all possible politeness. On entering the ring you should have all your harness on except your mask; this you should carry in your left hand until you are face to face with your antagonist. When in the ring, lay your helmet down on your left hand (side) and come to slope swords – your blade upon your right shoulder, your elbow against your side and your hilt in a line with your elbow, your knuckles outwards. Your body should be erect, your head up, your heels together, your right foot pointing straight to your front, your left foot at right angles to it pointing to the left.

Both men acting together now come to the engaging guard, and beat twice, stick against stick; then they come back to the "recover" by bringing the right foot back to the left, and bringing the stick into an upright position in front of the face, basket outwards, and thumb on a level with the mouth.

After a slight pause, salute to the left in quarte, i.e. extend the stick to the left front across the body, keeping the elbow fairly close to the side and the finger-nails upwards; then pause for a second and salute to the right in tierce (the back of the hand up); pause again, and salute to the front, by extending the arm in that direction, the point of the stick towards your left front. Now step forwards about two feet and come to the engaging guard, beat twice, draw the left foot up to the right, draw yourself up to your full height, and come again to the recover, drop your stick to the second guard (i.e. low hanging guard for the outside of the leg), making a slight inclination of the body at the same time (probably this is meant for a bow ceremonious), and then you may consider yourself at liberty to put on your mask and begin.

Don't forget, when you cross sticks, to step out of distance again at once. This salute, of course, is only usual at assaults-at-arms, which are modern tournaments arranged for the display of men's skill and the entertainment of their friends. At the assault-at-arms, as we understand it generally, there is no element of competition, there are no prizes to be played for, and therefore, so long as a good display is made, every one is satisfied, and nobody cares who gets the most points in any particular bout.

In competitions this is not so, and time is an object; so that as soon as the men can be got into the ring they are told to put their masks on and begin.

In assaults and in general play you cannot be too careful to acknowledge your adversary's hits. In a competition do nothing of the kind. The judges will see that every point made is scored, and you may safely relieve your mind from any anxiety on that ground. But in general play it is different, and you cannot be too liberal in scoring your adversary's points, or be too liberal in allowing them, even if some of them are a little bit questionable.

ACKNOWLEDGEMENTS

The ordinary form of acknowledgement (and a very graceful one it is) is accomplished as follows: - On being hit, spring to attention, with your heels together and body erect, at the same time bringing your sword to recover, i.e. sword upright in front of your face, thumb in a line with your mouth, and knuckles outwards.

The acknowledgement should only be a matter of seconds, and when made the player should come back to the engaging guard and continue the bout.

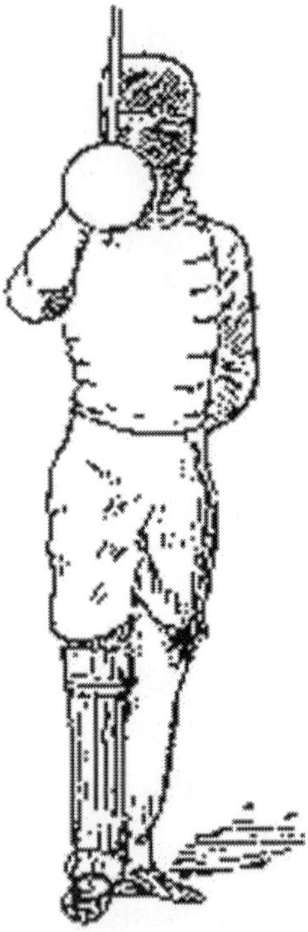

Fig. 11. The acknowledgement

FOUL HITS

Of course there are occasions on which the best player cannot help dealing a foul hit. When this happens there is nothing to be done except to apologise; but most of these hits may be avoided by a little care and command of temper. By a foul hit is meant a blow dealt to your opponent on receiving a blow from him – a hit given, not as an attempt to "time," but instead of a guard and, as a matter of fact, very often on the "blow for blow" principle.

This, of course, is great nonsense, if you assume, as you should, that the weapons are sharp, when such exchanges would be a little more severe than even the veriest glutton for punishment would care for.

If you only want to see who can stand most hammering with an ash-plant, then your pads are a mistake and a waste of time. Ten minutes without them will do more to settle that question than an hour with them on.

There ought to be some way of penalising the player who, after receiving a palpable hit himself, fails to acknowledge it, and seizes the opportunity to strike the hardest blow he is able to at the unprotected shoulder or arm of his adversary.

One more word and we shall have done with the courtesies of sword-play.

Don't make any remarks either in a competition (this, of course, is worst of all) or in an ordinary bout. Don't argue, except with the sticks. Remember that the beau-ideal swordsman is one who fights hard, "with silent lips and striking hand."

COMPETITIONS

Once a man has mastered the rudiments of any game and acquired some considerably amount of dexterity in "loose play," he begins to long to be pitted against some one else in order to measure his strength. Before long the limits of his own gymnasium grow too small for his ambition, and then it is that we may expect to find him looking round for a chance to earn substantial laurels in public competitions. Unfortunately the stick-player will not find many opportunities of displaying his skill in public. As far as the present writer knows, there are only two prizes offered annually in London for single-stick, and neither of these attract much attention. One of them is given at the Military Tournament at Islington, in June, and one at the German Gymnasium, in December .

The former of these prizes is only open to soldiers, militia-men, or volunteers, the latter to any member of a respectable athletic club, who is prepared to pay 2s. 6d. for his entrance fee. The attendance of spectators at both shows is very poor, which is to be regretted, as the interest of the public in any game generally goes a long way towards insuring improvement in the play.

It is just as well, before entering either of these competitions, to know something about the conditions under which they take place, and the rules which govern them. The bouts are generally played in a fourteen foot ring, at least that is the statement in the notice to players, and it is as well to be prepared to confine your movements to such a limited area. As a matter of fact, no objection ever seems to be raised to a competitor who transgresses this rule, and we remember to have seen a nimble player skipping about like an electrified eel outside the magic circle, until stopped by a barrier of chairs at the edge of the big arena.

At the Military Tournament the play is to the best out of three hits, i.e. the man who scores the first two points wins. At the German Gymnasium the competitor who first scores five wins the bout. This is better than at the Tournament, although it will seem to some that even this is hardly a sufficient test of the merits of each player. The bouts seem too short, but probably this is unavoidable; that which is to be regretted and might be remedied, being that no points are given for "form:" the result is that, in many cases, the anxiety to score the necessary points as soon as possible results in very ugly and unscientific rushes, in which no guards are attempted and form which the most reckless and rapid hitter comes out the winner. This, of course, is the same for every one, and therefore perfectly fair, but it does not tend to elevate the style of play.

But the great difficulty at these competitions appears to be the difficulty of judging. And here let me say once that it is as far to find fault with any individual judge as it possibly can be. Being English, I believe them to be above suspicion; being sometimes a competitor myself, it would not be for me to impugn their honesty if they were not. Whatever he does, I would advise the athlete to preserve his faith in the judges and a stoical silence when he does not quite agree with them.

All I would suggest for the benefit of the judges and judged alike in these trials of skill which test the eyesight and quickness of the umpires as much as the eyesight and quickness of the competitors, is that some definite code of scoring should be established and recognised amongst the different schools-of-arms in England.

In order to facilitate the scoring they have a very good plan at the Military Tournament of chalking the competitor's sticks. This precaution ensures a mark upon the jacket every time the ash-plant hits it; but even this is not always sufficient, for it is quite possible for a true guard to be opposed to a hard cut with a pliant stick, with the result that the attacker's stick whips over and leaves a mark which ought not to be scored, for had the weapons been of steel this could not have happened.

This, however, is a point which would generally be detected by one of the three judges in the ring.

What gives rise to a question in the players' minds is not any small point like this, so much as the question of timing and countering.

To take the last first: If A and B lunge together, both making direct attacks, and if both get home simultaneously, it is generally admitted that the result is a counter, and nothing is to be scored to any one.

But if A makes a direct attack, and B, ignoring it, stands fast and counters, this is a wilful omission to protect himself on his part; and even if his cut should get home as soon as A's it should not count, nor, I think, should it be allowed to cancel A's point, for A led, as the movement of his foot in lunging showed, and B's plain duty was to stop A's attack before returning it. This he should have done naturally enough if he had had the fear of a sharp weapon before his eyes.

I even doubt whether a time-thrust or cut should ever be allowed to score, unless the result of it be that it would have rendered the direct attack ineffectual in real fighting. Should not the rule be, either that the point scores to the person making the direct attack, as shown by the action of his foot in lunging (unless, indeed, the attacked person has guarded and returned, when, of course, the point is his), or, to make the rule a harder one, but equally fair for every one, to say no hits shall count except those made clean without a counter, i.e. to score a point the player must hit his adversary without being hit himself?

Of course bouts would take longer to finish if this were the rule, but such a rule would greatly simplify matters.

The really expert swordsman is surely he who inflicts injuries without receiving any, not he who is content to get rather the best of an exchange of cuts, the least of which would with sharp steel put any man hors de combat.

In connection with public competitions, I may as well warn the tyro against what is called "a surprise." On entering the ring the men face each other, come on the engaging guard, and begin at the judge's word of command. The sticks must have been fairly crossed before hits may be counted. But it is as well the moment your stick has crossed your opponent's to step out of distance again, by taking a short pace to the rear with your left foot and bringing the right foot after it. You can always come in again at short notice; but if you do not keep a sharp look out, a very alert opponent may cross swords with you and tap you on the arm in almost the same movement. If he does you may think it rather sharp practice, but you will find that it scores one to him nevertheless. As no word of practical advice founded on experience should be valueless, let me add one here to would-be competitors. Do not rely upon other people for masks, aprons, or other necessaries of the game. You cannot expect a gymnasium to which you do not belong to furnish such things for you, and even if they were provided they probably would not fit you. Bring all you want for yourself; and if you value your own comfort or personal appearance when you leave the scene of the competition, let your bag, on arriving, contain towels, brushes, and other such simple toilet necessaries as you are likely to require.

http://ejmas.com/jmanly/articles/2001/jmanlyart_Phillipps-Wolley_1101.htm

Appendix J

Walking Stick Techniques

Journal of Non-lethal Combatives, February 2000

Self-defence with a Walking-stick: The Different Methods of Defending Oneself with a Walking-Stick or Umbrella when Attacked under Unequal Conditions (Part I)

by E.W. Barton-Wright

From Pearson's Magazine, 11 (January 1901), p35-44. Contributed by Ralph Grasso.

Introduction

It must be understood that the new art of self-defence with a walking-stick, herewith introduced for the first time, differs essentially from single-stick or sword-play; for a man may be a champion in the use of sword or single-stick and yet be quite unable to put a walking-stick to any effective use as a weapon of defence. The simple and sufficient reason to account for this is that both in single-stick and sword-play a cut is always taken up by the hilt of the weapon, whereas if you attempted to guard a blow with a walking-stick—which has no hilt—in the same way as you would with a sword, the blow would slide down your stick onto your hand and disable you. Therefore, in order to make a stick a real means of self-defence, it has been necessary to devise a system by which one can guard a blow in such a way as to cause it to slide away from the hand instead of toward it, and thus obviate the risk of being disarmed by being hit upon the fingers.

After some fifteen years of hard work, such a system has been devised by a Swiss professor of arms, M. Vigny. It has recently been assimilated by me into my system of self-defence called "Bartitsu."

In the art of self-defence with a walking-stick, the stick is held in the hand with the thumb overlapping the fingers, and not, as in single-stick or sword-play, with the thumb resting on the blade. The stick is therefore manipulated with the wrist—and not with the fingers as in sword-play—and the blows are given by swinging the body on the hips—and not merely by flips from the elbow. In this way blows can be made so formidable that with an ordinary malacca cane it is possible to sever a man's jugular vein through the collar of his overcoat.

No. 1. -- The Guard by Distance—How to Avoid any Risk of being Hit on the Fingers, Arm, or Body by Retiring out of the Hitting Range of your Adversary, but at the same time Keeping Him within the Hitting Range of your Own Stick.

The mode of defence I am about to describe I have called "The Guard by Distance," to distinguish it from "Guards by Resistance." It will be noticed that in this method of defence the man attacked does not attempt to guard a blow by raising his hands to stop it, but simply by changing front from left to right foot—in other words, by swinging round from his original position, in which his left foot is advanced in front of his right, to a position in which his right foot is in front of his left. By so doing, he avoids being hit himself, with the certainty of being able to hit his adversary.

When guarding by distance, you take up the position of rear-guard—that is to say, you stand with left foot forward, slightly bent knees, right arm held above the head, and left arm thrown well out in front of you. I ought to state here that this is not a very easy attitude to assume, and that a certain amount of training in physical culture is necessary before it can be adopted with ease; but when you have acquired the requisite suppleness of body it is a very safe and reliable position to take up.

You must be careful to maintain the same distance between yourself and your adversary, which you originally take up, by retiring (right foot first) as he advances, and advancing (left foot first) as he retires. Then play a waiting game, and entice your opponent to strike at your arm or head by exposing one of the two, so that you are prepared to retire instantly upon the first sign of danger.

Your opponent, encouraged by the apparently exposed position of your left arm, naturally strikes at it, but you, anticipating the attack, withdraw it very quickly, and swing it upwards behind you. This upward sweep of the arm automatically causes you to swing your left foot well behind your right, and to draw in the lower part of your body out of your opponent's reach; at the same time it imparts the initial momentum to your right arm, and assists in bringing your stick down very quickly and heavily upon your adversary's head before he has time to recover his balance after over-reaching himself in trying to hit you.

No. 2. -- Another Way to Avoid being Hit by Retiring out of Range of your Adversary's Stick.

It is always most desirable to try to entice your adversary to deliver a certain blow, and so place yourself at a great advantage by being prepared to guard it, and to deliver your counter-blow. To induce your opponent to aim a blow at your head you take up the same position of rear-guard as described in the last trick, but instead of exposing your arm so much, you push your head more forward, leaving it apparently quite unguarded. Your assailant foolishly accepts the invitation, and you promptly draw yourself out of danger by swinging your left foot behind your right. This movement gives an automatic counter-movement to the right side of your trunk and helps you to swing in a very heavy right-handed blow across his wrist, which might thus easily be broken.

No. 3. -- Double-handed Stick-play—Showing the Best Way to Handle with Two Hands a Stick which is too Heavy to Manipulate Quickly with One Hand, when Attacked by a Man Armed with a Light Stick.

In mastering the art of self-defence with a stick it is important to learn how you may best wield your weapon with two hands, otherwise you might be at a serious disadvantage when carrying a heavy stick which you could not use freely with one hand, if attacked by a man carrying a lighter cane with which he could make quick, one-handed play. Your assailant's movements in this case would be so much quicker than yours that you would be at a very serious disadvantage with your heavier weapon.

The preparatory position for delivering a double-handed blow at your adversary's head is a position of guard, in which you hold the stick with both hands horizontally above your head, with thumbs away from your face and hands at the ends of the stick. The beauty of this position lies in the fact that your opponent does not know which end of the stick you intend to use to hit him with. We will suppose that you are holding the stick with the heaviest end in your right hand, and that you propose to hit him with this end.

The blow is delivered thus—you slide your right hand quietly off the right-hand end of the stick, and bring it back again, holding the stick with the thumb on the side nearest your face. Then, using your left hand as a pivot, you slide your right hand up to your left with a circular motion, thus delivering a strong side blow at your adversary's face.

Should you wish to strike our opponent with the opposite end of the stick—the lighter end—you would slip your left hand off the left end of the stick, bring it back with the thumb on the side nearest your face, and then slide your left hand towards your right, to impart a circular motion to the stick as before.

A person requires to be very supple in the shoulders to work a stick gracefully and well with two hands.

No. 4. -- How to Defend Yourself, without Running any Risk of being Hurt, if you are carrying only a Small Switch in your Hand, and are Threatened by a Man with a very Strong Stick.

Imagine that you are walking in a lonely part of the country, carrying a light switch or an umbrella, when suddenly a foot-pad bars your way, carrying a stout stick, with which he threatens you.

It is obvious that under these conditions if you gave your assailant time to assume the offensive, he would have no difficulty in breaking down any slight guard you might offer, and in felling you to the ground. Knowing this disadvantage, and without giving him time to realise it, you must at once attack.

You should aim a vicious blow at your assailant's head, holding your hand very high in order to force him to guard high.

Simultaneously, you should jump forward from the attacking position, shown in the second photograph, to the position shown in the third photograph, and strike him with the open hand high up on the chest, pulling his foot away from beneath him at the same time—in order to disturb his balance, and destroy his power to hit you. You could now strike your adversary such a blow with your fist on the face as to render him unconscious, or, of course, you could belabor him with your stick if it were suitable for the purpose.

No. 5. -- Another Way to Defend Yourself when your Adversary is Armed with a Stout Stick, and you are Carrying only an Umbrella or an Unreliable Cane.

In case the student of the art of self-defence with a walking-stick finds difficulty in mastering the preceding method of defense, here is an alternative, equally effective, and, perhaps, somewhat safer for beginners to practise.

As before, appreciating the unreliability of your weapon, you assume the offensive at once before your opponent has time to discover your disadvantage. You begin operations precisely as described in the last trick, by striking high at your assailant's head, and forcing him to guard high. Simultaneously you spring into the position shown in the third photograph, seizing your opponent just below the elbow, thereby completely disturbing his balance, and so preventing him from hitting you. You can now deliver a heavy right-handed blow with your fist upon his chin, or over his heart, which will render him unconscious.

A nine-stone [126-pound] man who is active, and who timed this movement nicely, could completely upset the balance of a man twice his weight and bring him to the ground in a second. [Judoka

Yukio Tani worked for Barton-Wright, and was quite capable of accomplishing this feat.]

In case you are carrying a stick which might be strong enough to deliver a heavy blow, another method of attack is as follows: After you have disturbed your assailant's balance by seizing him by the elbow, you retire quickly, by withdrawing your left foot well behind your right, and then, holding your head and body well on one side out of possible danger, you deliver a heavy blow with your stick across your assailant's kneecap is very dangerous, and would utterly incapacitate a man if well delivered. It is advisable, therefore, not to hit too hard when showing the trick to a friend.

No. 6. -- A very Safe Way to Disable a Boxer who Attempts to Rush You when You are Armed with a Stick.

Imagine the case of a man armed with a serviceable stick being attacked by a skilled boxer. One of the safest and most reliable methods of defence against a boxer's fists is as follows:-

The man with the stick faces the boxer in the back-guard position—that is to say, with his left foot and arm extended, and his right arm guarding his head. His left arm is thus free to guard his face or body, if, by any chance, he should fail to evade the blow.

As soon as the boxer opens his attack with a direct blow upon the man with the stick, the latter jumps with one movement to the former's left, bending well forward in a crouched position, so as to avoid any possibility of being hit. Then, turning half round on his left toe, and drawing his right foot in a line with his left, he makes a low, back-handed sweep with his stick, and strikes the boxer across the knee, disabling him, and bringing him to the ground.

But for the sake of argument, we will suppose that in the

excitement of the engagement the blow missed the boxer's knee, and struck him on his shin, in which case he might still be able to show fight. Quickly recovering his balance, the boxer turns on his left toe by stepping to the right with his right foot, faces his opponent, and puts in another blow. But here, again, the man with the stick anticipates the move, and bayonettes the boxer in the heart before the blow can fall. As his stick gives him a longer reach than the boxer's, he runs no danger, and the strong, upward thrust with the stick should completely incapacitate his adversary.

I should like the reader to thoroughly understand that in every form of self-defence the first and most essential thing is to have a well-trained eye. This trick is entirely dependent upon the quickness of the eye in judging the right moment to jump on one side, so that the boxer does not become aware of the fact until he has struck at you and overreached himself, when it is too late for him to make good his disadvantage.

No. 7. -- A Safe Way for One Man to Disable Another when both are Equally well Armed with Sticks.

Supposing that you are attacked by a man armed, like yourself, with a stout stick, here is a very pretty way to disable him.

Standing in the position of front guard, right foot forward, knees bent, right arm extend, you invite an attack at your head by holding your guard rather low. Your opponent accepts the invitation, and leads off at your head. You parry—an easy matter, as you are prepared for this blow—and simultaneously jumping well to your opponent's right, you crouch down and make a low, sweeping cut at his knees, which will bring him to the ground.

If, however, by any chance this result is not achieved, because your blow has fallen upon your opponent's shin instead of upon his knee, you will still have the best of the situation. Finding that you have got under his guard, your adversary will draw back his right foot and prepare to give you a back-handed cut across the face. You, however, foil this attempt by keeping too close to him to admit of this, and bayonette him with the point of your stick.

I specially recommend this, as well as the foregoing trick, to the attention of the reader, whether lady or gentleman, both being very easy and most effective. The most difficult part of the trick is to learn how to make your opponent lead off in the way you wish. But this becomes very simple with a little practice.

No. 8. -- One of the Safest Plans of Defence for a Tall Man to Adopt, who has not much Confidence in his own. Quickness and Knowledge of Stick-play, when Opposed to a Shorter and more Competent Opponent.

A tall, slow-moving man, attacked by a quick, short opponent, is at an immense disadvantage, as the short man delivers his attacks at lightning speed in unexpected quarters, and so reduces any possible advantage the other may hold in size and reach. Under the circumstances it would be advisable for the tall man to try to induce his opponent to deliver a blow for which he will be fully prepared.

This he will best do by taking up the rear-guard position, standing with his left foot forward, left arm extended, and right arm above the head, as previously described. He then throws his left arm forward as a bait. In ninety-nine cases out of a hundred the bait will prove irresistible. No sooner, however, does the short man begin to move his stick, with the intention of bringing it across the tall man's arm, than the latter must jump within the former's guard, in order to break the force of his blow as it falls, then seizing the other's stick, the tall man can belabor this opponent's head.

Of course, it is understood that if the tall man has only got a weak stick or umbrella in his hand, which would only be of use in making the necessary feint to get an opening, directly he obtained the advantage shown in photo No. 2, he would use his fist to strike his opponent in the face or over the heart in order to disable him.

No. 9. -- How to Defend Yourself with a Stick against the most Dangerous Kick of an Expert Kicker.

The student of the art of self-defence with a walking-stick might think it hardly worth while to study any particular method of defending himself which might insure him against an attack by a savater, or foot-boxer. You might suppose that there would be no great difficulty in guarding a high kick, provided you carried a stout stick in your hand. Those who have seen savaters at work, however, and realise the extraordinary swiftness of the kicks which they plant on their opponents' bodies, will understand that scientific kicking can only be guarded with certainty by a scientific method of defence.

Taking up a position of rear-guard, with left arm extended to ward off a possible kick at the small of the back, hip, or left side, you describe circular cuts in a left to right downward direction with your stick. Your opponent, standing well out of reach, prepares to do what in French boxing, or la savate, a called a "chassé"—that is, from his original position, with his left foot and left arm extended, he places his right foot behind his left so as to enable him to approach within kicking distance if the opportunity presents itself, and, at the same time, to keep his body and head well out of danger. Then, seeing an opening, he places his right heel firmly on the ground and aims a kick with his foot at your heart.

Anticipating the danger, you transfer the whole weight of your body from your left to your right leg, which enables you at the critical moment to withdraw your foot very quickly—to avoid a kick on the shin in case of a diversion in the attack—and at the same time assists you to draw your body out of danger. You then bring your stick so heavily down on your adversary's ankle as to break it.

If you wish to defend yourself against kicks lower down on the body, you employ exactly the same means of defence, but as it is not necessary to hold the arm so high in describing the circular cuts, it is very much easier to defend yourself. The objects of describing circular cuts, by the way, as opposed to a direct cut, is that you are very apt, in the latter case, to miss the kicker's leg, whereas in the former case you cannot fail, not only to deliver your blow, but also to ward off and divert the kick.

No. 10. -- One of the Best Ways of Knocking Down a Man in a General Scrimmage, when there is not Room to Swing a Stick Freely.

When a man finds it necessary to defend himself in a street fight, or the like, he may not have room to swing a stick freely. One of the best methods of using a stick as a weapon under these circumstances is to pass it between the legs of the assailant, and, by pressing it sharply against the inside of one of his thighs, to cause him to lose his balance.

In order to carry out the trick effectively on a single assailant, when there is no crowd, you should stand in the front guard position, and make a cut at the side of your opponent's face. While he raises his hand to guard his face, you seize his uplifted with your left hand, crouch down and pass your stick through his legs, exerting sufficient leverage to throw him on his back.

Another method is to take up the back position guard, standing with your left foot forward and your right arm above your head, which you must purposely expose in order to induce your opponent to strike at it. At the moment when he attempts to hit you on the head, you must slip under his guard, and seize his right wrist. Now pass your stick between his legs, and throw him upon his back.

To employ the same trick in a crowd it is only necessary to stoop, cover your face well with your arm and hand, and to keep diving with your stick between people's legs, upsetting them right and left.

http://ejmas.com/jnc/jncart_barton-wright_0200.htm

Appendix K

The Iaido Journal Nov 2000 - Making Your Own Wooden Weapons

By Kim Taylor

Based on an article that first appeared in The Iaido Newsletter #74 8/10, October 1996.

Introduction

I've been making wooden weapons for twenty years now and as I'm still not bored, I thought perhaps some readers also might get some enjoyment out of the hobby. Therefore I've provided some instruction here. Those who read this but still don't want to try making their own can get information about buying these weapons by looking at the Sei Do Kai catalogue. You should also check out the EJMAS shopping pages under equipment for photos of wood for weapons, you can buy them there as well.

Since I practice Japanese martial arts, my experience lies mostly in making Japanese weapons (bokuto, bo, jo, and other such things). However, wood is wood and the suggestions given below apply to any wooden weapon, whether a French cane, an Irish bata, or a Zulu knobkerrie.

I hope these notes will spur some of you to try your hand at the process. There's nothing like using a weapon you made for yourself.

Design Considerations

A good stick should last years. Therefore it should be chosen carefully. Factors to consider include the following:

- The shape and colour of the weapon should be pleasing to the eye.
- The grip should be smooth. (Stickiness or roughness will cause blisters.)
- The grip should be large enough so that the fingers don't touch the palm. (A badly sized handle can cause excessive cramping in the hands and a poor pattern of callus formation on the palm.)
- The wood grain should run straight from the handle to the tip. The wood must have no knots. Grain should be tight and closed. No warps or cracks should be seen.
- The weight should allow easy completion of a two-hour practice involving several thousand strokes. To avoid muscle strain and problems during partner practice, students should consider beginning with a lighter weapon and then moving to a heavier version once arm and shoulder strength have developed.

Recommended Woods

If buying a custom-made weapon, price may be a consideration, but if you are making your own price is essentially irrelevant. After all, the most expensive North American hardwood sells for less at the lumber store than the cheapest junk from the martial art store. Factors that are important, however, include weight, strength, and crush resistance.

- Weight is crucial for students who go up against their teacher not having the faintest idea what he is going to do. If due to its heavier weight, your weapon is slower than your instructor's weapon, then you will get clunked. As a result, I always tried to make sure my weapon was lighter than my teacher's. Gifting him with a heavy one usually worked.
- Strength is a combination of the "absolute" strength of your wood and the "relative" strength of your weapon compared to your partner's. A good Brazilian blackheart weapon will destroy a red oak weapon within about three hits. (Please note that I haven't been able to get blackheart for several years now, so don't ask.) James Goedkoop has a nice article describing the impact strength of various weapon-grade woods at http://www.aikiweb.com/weapons/goedkoop1.html.
- Crush resistance is the ability of the wood to dent without the fibres breaking causing splintering. Goedkoop's article also gives insight into this.

Other factors that may need to be considered include historical accuracy—Irish sticks, for example, were typically made of blackthorn roots—and appearance. The latter is not too important for everyday weapons, but can be critical for weapons intended to be given as gifts.

Grain Traits

Grain affects both strength and appearance. Basically, a wildly irregular grain usually looks better than a straight tight grain, but a straight tight grain is usually stronger.

Grain refers to the stratification of wood fibres. Although

climatic conditions affect grade, in general trees have a tighter grain toward the outside than in the centre. The reason is that the grain is a function of how much wood relative to the whole cross section the tree can produce in a season, and older trees put down tighter rings at their edges.

However, how much old growth is still around? Not much. As a result you have to be careful with wood selection, as young trees commercially harvested are rarely as tightly grained as the old stuff.

Desirable grain traits include:

- No knots.
- A smooth grain that doesn't run out less than halfway along the length of the stick.

The reason for no knots is obvious, as is the reason grain must run the length of the shaft or blade. However, it is not so obvious that the grain also must line up so that it runs from back to edge. Yet this is the reason that some "ironwoods" (a loose definition of any wood that is hell to work with) are no good for weapons—the grain goes all over and you're likely to get some that goes the wrong way about half way down the length. It is also why blocking should be done with the "edge" of the wooden sword since the strength of a wood is usually greater in this direction to the grain. (The wood is also thicker in this direction which doesn't hurt the strength any either. For those who are familiar with wood terminology, this is the radial face.)

In technical terms, assume a 40"-long board 1" in diameter. If the grain runs out at 20", the board is said to have a grain slope of 1 in 20 and it retains at least 93% of its strength along its length. If the grain runs out at 10", then the board has a 1 in 10 slope and it retains 81% of its strength. On the other hand, if the grain runs out 5 inches along the blade, it is down to 55% of its strength, and if the grain runs at 45 degrees (a 1-to-1 slope), then the wood has less than 10% of its potential strength.

North American Hardwoods

If you buy a commercial stick, it is likely made of ash or red oak, both of which are fairly cheap but neither of which is very dent resistant. Since you are making your own stick, you aren't worried about pinching pennies, instead you want a stick that looks spectacular, is strong as hell, or both. The following are my recommendations, these woods are all readily available throughout North America, and probably Europe, too. Latin names and technical descriptions are easily available via the Internet, so are not given here.

Ash: White ash is the light, strong wood used to make most commercial tonfa. Unfortunately its open pores make it "crushable" like oak. Nevertheless a tight-grained piece makes a good weapon for smaller students or beginners who can't safely use heavier weapons.

Hickory: Hickory often shows heartwood and sapwood of two different colours, one slightly harder than the other, and can be quite attractive. The First Nations peoples made their war clubs from hickory, and it is also my personal favourite. The wood has excellent crush resistance and strength plus comparatively light weight. It is suitable for heavy practice because when it breaks, it tends to split without letting pieces go flying about. Indeed, hickory's only drawback is that it is slightly "shaggy" and so may need to be sanded once in a while as the hairs lift with moisture from your hands.

Oak: Tight-grained pieces of old growth white oak make excellent weapons. However, the fast growing cycles and small diameters of some modern oak result in poor crush resistance due to porous grain. Red oak, pin oak, etc. are not suitable for high impact practice due to their open grain, but the pores in white oak are filled with waxy tylose residue that reduces crushing. The "magical" (some people think they're indestructible) wooden weapons one gets from Japan (shiro kashi or aka kashi, white or red oak) are Quercus mongolica, whereas North American white oak is usually Quarcus alba. Quarcus mongolica is more tightly grained than North American white oak, but more importantly, has a greater infill of the cells and as a result seems "heavier" (denser) and less liable to crush and dent.

Maple: Hard maple has good crush and dent resistance and a tight grain, and has sufficient strength and weight for everyday practice. Unfortunately, it is not suitable for heavy practice because when it breaks (and ALL wood eventually breaks), pieces go flying across the room. Nevertheless it is beautiful to look at and hold. Beech is like maple, just not as pretty.

I've used other woods such as cherry but while it is very pretty the suitability depends more on the piece of wood than the species. Meanwhile our local ironwood is hophornbeam, sometimes called muscled (or rippled) beech. It's a very white wood, light but with a lot of strength. I've been using it a bit lately when I can find a good piece.

Exotic Woods

Here are some of the more exotic woods I've used to make wooden weapons. WARNING: There is such a thing as carpenter's cancer (nasal cancer) and these exotics with their resins are probably great for causing it. Some of these woods can cause an almost instant irritation so be careful. I mention this here because ipe sent me into sneezing fits almost immediately (as opposed to purpleheart, which took a while). Macassar ebony dust has the same effect as inhaling chilli peppers. Wear a proper dust mask.

Afromosia: An attractive brown with yellow stripes, this West African hardwood is moderately heavy and is a bit brittle, therefore it could give splinters.

Bloodwood: This wood from the Amazon region has to be one of the nicest "weapon-grade" hardwoods I know. It is a joy to work with.

Brazilian Blackheart (redheart): This used to be imported as an ebony substitute, but it has a bad habit of dulling tools. This is the strongest wood I've ever seen, I weigh 230 pounds, my Tachi Uchi no Kurai (iaido partner practice) partner weighs at least that much, and we use a pair of these to demonstrate full stop blocks against full strength strikes. These things don't even dent, though I did once accidentally slice a piece off one of them using a "semi-sharp" aluminum iaito. Before the clamour to find and import this wood begins, I should mention that it is not really the perfect wood for weapons because it also has a tendency toward checks (cracks in the face). It's also heavy as blazes.

Bubinga: This wood from equatorial West Africa has light-yellow sapwood with red-violet stripes. It's fairly light and great fun to work with. Sadly, it is not so popular with the customers.

Cocobolo: Deep red with black stripes and swirls, and very heavy, cocobolo is a Central American true rosewood (Dalbergia sp.), as are kingwood and tulipwood. The grain tends to be screwy but it is so tight it usually doesn't matter. When working with cocobolo, tools must be kept very sharp as the wood can literally bounce a spokeshave off of itself. It is a great weapon wood, and I've sold every weapon I've ever made with this wood.

Ebony, African: African ebony comes from Madagascar and West Africa. On those rare occasions I find a piece big enough for a weapon I have to charge a couple hundred dollars for it! A beautiful wood though.

Ebony, Ceylon: Ceylon ebony is a VERY expensive black wood from southern India. It is hard to find in suitable grain patterns (as if you could see the grain in some pieces), and due to unseen stress cracks inside the wood I've seen Ceylon ebony weapons literally explode on contact. But anybody who takes a stick whose wood costs this much and smacks it against something hard deserves to have it break.

Ebony, Makassar: Makassar ebony is a moderately heavy wood from SE Asia that is coloured black with brown stripes. The wood is fairly strong, but due to cost—enough for a sword costs over CDN $100—ebony weapons are more suited for lone practice (suburi) than partner practice.

Ipe: Another very hard South Central American wood. This one is a light to dark brown that, with a good finish, shows rainbow flecks that make it look like you are actually seeing into the wood. It's not as heavy as blackheart, but not much is. The sanding dust from this wood is green and turns blood red when you wash with soap. Ipe ranks among my current candidates for "toughest weapon material".

Kingwood: Very pretty, very expensive, and from Brazil, this wood is more for looks than for partners. It is not as flashy as cocobolo or tulipwood, but very elegant.

Lignum Vitae: This slightly greenish wood from South and Central America is the heaviest wood around. It's fairly strong, too and is used in steamships as a bearing for the underwater propeller shafts. Unfortunately due to poor forest practices it has become an endangered species and as a result pieces large enough to make into weapons are becoming hard to find. Still, I made a weapon with it once, and even with a crack it would pound anything else to pieces. Recently I've found some larger pieces and should be able to make a bokuto or two in the next couple of years.

Osage Orange: The Indians of the Southwestern United States used to make lances and bows from this deep yellow wood. Unfortunately it is a real bear to work with, the grain wanting to rip out no matter which way you work it. Good pieces are somewhat hard to find.

Padauk: A deep red wood from Central and West Africa, padauk is not too bad to work with but quite a bit more splintery than bloodwood.

Pau Ferro: Although the dust from this Brazilian wood is toxic, it is so good looking that I occasionally make weapons of it. It's the local "ironwood" of its range and it earns the name, very hard.

Purpleheart: This Central and South American wood has a deep red colour and a nice straight grain. It can be a bit crushable because it's so stiff, but still makes an excellent weapon wood, especially if you want a bit more weight.

Teak: Heavy and strong but too soft, it dents easily. Nice and waxy so finishing is not too important. It's from Burma and Thailand.

Tulipwood: Not the North American wood that is actually poplar (Liriodendron tulipfera), but instead the Brazilian hardwood that (legend has it) some company in England made sports car frames out of. The wood is red with cream stripes and has good properties but it is expensive and hard to find a good piece.

Wenge: I have made exactly two bokuto from this Central African wood, no more. I've never met a more irritating dust or more painful splinter. The only thing that ever came closer to instant rejection was mansonia, which stinks something awful when you cut it.

Ziricote and Bokote: These are often called rosewoods but are

Cordia sp. rather than Dalbergia sp. Both are brown woods with black grain, the ziricote tending to be blacker and harder. Ziricote also produces a very irritating dust, and as a result I prefer working with bokote. Both woods are best used for show but will stand light partner work. (Well, heavy work if used only against anything bought in the local martial arts store). Both are from Mexico and Central America. Zebrawood looks very much like bokote, but is lighter and not as resinous.

I've probably tried a few more woods but can't remember them right now. If anyone wants to try another let me know and I'll tell you if I've used it.

Stuff That Is Not Wood

Rattan is a vine rather than a wood. It does not have much fibre connection and so tends to go floppy when used rattan-on-rattan, and to shred when used against hickory or other hardwoods. As it has to be replaced frequently and usually has to be shipped rather than purchased locally, rattan is often more expensive in the end than a good wooden stick.

I'm not a big fan of rattan for working weapons, but it's fine to whack partners with.

Selecting Wood at the Store

For making a first weapon I'd recommend maple. It's a nice wood to work and can be found easily. Hickory is a bit more difficult to find since it isn't really a woodworker's wood. (More a toolmaker's wood, used for ax handles and whatnot). Poplar is showing up in some of the lumberyards around here, but it's a bit soft.

If you're wondering about a new wood, try the thumbnail rip and bend test. If this sounds painful, let go of your thumbnail.

- Press your thumbnail into the wood at a corner. Does the wood crush easily? If it does, this isn't a good wood for a stick.
- Take a loose sliver of wood and rip it down. Is the fibre long or short? Does the fibre break easily or does it bend? Short is better than long and strength is important. It also makes a difference how hard it is to rip the fibre off the rest of the board. Why? Well, I once made a bokuto out of a wood called ramin. It had very long, strong straight fibers and seemed to have good crush resistance. The first time the student who bought it used it, the damn thing split right down the long axis. I swear that wood had absolutely no cross connections at all.
- Take a board and put one end on the floor while holding the other end. Look around and make sure nobody's in sight. Now lean on the board. If you hear it start to crack it's probably not very strong.

If the wood passes all these tests, then find a piece with good grain and start cutting.

Selecting Branches and Roots

Branches, saplings, and roots can be stronger than turned sticks, but it depends on knots, grain, and other factors and is not a guaranteed thing. Considerable experience is required to know the difference, and therefore beginners should stick to wood they buy from the store.

But if you're cheap, go to the woods and find a suitable hardwood sapling. Be sure to obey all forest laws! If you want the knob for a knobkerrie or whatever, then pull it up so that the root remains. In any case cut it off longer than you need.

Next, let the wood dry for a year or so. To prevent cracking, paint or wax the ends before putting it away to dry. (It's the faster water loss out of the end grain that causes splitting.)

Some people try to speed the drying process by using polyethylene glycol to displace the water. However, this is not recommended because the stick still retains the qualities of green wood rather than dry, and wood gains strength as it gains density (as it dries and shrinks).

Other people try heat. Note, however, that under ideal conditions air-dried wood is a bit tougher to break than kiln-dried wood. The reason is that the air-dried wood retains a slightly greater percentage of moisture. (The percent moisture for air-dried hardwoods of medium density is 15-20% while the percent for the same wood dried in a kiln is 12-15%.) This increased moisture means that the wood retains some of the properties of green wood. That is, it's more flexible, less brittle, and therefore less likely to snap.

However, under less-than-ideal situations, air-dried wood is subject to fungal growths that destroy the wood.

Therefore it is all a balance of properties. Drier wood is harder and won't dent as easily; wetter wood is more flexible and not as subject to splitting and breaking. Wetter wood is heavier and so has more impact power, drier wood is lighter and can be moved faster.

No matter how you decide to dry your stick, be sure to store the green wood out of the direct sunlight, as even a few hours can cause one side to dry faster than the other, thus resulting in a permanent warp. Direct sun on properly sealed and dried sticks is less of a problem, but can still result in hairline cracks called checking, and these in turn lead to unexpected breaks.

Finally, make sure that you store your drying wood flat. Wood that is dry resists bending, so wood that is bent during drying stays bent. Yes, small pieces can be subsequently unbent using steam, ammonia, heat, and presses applying pressure for weeks, but it is much easier to dry the wood straight in the first place.

Making the Weapon

With a few basic tools it is not hard to make a complex-shaped wooden weapon such as a curved sword or war club.

The first consideration is which wood to use. The choice will depend on what style of weapon is being made and whether or not it is to be used for partner practice. Once a source of suitable wood is found the actual piece must be chosen. Use a board that is about one inch thick and at least two inches wide for a Japanese sword. As noted above, the grain must be straight and preferably run along the wide dimension of the end of the board rather than across it.

Next you have to condition your wood. If at all practical, buy your wood and store it for several months to a year in conditions similar to your practice place. This will ensure that the wood is at a proper humidity level and any faults that are going to develop will do so before you start working.

Third, lay out a pattern. Here I'm describing how to make a bokuto, which is a wooden weapon made to resemble a Japanese sword. But the idea applies regardless of what kind of weapon you have in mind.

The easiest way of laying out a pattern for the curve is to copy a weapon you like. If you don't have a pattern then cut the board to about 41 inches long and at least two inches wide. Check grain patterns to determine which end of the board is weakest, that will be your handle. If the grain has a curve then the curve of the sword will follow it. Decide how far along the blade the bottom of the curve will be. For koshi-zori blades the point of maximum curve is close to the handle, for other styles (tori-zori) it is closer to the middle of the blade. Saki-zori blades have the maximum curve toward the tip. Mark out a curve so that the bokuto is about one and a half inches tall (from ha to mune, edge to back). The top of the handle and the point will touch one side of the board. The point of maximum curve on the edge touches the other side if the board is 2" wide. Cut out this sword blank using a band or sabre saw. (I even used a 5-1/4 inch circular saw for a few blades when I had nothing else. The small blade will make this curve.)

Now decide what tip shape you desire. Some sword styles leave the point blunt while others use a modified point. The commercial bokuto mimic the point of the katana. If you want a point, cut the end at the angle preferred.

If your bokuto is going to taper toward the tip (it should to look good), and you have access to a jointer, mark the taper on the concave and convex sides and by using a series of longer and longer passes over the blades, create the taper on the sides of the blade. If you don't have a jointer you'll simply do this by hand when shaping the blade.

To carve out the shape some people prefer a wood rasp, some a plane. I prefer a combination of a spokeshave and a Stanley Surform® rasp depending on which wood I am using. I have a Black & Decker Workmate® bench that is about the correct height for me to work on. If you don't, well, adjust according to what you have.

Start with the blade first and do the handle last. The reason is that the squared handle will allow you to keep the blade in the correct orientation while creating the long straight lines needed to produce a good looking bokuto.

Clamp the wood so that you can cut out the back ridge. For this you also need to have the blade clamped straight up and down. Hold the spokeshave at the chosen angle and use long smooth strokes to cut the shoulders. A 45-degree angle will make a round looking blade while an angle more toward vertical will create a thin blade. Which you prefer is a matter of taste.

Once you have cut these shoulders to a straight pleasing line, then you can start on the edge. To make the edge, turn the wood over and work the curve into the bottom of the blade. A more rounded edge will create a stronger sword with a more resistant striking surface while a sharper edge will create a more visually pleasing shape. Whichever edge you choose, make sure that the edge lines up with the top of the blade. Clamping the squared handle will help with this. The edge will want to wander as you cut so be careful.

The way you taper the blade toward the tip determines the sword's balance. If you want to replicate the katana point use a Surform® to cut a plane in from each side at the tip. If there is to be no point or a modified point then use the Surform® to round off the edges of the tip and the base of the handle.

Next, even out any wavers in the lines along the back.

Once that is done, carefully clamp the blade. Be sure to put pieces of scrap between the clamps and the blade, otherwise you will leave unwanted indentations. Now carve out the handle. This is an important step since the handle is what you grip and the angle must agree with the curve of the blade. As a rule the handle should be an oval shape with the long axis arranged so that you know where your blade edge is facing. In other words, the top and bottom of the oval must line up with the back of the blade and the edge. For a more sophisiticated grip use an egg shape with the narrower curve on the edge side.

If you have access to a fixed belt sander, you can use both hands to smooth the wood. Your straight lines will be straighter that way, and a lot of shaping can be done using the 36-grit belt. If the sander has a large flat bed you will have to create a padded "hump" on the bed with foam and masking tape so that the belt moves in a curve to fit the concave mune.

If you don't have a sander, then you can use hand tools. However, you will also have to work much more carefully to prevent blisters on your hands. Use several grits of sandpaper to smooth the wood and close the pores.

After sanding, apply boiled linseed oil or tung oil. Do not use surface finishes like varnish or urethane; even Danish wood oil is a bit much. These create a sticky surface that will give you blisters while an oil finish allows the wood to soak up the sweat on your hands without causing the grain to lift too much.

If you use linseed oil make sure it is boiled—raw oil will never dry. I prefer tung oil.

Making a Cane, Stick, or Staff

The previous advice was for people making weapons that resembled swords.

The following advice is for people who want to make tapered round sticks but do not have lathes. You'll need (ideally) a band saw, a table saw, a spokeshave and a plane. By the way, this took me a lot of years to figure out, so anyone who thinks they may make a round stick for themselves one day, pay attention and save yourself a lot of work and thought.

On the table saw, cut the wood square to the maximum width you want. Usually this is 1” (yes I do work in English measurements in a metric country, 1” is 2.54 cm, 1000 mils, and 0.85 sun) or sometimes $1^1/_8$”. I’ll assume you want to make a six-foot staff measuring 1” in the centre and $3/_4$” at the tips.

To taper the wood, mark the piece from the maximum width in the centre (or 6” either side of the centre or whatever you prefer) to $^1/_8$” in from each side at the tips. Draw lines and then plane this taper into the four sides. Make the lines as straight as you can get them. That’s 8 surfaces to plane in all.

Now carefully mark out lines on opposite sides. The ratio is 3-4-3. For those of you less mathematically inclined:

- In the centre, make a mark 4.8-16ths of an inch in on each side. (0.3 of an inch)
- On each end, make a mark 3.6-16ths of an inch in on each side. (0.3 times $3/_4$”)

Then make a line between these marks.

Set the band saw to make a 45-degree cut and cut along the lines. This will give you an octagonal shape with almost equal sized planes.

Go to the spokeshave and round the edges off the octagon as smoothly as possible.

Then go at it with sandpaper and finish the job.

If you don’t have the table saw and band saw:

- Get a piece of the right square size from a local lumberyard.
- Mark the 0.3 lines on all four sides.
- Use the plane to cut the four planes into 8 planes before switching to the spokeshave. (It’s hard to cut a straight plane with a spokeshave unless you have a lot of practice.)
- Now work away at the corners to round it off, trying not to cut

into the centre of each of the original 8 planes.

Care of a Wooden Weapon

If the weapon feels good in your hands and is the right weight, then appearance is not important. It is a tool and it will soon be banged up so don't worry if it is not a museum piece. Meanwhile, if you treat it with the proper care it will be useful for many years of hard service.

The most important advice is to keep your stick out of the sunlight and away from heat sources, and to reapply a tung oil or boiled linseed oil finish every few months. (Hard surface finishes such as varnish make the handle sticky while mineral oil requires frequent applications and feels slimy.)

It is also important to pay attention to relative humidity, as sudden changes may cause the wood to warp, crack, or check (small cracks in mid-board). Note that air-conditioning creates a very dry environment, so a weapon flown from an indoor training area in Arizona to an outdoor training area in Hawaii is at slight risk. Ideally you would not take your Arizona weapon out of its bag for a month or two upon arrival, but if that's impossible then it might be better to take a less-favoured stick.

All wooden weapons are ideally stored flat rather than stood in the corner, but there is no reason that a properly dried stick cannot be stood in the corner for a few weeks without noticeable warp. Weapons made of green wood are another matter altogether.

Finally, consider transporting your weapon in a bag. Not only does this protect its finish from nicks caused by car trunks and windows, but it also provides some protection from sudden changes in humidity and more importantly, heat. Whether this bag is cloth, leather, nylon, or vinyl is mostly a matter of esthetics.

Conclusion

There you have it—how to select the proper wood, how to make a complex wooden weapon having lots of curves, and how to make a round tapered stick. For photos of some weapons that I've made, check out http://sdksupplies.netfirms.com/thumb.htm

Have fun making your first weapon. Write and tell me how it went.

kataylor@ejmas.com TIJ Nov 2000

Appendix L

The Danmyé in Martinique

Historical background

Danmyé, also called Ladja, is the first martial art to be practised in Martinique. It was born from the impact of two worlds meeting each other. The slaves from Senegal and elsewhere who passed intransit through the island of Gorée created an art of fighting inspired by the initiation ceremony of "N'golo" which symbolised the passing from adolescence to adulthood and consisted of a confrontation which took the form of a fight. The main source of inspiration is unquestionably the Lamb (Senegalese fight).

The cultural melting pot confirmed the transformation of modes of expression. The quadrille, a traditional Martinican dance, is inspired by the dances at the King's court.

The owner (béké) used his black stallion, usually a Mandingo (African tribe) as a fighting cock that he could exhibit during celebrations. Yet, the loss of his best slave or his being temporarily disabled lead the béké to put an end to this kind of events. Still, fights between "majors" went on at the occasion of village fairs or appointed fights. After the 1947 "departmentalisation" however, municipal decrees banned the practice of Danmyé.

The growing importance of folk ballets during the sixties, with the notable contribution of Le Ballet Martiniquais (Martinican Ballet) and its choreographic contests brought this martial art into fashion again. With the seventies and the emerging independence movement, the phenomenon became more extensive to the point of getting more and more concrete thirty years later. Nowadays such cultural associations as the AM4 are working to update the knowledge connected with this activity. Furthermore, Sully Cally, working in partnership with Jacqueline Rosemain, has been carrying out thorough research on this subject.

It is worth noting that Danmyé only developed in Martinique. As for Guadeloupe, it gave birth to a dance called "Le Lérose" and a fight with sticks known as "Mayolet". There are many places for practice: "pitts" (cockpits), a spot in front of the BNP (a bank) in Fort-de-France during Carnival, and bèlè events. Traditionally, the evening starts with Danmyé fights then the bèlè takes over and the attendants keep in communion through the night. The event ends at daybreak with the "ting-bang".

Danmyé at school

At Lorrain High School, an educational experiment was born from three summer schools and enabled the definition of contents of this martial art. What does this activity consist of? A wrestler has to get the upper hand of his opponent while respecting the drummer's pace.

How to win the fight? There are many solutions: it comes either from the referee's ruling after a decisive blow or from one of the opponents being hit once more than the other, or from his being immobilised on the ground. The Danmyé has the distinctive feature of being the only martial art which combines prehension (seizing) with percussion (blows).

The sound

It is composed of several elements, which play a deciding part in the proper course of the fight. It acts as an incentive on the wrestlers as in Capoeira (Brazil).

drum (cocoyé)	
ti-bwa	
singing	The singer spurs on the wrestlers by means of provocative lyrics. These lyrics are derived from the history of Martinique. They either praise a famous "major" or highlight the qualities of courage, strength or even wickedness of one of the wrestlers.
the chorus	
(la vwa):	The chorus is made up of the attendants who take up the refrain, with the effect of stimulating the wrestlers.

The ring (The fighting space)

The wrestlers determine the fighting space by dancing round in a ring to the rhythm of the drum (introductory stage of the fight). Then each wrestler in turn draws an invisible circle which represents a magic space. Any person entering that circle is an opponent.

Rising to the drum

After dancing in a ring each wrestler comes to the tambouyé to size him up. That's the moment when the collusion between tambouyé and wrestler can become effective and enable him to win the fight more easily.

During the rise to the drum each wrestler tries to impress his opponent and outdo his litheness, strength and agility.

The fight

Danmyé is the only martial art which combines prehension with percussion. The strokes must be restrained and given without intending to hit. As a matter of fact they must be shown rather than given except when it is necessary to drive back the opponent to refuse a hand-to-hand fight.

How to win?

- After the referee's ruling, if he considers a blow was decisive because it might have led to a KO if it had really been carried out (cou lan mô).
- Lifting the opponent off the ground (lévé féssé)
- Counting the amount of points that were scored during a two-minute fight.
- Immobilising the opponent (Kakan)

How to fight?

- Being in harmony with the sound :
  The wrestler has to hit and move in harmony with the duple time rhythm. If this condition is not respected the fight is stopped and the guilty wrestler is disqualified.
- Using the opponent's strength.

The score

The body is a target. Thus:

- a kick at the face means 5 points
- a kick at the chest means 3 points
- a kick at the leg means 1 point
- a punch means 1 point
- a series of punches means 2 points
- a sweeping blow means 5 points

The aim is to score more points than the opponent does and hit without being hit.

http://www.european-schoolprojects.net/festivals/Martinique/danmye/danmye_e.htm

Appendix M

KALENDA - AFRICAN STICK DANCE / FIGHT

Dennis Newcome

Dennis Newsome is the first and only African-American Master in the art of Capoeira in the world (an African Brazilian combat dance), and a pioneer of Capoeira in San Diego, California, USA. Newsome has traveled to many countries working as technical advisor, stunt actor and fight choreographer on several motion picture films. He has served as a technical advisor and fight choreographer for "Lethal Weapon" and other movies. He is one of the leading African martial artists and leading exponent of "Kalenda" (African American & Caribbean Stick Dance/Fight) in the U. S.

There is a Kalenda style (stick fight/dance found in the U.S. and Caribbean South America under the same or different names) that resembles the Maculele in Brazil imagine Maculele done much more fight like. I know a little of this style of Kalenda and I practice the Maculele that is in Brazil and in my opinion they are the same thing except that this two stick Kalenda method has retained more of the fight than Maculele. There is also a Kalenda that is done with two sticks except that the sticks are clasped in the middle of the sticks. Just like the defense stick is held in Zulu Impi (Zulu Stick fight) or like the way of some Ethiopian stick fighters.

The old Capoeira method that relied heavily on head butting and utilized kicking is very similar to the methods in the deep south of the United States, Jamaica, Barbados, Trinidad and Grenada. In modern Capoeira the feet are far and beyond the main weapon. The Cabecada is on the back burner in today's jogo. I do Reisy or Testa, which is Eritrean Head butting and to me in comparing the butting of Capoeira and the butting of Reisy I consider Reisy inside butting and Capoeira outside butting which probably won't make any sense except to another butter.

The martial arts of the world differ in their vocabulary of movements and the strategic use of even commonly shared movements. They differ in philosophy and or religious content. They differ in efficacy in different environments. They differ in origins. http://stickgrappler.tripod.com/52/newsome.html

I was giving a lecture / demonstration on TESTA (an African Head Butting art from Eritrea) and DULA MEKETA (an African Stick fighting art from the Ethiopian Oromo's) when at the conclusion of the Lecture / Demonstration an elder brother approaches me and says "I know how to stick fight too." I assumed that he knew how to do DULA MEKETA so I said "You know Dula Meketa too?" and then he replied "No... I know another form of stick fighting." Of course I asked was it Black and he said yes! Now my interest was really peaked and I asked if he would teach me. He accepted me as his student and taught what he had learned from his grandfather. His name was Mr. Harrison a man old enough to be my father. In fact one of his son's is the same age as me. Mr. Harrison learned the art from his grandfather. I was fortunate enough to be in the right place at the right time to learn this art which I had only heard of before. The name of this art, he knew naught, so we used to refer to it as "New Orleans" after the city in which he grew up, in the state of Louisiana. Why hadn't his grandfather told him the name of the art? Perhaps he didn't think it important. The musical and dance side of the art he also neglected to teach him. What he taught him was the fight aspect of this multi-dimensional art form. I later learned these aspects of the art from other Kalendas. Even the name Kalenda I learned from meeting other Kalendas. The oldest name in reference to Kalenda I know of is MOUSONDI. MOUSONDI is from the Kongo Africa.

There were four styles of Kalenda in the U.S. Now today their is only one that I know of which is our style, the long staff style. Fortunately for the African peoples of the Americas, that which is Black may die out in one place and live on in another place. In the Caribbean, the other styles still exist in all their African glory.

Since the inception of slavery to the present times in the Americas, Africans in the Diaspora have been traveling and relocating from one country to another and bringing with them their musical, religious, artistic and martial traditions. Our Kalenda style was probably brought to New Orleans by the influx of African Haitian slaves who were of the Kongo nations. What gave me the idea to research this was when a friend and room mate of mine discovered that our styles of Stick Fighting were the same. One day while I was training the Kalenda my room mate was watching me. Then he interrupted my training and asked to see my stick. He then proceeded to use the stick in the same manner to both our dismay! His street name was Legba. He was from Haiti. He explained to me that as a child growing up the men would do this dance / fight also. They had the same licks. Another interesting brother I took time to study with was Steve from Trinidad. He knew our style plus three others and Savate (Original French foot fighting). It was from him that I learned the dance aspects of the fight. Finally I met and studied with the irrepressible "Reverend Baptiste"! He is from Trinidad also and he practiced the medium stick style. In addition to this he is a Head Butter. One day I will tell you of the time that he Head Butted Jesus into a hoodlum who later became a minister of God! I also learned a few Kalenda songs from him.

It is paramount that we continue the practice of Kalenda because every time an African tradition stops being practiced by us a little bit more of our national and international African soul dies. A little bit more of our identity, history and dignity dies.

Kalenda a beautiful dance! Kalenda a beautiful fight! It is a dance of war! An African cultural game of ritual war strategy. We will inform you of more things related to Kalenda later.

http://www.malandros-touro.com/generic.html?pid=10

Bibliography

Almeida, Bira. *Capoeira: A Brazilian Art Form*, North Atlantic Books, 1986

Allsopp, Dr. Richard. *Dictionary of Caribbean English*, Oxford University Press, 1996

Anderson, Jack. *Pugilistic Prosecutions: Prize Fighting and the Courtsin Nineteenth Century Britain.* http://www2.umist.ac.uk/sport/SPORTS%20HISTORY/BSSH/The%20Sports%20Historian/TSH%2021-2/Art3-Anderson.htm

Anderson, Jack. Queensbury rules - *Pugilistic Prosecutions: Prize Fighting and the Courtsin Nineteenth Century Britain.* (Extract) - School of Law, University of Limerick, Ireland

Anderson, Jack. Tom Johnson Rules - *Pugilistic Prosecutions: Prize Fighting and the Courtsin Nineteenth Century Britain.* (Extract) - School of Law, University of Limerick, Ireland

Bare Knuckle Boxing, http://www.georgianindex.net/Sport/Boxing/boxing.html

Barton-Wright, E.W. *Journal of Non-Lethal Combatives*, February 2000, "Self-defense with a Walking-stick: The Different Methods of Defending Oneself with a Walking-Stick or Umbrella when Attacked under Unequal Conditions (Part I)", From Pearson's Magazine, 11 (January 1901)

Beckles, Prof. Hilary. *For Love of Country*, Foundation Publishers, NCF, Bridgetown, Barbados, p 16

Brathwaite, Kamau. *Sun Poem*: "Hereroes"

Conley, Carolyn. "The Agreeable Recreation of Fighting" (Extract),

Journal of Social History, Fall, 1999 University of Alabama at Birmingham

Courlander, Harold. *The Drum and the Hoe*, University of California Press, Berkeley and Los Angeles 1960

Cowley, John. *Carnival, Canboulay and Calypso: Traditions in the Making*, Cambridge university Press, 1996

Danmyé in Martinique, YouTube videos. www.youtube.com

de Barros, Dr Juanita. *Order and Place in a Colonial City*, McGill-Queen's University Press, 2003

Dookhan, Professor Isaac. "A History of the Virgin Islands of the United States"

Gerstin, Julian. *Tangled Roots: Kalenda and other New-African Dances in the Circum-Caribbean.* http://kitlv.library.uu.nl/index.php/nwig/article/viewFile/3539/4300

Highland Officer. *The Science of Defense Exemplified In Short and Easy Lessons for the Practice of the Broad Sword and Single Stick.* http://www.geocities.com/cinaet/anti-pugilism.html

Filipino Stick Fighting. http://www.youtube.com/watch?v=ne7cALRIlBw

Filipino Stick Fighting. http://www.youtube.com/watch?v=-GzVpSypCFY

Hill, Dr. Donald R. *Calypso Calaloo Early Carnival Music in Trinidad*, University Press of Florida, 1993

Hill, Dr Donald R. *Tradition and Trinidad: The 1971 Carnival in Cariacou*, Grenada

Lang, HG. *The Walking Stick Method of Defense*, 1923. http://www.the-xiles.org/manual/lang/lang.htm

Mbiti, John. *The Contributions of Africa to the Religious Heritage of the World.* http://www.wcc-coe.org/wcc/what/interreligious/cd37-14.html)

Moore, Brian L. and Michele A. Johnson. *Neither Led nor Driven: Contesting British Cultural Imperialism in Jamaica*, 1865-1920,

Newcome, Dennis: *Kalenda - African Stick Dance/Fight*

Phillipps-Wolley, C. *Journal of Manly Arts*: "Single-Stick". http://ejmas.com/jmanly/articles/2001/jmanlyart_Phillipps-Wolley_1101.htm, Nov 2001.

Rivera, Raquel Z. http://www.allhiphop.com/features/?ID'55

Rohlehr, Gordon. *Calypso and Society in Pre-Independence Trinidad*, Gordon Rohlehr, Trinidad 1990

Senior, Olive: *Encyclopedia of Jamaican Heritage*

Stuempfle, Stephen. *Steelband Movement - The forging of a National Art in Trinidad and Tobago*, The Press of the University of the West Indies, 1995

Walking Stick techniques

Warner-Lewis, Professor Maureen. *Central Africa in the Caribbean*, University of the West Indies Press, Jamaica, 2003

Welch, Pedro. *Slave Society in the City*, Ian Randle, 2003

Index

28644807R00221

Made in the USA
Charleston, SC
18 April 2014